MASTERCLASS:
WRITE A
BESTSELLER

Jacq Burns

Teach Yourself®

Masterclass: Write a Bestseller

Jacq Burns

First published in Great Britain in 2014 by John Murray Learning, an Hachette UK company.

First published in US in 2014 by The McGraw-Hill Companies, Inc.

This edition published in 2014 by John Murray Learning.

British Library Cataloguing in Publication Data: a catalogue record for this title is available from the British Library.

Library of Congress Catalog Card Number: on file.

Paperback ISBN 978 1 473 60003 4

eBook ISBN 978 1 473 60005 8

10 9 8 7 6 5 4 3 2 1

The publisher has used its best endeavours to ensure that any website addresses referred to in this book are correct and active at the time of going to press. However, the publisher and the author have no responsibility for the websites and can make no guarantee that a site will remain live or that the content will remain relevant, decent or appropriate.

The publisher has made every effort to mark as such all words which it believes to be trademarks. The publisher should also like to make it clear that the presence of a word in the book, whether marked or unmarked, in no way affects its legal status as a trademark.

Every reasonable effort has been made by the publisher to trace the copyright holders of material in this book. Any errors or omissions should be notified in writing to the publisher, who will endeavour to rectify the situation for any reprints and future editions.

Typeset by Cenveo® Publisher Services.

Printed and bound in Great Britain by CPI Group (UK) Ltd., Croydon, CR0 4YY.

John Murray Learning policy is to use papers that are natural, renewable and recyclable products and made from wood grown in sustainable forests. The logging and manufacturing processes are expected to conform to the environmental regulations of the country of origin.

John Murray Learning
338 Euston Road
London NW1 3BH

www.hodder.co.uk

Also available in ebook

Dedicated to Michael and Richard Mcdonald,
and Johnny and Tommy Williams whose stories
were cut short

Acknowledgements

Thanks to Bob, Fred and Mathilde, top scrappers, non-sulkers, big on love, patient throughout. To my mum, for my first job stacking books. To my sister Lee-Anne (and Claire) for introducing me to Random House. And to Paula and Miles for loving encouragement. To Adelaide Writers' Week, my first literary festival, and the best bookselling job ever (Alice Walker being one of my customers). Thank you to all the generous contributors. And to Lindsay Brodin, Stephanie Goldberg, Jamie Joseph, Robert Anderson, Kirsty Mclachlan, Victoria Roddam and Jane Ryan for their help in writing this book. To the authors I represent: I'll never again give you a hard time about meeting deadlines. And, last but not least, to all you writers who carry on writing for the love of it, never knowing if you'll get published but always working towards your bestseller.

Contents

About the author

Jacq Burns has over 25 years' experience in bookselling and publishing, including commissioning roles at Random House and HarperCollins. She now agents non-fiction including: personal development, business, how-to books, parenting and well-being. She co-founded London Writers' Club, offering advice and workshops for fiction and non-fiction writers. She has ghost-written titles on a range of subjects, from neurology to a novel about forced marriage, and wrote the humorous Handbag Girly Emergencies *series under a pseudonym.*

Introduction

Most bestsellers have about them a touch of the unpredictable. It would be nice to think that it is the intrinsic qualities of a book that will give it a leg up the charts, but it is just as likely to be luck, serendipity or timing. These things can only be influenced to a degree, yet they can help create a monster bestseller. Perhaps this isn't fair, but it could be argued that it makes publishing more interesting and perhaps more accessible to a wider range of writers.

In the current shifting landscape of publishing, authors need agility and determination. They must be strategic about their writing and focused on the action that needs to be taken before, during and after the publication of their book to increase the chances of creating a bestseller. This book will deconstruct bestsellers to see what makes them, and focus on the tangible, practical things you can do to nudge your book sales in an upward direction.

A key part of the thinking and the style of this book is around finding ways to build bestselling appeal into your writing in the inspiration and ideas phase, before you start to write. For those who have already started writing, there are ideas for road-testing and improving your ideas and your writing.

The suggested plan of attack is to become familiar with what sells and why, and to take key decisions and rough out a plan before starting a new project, but then to write freely, as far in 'flow' as possible, free of criticism or worry. Then, when the first draft is done, it's time to consciously evaluate that draft and to inject the vital things that are the markers of a bestseller.

About this book

This book is divided into five parts, in which we cover the following actions to creating a bestseller: planning, getting it done, getting it right, putting it out there in the best way for our book, making it visible and discoverable and approaching your writing and publishing in a businesslike way. Here's what we'll cover in the book.

PART ONE: PLAN

You will learn about:

- planning and how to make key decisions about your writing so that when you start you don't get tangled up by easily preventable mistakes
- how to find and nurture inspiration and get started
- the all-important aspects of understanding story and concept so that, when you have your idea, you can test it before you start to write so that you're clear *where* the story really is and to get a sense of *whose* story it is
- the practicalities: whether to make a structured plan or not; whether to use writing software, to write on a computer or in longhand and then which pen or stationery and where you'll write – café, desk or park bench.

PART TWO: WRITE

You will learn about:

- ways of starting and keeping going until the first draft is done, forgetting about the reader and the market, which at this moment don't exist. There's just you and your story, your first thoughts pouring out, and allowing your voice to come through loud and clear
- taking a break from your first draft, and then sorting out any technical or mindset problems you may have encountered along the way
- how to examine your first draft to see what you've achieved, evaluating and sizing up what you've produced
- ways of formulating a clear plan to rework your book, since a first draft is rarely, if ever, good enough to send out, let alone publish.

PART THREE: PITCH

You will learn about:

- agents and their role in the new publishing context, as well as what they are good for and how to get one
- your pitch package; your essential kit for pitching to publishers.

PART FOUR PUBLISH

You will learn about:

- rechecking your priorities for your book and figuring out the best route to market for your book and your writing career
- the differences between trade and indie or self-publishing, what to expect from each, and the pros and cons
- an inspiring new breed of hybrid authors who combine both.

PART FIVE: SELL

You will learn about:

- the mammoth ongoing task of publicizing and marketing your book to make it more discoverable by readers
- the way of the 'authorpreneur', and what you have to do – and keep on doing – to make it in the publishing business.

THE EXERCISES

The chapters have a practical outlook, with lessons, exercises and advice. You will find icons indicating several kinds of exercise, as follows:

Snapshot is a short exercise or task related to the main idea in the adjacent text.

Write exercises – self-explanatory – ask you to write about a specific aspect of the task of creating your bestseller.

Workshop exercises are longer exercises that ask you to do a bit more work – for example working out your marketing plan.

Edit is a reworking or review of a previous piece or exercise.

There are two other features within each chapter:

Key ideas distil the most important points and ideas.

Focus points at the end of each chapter distil that chapter's core messages.

PART ONE
Plan

1

The best-laid plans ...

Many a publisher, agent and author would kill for a crystal ball that could foretell a bestseller. Choosing what to publish is not an exact science and agents and publishers invest in books based on their strong belief in the project, a sense of what the market wants, past experience of what sells, and possibly a little gut feeling.

If it were possible to reduce a bestseller to a recipe or formula it might look something like this:

Good idea + great story + Zeitgeisty or timeless + fits genre conventions + good-enough writing + plausible and interesting characters + interesting setting + series of books + promotable author + luck + marketing strategy + author engagement + discoverability = strong word of mouth and high visibility = bestseller.

Not every bestseller has all these things, but they do share many of the elements that make a bestseller.

What is a bestseller and how do I write one?

It should help your understanding of what it takes to write and publish a bestseller if you spend some time looking at the books that readers are buying in any given period. Study the weekly bestseller charts in the newspapers over a number of weeks, or the charts in publishing industry magazines such as the UK's *The Bookseller*.

The Bookseller Official UK Bestsellers Chart is constructed from a weekly list of the top 5,000 bestselling books in the UK. Gathered by Nielsens BookScan, it captures 90–95 per cent of book sales in the UK from a huge range of outlets, including Amazon, Asda, B&Q, the BBC, Blackwells, ELC, The Eden Project, HMV, *The Independent*, the Imperial War Museum, Mothercare, art galleries. PC World, Play.com, the Saatchi Gallery, Sainsburys. Tesco, Tesco online, Waterstones and WHSmith. The figures don't include independent bookshops or digital sales.

Since 1998 the charts have reflected *actual* sales: point-of-sale data is gathered via the barcode on the back of a book. Before 1998, it was a matter of calling up a selection of 'representative' booksellers and asking them for their figures. And of course this was open to guestimates, mistakes and favouritism.

You can also check the biggest online platform, Amazon's top 100 chart (which, they say, is updated hourly based on sales) and you'll see that you can go into separate charts for hardback, paperback and Kindle, where you'll find a mix of trade-published and self-published books. From that page, you can then go into different genres to look at the list toppers for each genre.

Analyse a bestseller

If you find studying the charts useful, once you have decided on your idea and the genre you will write in, find a book in a similar genre to yours and unpick it to find out what it gets right, as well as analysing the marketing campaign that got it into the charts.

1   How is the book described?
2   What distinguishes the cover from others in the same genre?
3   What is the author's backstory?
4   Is it clear from the cover and blurb what genre the book is in?
5   Can you work out the book's target readership by looking at reviews and recommendation sites such as Goodreads?

Can we predict what will sell?

Generally, it is thought that it is not possible to write a bestseller to order, although, as we have seen, bestsellers often share many of the same elements.

The publisher most associated with writing to a formula is arguably Mills & Boon. So many people attempt to write a novel for that imprint that the publisher produces guidance for authors, where they advise: 'Innovate, don't imitate!' Writers who think that just knocking out 50,000 words can create a Mills & Boon bestseller are in for a shock. Of the thousands of submissions each year only 0.5 per cent are published. There is no formula – only a format, as with all genre fiction, which allows room for creative expression, unique writing and memorable characters. So throw those clichés out of the window!'

While a formula remains elusive, the ingredients – or words – that give you the greatest chance of achieving a bestseller have been calculated. Computer scientists at Stony Brook University studied 800 books over eight subgenres. Using an algorithm, they were able to predict the success of each title. These predictions were then compared with the actual success of each title. They found that:

- successful books tended to feature more nouns and adjectives, as well as a disproportionate use of the words 'and' and 'but', when compared with less successful titles
- the most popular books also featured more verbs relating to 'thought-processing' such as 'recognized' and 'remembered'
- less successful books featured topical, cliché words and phrases such as 'love', as well as negative and extreme words including 'breathless' and 'risk'
- books that sold poorly also favoured the use of 'explicitly descriptive verbs of actions and emotions' such as 'wanted', 'took', 'promised' 'cried' and 'cheered'. Books that made explicit reference to body parts also scored poorly. (That last point seems a little at odds with the popularity of erotic fiction, say, but we'll leave you to look at the full study for yourself.)

Key idea

Read more about this study at: http://www.dailymail.co.uk/sciencetech/article-2538517/Want-write-bestseller-Avoid-talking-body-parts-emotions-negativity-include-plenty-quotes.html#ixzz32jG3F5zW

Perhaps there is a formulaic route to a bestseller: could it be done by figuring out what people are buying, and combining this knowledge with the bestselling words spat out by Stony Brook's algorithm? Just when it seems within our grasp, however, there's another obstacle to overcome: it takes time to write a book, so unless you are speedy or assemble a writing team, by the time you write to your formula, the market may have moved on.

Publishing is a subjective business and it is also a victim of fashion, meaning that genres can go in and out of vogue. It is hard to pinpoint exactly why and when audience tastes change, but it is clear that they do. In terms of what is published, shifts can occur because there is (or is not) an editor to champion a particular genre. At other times, a genre can enjoy a renaissance, whether driven by one successful title that is swiftly followed by copycat titles riding on its coat tails, or by an editor with a passion and the imagination to publish something new. And, of course, the likes of the *Harry Potter* and *Fifty Shades of Grey* series have led, respectively, to the emergence of a whole new young adult genre and the resurgence of erotic fiction. When a genre does particularly well in the charts, agents see a surge of manuscripts submitted in those genres. And whatever they may say about the flood of submissions, for a time agents and editors will be looking for new authors in that genre in order to cut in on the bestselling action. When readers are wild about a book, they want to read more of the same, and publishers are happy to feed that appetite.

In publishing houses there's often much eye rolling at editorial meetings when a 'me too' title is presented but, eye rolling aside, a really good one may find a home. This is when timing is crucial. When a topic is hot, publishers need a fine sense of whether a genre is on the rise or in decline and to make a judgement call as to what the market will want in a year's time. Any book they commission can take a year or more to publish from acquisition. Digital or self-publishers can react more speedily and publish a digital 'me-too' title instantly and so it's less risky. Trade publishers have lost sales to self-publishing – broadly speaking because of the growth in digital and their speed to market – and many have reacted by launching digital-only imprints to take back market share.

 ## Key idea

Authors who don't write for the market but for their own interest are in a strong position to act when a particular genre becomes fashionable, because they are poised and ready to pitch their project at the opportune time.

If you really want to write for the market, then do your research and write, edit and publish fast. At London Writers' Club Live, our guest agent speakers often say they are looking for a new writer in a bestselling genre, but they are just as likely to say, and are more enthusiastic about, finding writers who sound unlike anybody else – who have an 'exciting and compelling new voice'. Your task is to write a story that gives people a reason to buy into you and your books, starting with the agent, then the publisher and, ultimately, the reader – you have to give them good reason to choose your book from all the others out there. You have to do everything you can to create confidence in your writing and in you as an author.

Andrew Crofts, ghostwriter

'Bestsellers come from giving something of real value. This need not necessarily mean your book has to be of literary merit, or even morally or politically correct. Whatever your view on it, even Fifty Shades *ticked this box, by acknowledging and covering a topic that women hadn't seen before in women's fiction.'*

What not to do

An important part of any undertaking is to remember that it is roughly two-thirds avoiding mistakes and one-third doing something right. This approach can help with both your writing and your publishing. Key mistakes to avoid, any of which can crush your chances of writing a bestseller, include the following:

1 Obsessing about perfect prose, thinking that's the key to writing a bestseller
2 Paralysis/waiting for an original idea, or waiting for inspiration to strike before you start writing
3 A weak story
4 Implausible characters
5 Poor editing
6 Use of cliché
7 Writing to an obvious formula
8 Sending your book to the wrong agent
9 A poor pitch package
10 Neglecting marketing and PR
11 Neglecting the reader.

THE TEN CHARACTERISTICS OF A BESTSELLER

1 **A bestseller 'knows' what it is and for whom it is written.**

It knows its audience. It is clear what the story is really about and conveys that clearly to the reader. It is written for an identifiable audience and genre, so making itself more easily discoverable.

2 **Bestsellers have a good backstory.**

This creates authenticity around a novel, as well as providing ready-made hooks and angles for publicity. It is also the why and the how of the book's creation, which readers are invariably fascinated by.

3 **Bestsellers either present a unique concept or a fresh spin on an old subject.**

The material is unique in some way; or, if not, it shows how it is demonstrably different from the competition. So, if, for example, it is important to the subject matter to be timely or contemporary, then it captures the Zeitgeist at just the right time. If it covers an old subject, the writing casts fresh new light that dazzles with its cleverness, or has such a clear stamp of a winning approach that everyone wonders why no one thought of it before.

4 **Bestsellers contain good enough writing.**

Bestsellers are well written: they're readable, not necessarily literary masterpieces, but written well enough to keep readers turning the pages. And, more often than not, they will have been improved through feedback and professional editing.

5 **Bestsellers have a strong and clear voice.**

They can be loud or quiet but they're distinctive and sound unlike any other writer. They're not dulled or swamped by being stuffed with every thought, opinion and idea the author has. If there is a cathartic aspect to the writing they make it work, taking Hemingway's advice to 'write hard and clear about what hurts'.

6 **Bestsellers engage with their readers to create powerful word of mouth.**

They speak to the reader by telling a story that readers will care about and enjoy enough to invest their money and time in it, and afterwards their energy in telling others about it.

7 **Bestsellers have impactful covers.**

Bestselling authors know that their cover is a key marketing tool that can create a winning first impression. They have covers that adhere to genre conventions and don't mislead the reader by having an off-genre cover.

8 **Bestsellers can grow out of being part of a series.**

Each book in a series helps to sell another. Publicity and marketing yield more return for effort because they benefit multiple books rather than a single one.

9 **Bestselling authors use brand and platform to make their book visible.**

They understand that visibility is everything and they work hard to build it. And they're switched on to the value of genuinely and effectively engaging with readers.

10 **Bestselling authors have bold and energetic marketing plans.**

Whether trade or self-published, bestselling authors market their books with gusto, and are guided by a clear PR and marketing plan. What's more, they start doing so well in advance of the publication date, and they keep on going well after it. They also measure and monitor what works and what doesn't for every book's campaign.

Focus point

In this chapter we covered what vital characteristics make a bestseller, to guide your action plan for taking the first steps towards writing one and achieving your own bestseller. In the coming chapters, we'll look at key decisions and get you ready to write, enabling you to:

1 Know the genre you are writing in

2 Learn the basic techniques of writing a bestseller

3 Have a clear sense of your story

4 Plot and plan your bestseller

5 Blast out the first draft

6 Get and act on feedback to refine your manuscript.

7 Be prepared to identify your weaknesses as a writer and work on them

8 Decide on the best format and route to market

9 Understand that writing is a business like any other, and it is a rare writer who achieves a bestseller without hard work

10 Be willing to get out and promote your book

11 Be patient and persevere.

Where to next?

The next chapter examines the next vital step in the quest for a bestseller: an understanding of the importance of genre.

2

Understanding genre

How many books will you read this month? This year? How about in the next decade?

There are only a finite number of books that we can get through in a lifetime. With millions of different titles stocked and available for purchase at any one moment, we have more choice than we can handle. As readers, we need to narrow down our options. We often do this by looking within our preferred genres.

In this chapter you'll learn how genre conventions can help readers, booksellers, publishers and authors; that the most popular genres change over time; and that changes can open up new markets. In light of this, you'll consider how you might change the genre profile of your own work in progress.

Why is genre important?

For the reader, genre fiction tells them what they can expect from a book. It makes it easier for them to find, to trust it will match their expectation, and so to purchase a book if they think they know what they're getting.

As the majority of books are now bought via online searching, writing to genre is increasingly important in the quest to write and publish a bestseller. Readers can not only search directly for their chosen genre but also refine their search to find subgenres of the genre.

Readers will look within specific genres to find the kind of books they like to read, and publishers use readers' understanding of genre to market their books to appreciative audiences. Bestsellers are books that have found a large appreciative audience, and a writer who hopes to create a bestseller needs to know how to handle genre.

A bestselling genre title draws writers to it, inspiring an 'I can do that too' reaction. It's often the extreme success of a particular book that motivates a non-writer to start writing in the first place, or that influences a writer in his or her choice of subject matter.

Genres are book categories. The categories are known by names such as 'romance' or 'thriller'. These names provide a shorthand description of the kind of book on offer, and provide a good indication of the story conventions followed within any particular book. The conventions within a genre often define key elements of the writing. For example, genre will influence the types of character and their relationships with one another, the events that unfold and a story's settings. Genre affects the tone of the writing and the language used. Genre conventions are applied to aspects of book design, such as the title, the cover art, and even the length of the story, not to mention the author's choice of name. It's unlikely that a browsing reader would mistake a romance on the shelf for a thriller, for instance. Genre fiction tends to be considered as distinct from literary fiction. In the twentieth century, some critics regarded literary fiction as good and worthy of merit and genre fiction as a poor alternative. Although this attitude can still be found, it's not helpful. Whether genre or literary, books are part of the entertainment industry and so have an important role in readers' lives. However, the overwhelming presence of genre fiction in bestseller lists seems to indicate that readers prefer it; literary fiction sales are consistently significantly lower.

Your genre

What's your favourite reading genre? For the purpose of this exercise, you can regard 'literary fiction' as a genre in its own right.

- Take some time now to write down the names of the books that you've read within the last six months to a year. Identify which of these books are from your favourite genre, and which are not. Does your recent reading support your choice of genre or does it suggest that your favourite genre has changed? If there's been a change, why has that happened?

- Write down the names of the five books published within the last ten years or so that you wish you'd written. Identify what it is about those books that you most admire. For example, in one book you may like the subject matter, in another the quality of the writing. Are these books within your preferred genre? If not, do they suggest an alternative genre for you to try?

- What's the genre of your recent writing, or your work in progress? Are you writing within your favourite reading genre? If not, do you have enough experience of the genre that you're writing in?

- Consider your writing strengths and weaknesses. If your writing is praised for its quiet restraint but you write action and adventure, make this a USP of your style while sticking to the conventions of the genre, or try shifting to a genre that suits your writing (as with the quiet intensity of the *Wallander* crime novels, for instance).

Don't worry if you can't quite identify your writing genre at the moment; there's more information about the various popular genres later in this chapter. Just pick one that feels close enough for now. You may have to wait until you've finished a complete first draft to identify exactly what you've written. And sometimes writers are so close to their story that they can't see the bigger picture – an agent or an editor may have a different opinion entirely about your book's classification. Some beginning writers think that they're writing literary fiction when they just haven't recognized their true genre yet; contemporary fiction may be a strong contender. Do try to write in a genre you have experience of from your own reading.

The bestselling genres

Based on Neilson BookScan data, the *Guardian* website detailed the top one hundred bestselling books in print format in the UK from January to mid-December 2013. (www.theguardian.com/books/2013/dec/27/bestselling-print-books-2013). The hundred books sold a total of over 17 million print copies. Just over a quarter of them were non-fiction, including the overall bestseller, *My Autobiography* by Alex Ferguson, with almost 650,000 copies sold. Number 100 on the bestseller list, the crime novel *11th Hour* by James Patterson, sold more than 104,000 copies – and it was one of six Patterson books on the list.

There were more individual children's titles on the list than any other classification. Of the 21 children's books, five were written by David Walliams, together netting him well over a million sales.

There were more than 20 different genres represented in the bestseller list. Of the hundred, only a handful can be regarded as literary fiction.

 ## What's selling?

Check out recent bestseller lists. With a few clicks, you can find out what's selling well right now on Amazon, both in general and in your genre. Covering all retailers in the UK and Ireland, the Nielson BookScan website gives top ten lists for the current month for all books – fiction, non-fiction and children's books. *The Bookseller* produces an overall Top 50 list every Friday as well as segmented charts for fiction and non-fiction. *The New York Times* website also carries weekly bestseller lists. A quick Internet search will take you to websites, such as the *Guardian*, carrying articles listing the previous year's bestselling books.

How well is your genre represented in the bestseller lists? Do you think there's a good market for the kind of books you want to write?

Defining genres and subgenres

There is no definitive list of genres. For example, some booksellers will link 'action and adventure' as one genre, and some will separate the two elements. And it's difficult to define the conventions for a particular genre. They evolve over time, following fashion and responding to social change; consider the significant differences between what's acceptable in the romance category now and what was acceptable a generation ago.

Conventions are usually built up tacitly, based on an unspoken understanding between writers, publishers and readers. Some publishers create submission guidelines that make the conventions explicit for their imprints, but these cannot necessarily be applied to the genre as a whole. Writers must find out for themselves the current conventions within their own genre.

Subgenres add another layer of complication. As more books are published within a given genre, trends may grow around certain topics, particular character types or specific milieus. If these trends attract readers and writers, they may crystallize into defined sub-categories of the genre, or subgenres. The most popular genres, such as crime, romance and science fiction, have many subgenres; at the time of writing, the Best Science Fiction Books website (bestsciencefictionbooks.com/) categorizes sci-fi books according to 55 different subgenres. Each subgenre has its own conventions; these can be very prescriptive and may even contradict the conventions of the overall genre. For example, while sci-fi stories are normally strictly based upon scientific possibilities, the steampunk subgenre can tolerate supernatural elements of the fantasy genre. And subgenres may have their own subgenres: there's a fae (fairy) subgenre of the paranormal romance subgenre of the romance genre.

However, it's worth remembering that, deeper into subgenres, books may have less appeal for the general reader. The market is smaller. To achieve bestseller status in niche subgenres, a writer needs to have many books on the market, whether they are stand-alone or series titles.

The list below contains some of the most popular genres of fiction and non-fiction. Each listing has:

- a short definition of the genre
- examples of bestselling authors
- a recent bestseller
- where to find out more
- some examples of its subgenres – there are many more and new ones pop up regularly.

ACTION AND ADVENTURE

Action and adventure can be regarded as a single genre, or may be divided into its two elements. The main characters face significant personal risk. In carrying out their mission or quest, characters in action stories are embroiled in exciting action sequences, whereas characters in adventure stories often journey to exotic locations.

- James Patterson, Tom Clancy, Clive Cussler
- *Inferno* by Dan Brown (Bantam)
- *How to Write Action-Adventure Novels* by Michael Newton (Classic Wisdom on Writing Series) is available on Kindle. It's somewhat elderly advice now, but still relevant. Try searching for action-adventure film-script advice and apply the same principles to fiction.
- Espionage, westerns, epics

BIOGRAPHY, AUTOBIOGRAPHY AND MEMOIR

As non-fiction books, biographical stories relate events from the subject's life. They aim to tell the truth. However, even autobiography and memoir – written by the subject – cannot be regarded as completely true, as they are filtered through the writer's awareness and memory. These life stories may be interpreted in a way that foregrounds elements from other genres, such as using a love story for the main structure, or a thriller.

- Martin Sixsmith, Walter Isaacson, Lucy Hughes-Hallett
- *My Life* by David Jason (Century)
- In *Write Fantastic Non-Fiction – and Get It Published* by Claire Gillman (Hodder Education), as well as information on how to get started, the craft of writing, and how to publish and market your work, there's a chapter on 'Writing personal histories' which covers biography, memoir and family history. See also *Write Your Life Story and Get It Published* by Ann Gawthorpe (Hodder Education).
- Tragic life story ('misery memoir'), crime, historical

CHILDREN'S

Children's fiction and non-fiction books are appropriate to the age category, usually regarded as up to 12 years. They reflect children's level of reading development and their interests, with the genre being subdivided in narrower age categories (such as babies' picture books) as well as subject categories. A strong convention is that the main character in children's fiction is slightly older than the target reader. Most genres for adults also have children's versions.

- J.K. Rowling, Michael Rosen, Julia Donaldson
- *Demon Dentist* by David Walliams (HarperCollins Children's Books)

- *Children's Writers' and Artists' Yearbook* (A & C Black), published annually, is an excellent source of information, including many articles about writing within this category and professional contact details.
- Children's comedy, espionage, historical

CONTEMPORARY FICTION

This is an extremely broad category, covering fiction set in the modern day (traditionally regarded as after the Second World War, but there are suggestions that more than ten years before writing is more appropriate) or in the deliberately undefined 'eternal present'. The genre accommodates stories that do not fulfil the criteria for other genres. A significant sub-category is women's fiction: stories featuring strong female characters that focus on relationships with lovers, families or friends.

- Jodi Picoult, Yann Martel, Khaled Hosseini
- *The Hundred-year-old Man Who Climbed Out the Window and Disappeared* by Jonas Jonasson (Hesperus Press)
- This is such a wide genre that it's impossible to find specific advice. Try individual authors' websites for information.
- Urban fiction, hen lit (more mature version of chick lit), coming-of-age

CRIME

The plot is driven by a crime that has been or is being committed. The story may be told from the point of view of the criminal, concerned with the successful execution of the crime. More frequently, the focus is on a character acting as a detective, finding out who is responsible for the crime and bringing them to justice. Conventions include protagonists who use their superior observational skills and logic to either commit or solve the crimes, multiple suspects, misleading 'clues', plot twists, and real clues hidden throughout the story. The story may extend into the legal process. Stories often end with justice being delivered, either by the legal establishment or by other means. There's often significant overlap with other genres, such as thriller, suspense and mystery; these are sometimes regarded as subgenres of crime fiction.

- Jo Nesbø, Tess Gerritsen, Ian Rankin
- *Criminal* by Karin Slaughter (Arrow)
- The website of the venerable Crime Writers' Association (www.thecwa.co.uk) has information about their famous

Dagger Awards and news of recent publications. The Crime Readers' Association (www.thecra.co.uk) was set up by CWA members in 2012. Its website has an informative blog and details of author events.

- Legal, historical, police procedural

EROTIC FICTION

Plots in erotic fiction are driven by and concentrate on sexual behaviour. These books have explicit sexual content and often use frank language. There are erotic versions of the other genres, such as erotic thriller. Conventions are very specific to each subgenre: the sexual behaviour driving a story in one subgenre may run counter to the conventions in another. For example, in erotic romance, convention dictates that characters are not sexually active outside the central romantic relationship from the moment that the lovers meet, while other sub genres allow multiple sexual partners.

- Tiffany Reisz, Evie Blake, Sadie Matthews
- *Entwined with You*: a Crossfire Novel by Sylvia Day (Penguin)
- *Get Started in Writing Erotic Fiction* by Judith Watts and Mirren Baxter (Hodder Education) is a comprehensive introduction to the genre, with information for complete beginners and more experienced writers.
- Erotic romance, gay and lesbian, ménage

FANTASY

Fantasy fiction is often linked with science fiction; both deal with elements of story and setting not found in the real world. In fantasy fiction, these unreal aspects have supernatural causes. For example, mythical creatures may exist in fantasy worlds and magic is a common element of stories and settings. Traditional fantasy stories are often set in pre-industrial societies, but many contemporary fantasy bestsellers set myth and magic in the modern day.

- Neil Gaiman, Lauren Beukes, Terry Pratchett
- *Game of Thrones: A Song of Ice and Fire* by George R.R. Martin (Harper Voyager)
- The Science Fiction and Fantasy Writers of America is a professional organization for recognized authors. Its website (www.sfwa.org) has an up-to-date list of American publishers and magazines, and details of the famous Nebula Award.
- Urban fantasy, high fantasy, sword and sorcery

HISTORICAL FICTION AND NON-FICTION

Historical fiction can encompass many other genres, such as historical mystery. It traditionally covers books set in any time period before the end of the Second World War, but is now expanding to include post-war fiction that follows historical conventions. Conventions often have fictional characters involved with real historical characters and events. As a non-fiction genre, history books may investigate a particular period (for example the Russian Revolution or the events of 1665) or recount incidents in the life of real historical characters (such as a study of the Bloomsbury Group or Anne Boleyn).

History and historical fiction require thorough research so that the historical period can be accurately described. For example, the writer may wish to highlight comparisons with the present day in terms of clothing and architecture, social structures and attitudes, and language and the arts.

- Fiction: Bernard Cornwell, Philippa Gregory, C.J. Ransom; non-fiction: Max Hastings, Bill Bryson, Antonia Fraser
- Fiction: *Citadel* by Kate Mosse (Orion); non-fiction: *Vikings: Life and Legend* by Gareth Williams and Peter Pentz (British Museum Press)
- *Writing Historical Fiction: A Writers' and Artists' Companion* by Celia Brayfield and Duncan Sprott (Bloomsbury) includes an introduction to the fiction genre, links to resources and thoughts from many bestselling writers about working in the genre.
- Any specific time period, alternative history, military history

HORROR

Horror fiction is designed to frighten the reader; the thrill of being scared keeps readers turning the pages. Traditionally, horror convention said that the main character is threatened by supernatural or paranormal characters or events. The threat can be physical or psychological. In modern horror, the menace may be malevolent, but it does not have to be supernatural in origin. For example, Stephen King's *Cujo* (Hodder Paperbacks) is a rabid dog. Horror's key ingredient is suspense. Isolated, creepy settings lead the reader to expect that the worst will happen.

- Dean Koontz, Anne Rice, Susan Hill
- *Doctor Sleep* by Stephen King (Hodder & Stoughton)
- *On Writing Horror: A Handbook by the Horror Writers of America*, ed. Mort Castle (Writers' Digest) is packed with

articles by established horror fiction writers, covering all aspects of the craft. Look for the latest edition.

- Ghosts, gothic horror, zombies

HUMOUR

If horror writers seek to scare the readers, humour writers are trying to amuse them. Again, humour is a genre that can encompass many others, both in fiction and non-fiction (for example humorous essays by writers such as Charlie Brooker). Humour tends to be based on exaggeration, for example of situations, characters and their behaviour, or mannerisms and attitudes.

- David Sedaris, Jenny Colgan, Christopher Brookmyre
- *Bridget Jones: Mad About the Boy* by Helen Fielding (Jonathan Cape)
- *The Secrets to Writing Great Comedy* by Lesley Brown (Hodder Education) takes writers step by step from comedy basics, through an analysis of humour, to generating, publishing and performing their own work.
- Romantic comedy, parody, satire

LITERARY FICTION

If you favour literary fiction, you were asked to regard it as its own genre for the purpose of the exercises in this chapter. Literary fiction may have subject matter that can be found in the other genres, but the key difference is in the way the stories are delivered. It tends to be more serious (intellectually challenging, fewer conventionally happy endings), concentrating on complex characters rather than plot, and it is often written using more stylized, eloquent language. Compared with genre fiction, its less of an 'easy read'. There are no conventions that must be observed, and radical innovation is accepted. It can be difficult to find points of similarity between radically different bestsellers.

- Kazuo Ishiguro, Siri Hustvedt, Jim Crace
- *Bring Up the Bodies* by Hilary Mantel (Fourth Estate)
- As with contemporary fiction, this is such a wide genre that it's impossible to find specific advice. Try individual authors' websites for information.
- Sub-categories include century of publication, geographical area and culture

MYSTERY

Part of the same stable as crime fiction, mystery is often regarded as one of crime's subgenres and it shares many of crime's conventions. Mystery stories are concerned with discovering who or what is behind perplexing events, often events that initially seem unconnected. A significant piece of information or a leap of logic is required to finally solve the puzzle. The solution may be related to criminal activity, to other causes such as the supernatural, or to anything that the 'detective' doesn't yet understand (an example is Mark Haddon's *The Curious Incident of the Dog in the Night-time*, published by Vintage). By its nature, the main storyline of a mystery is usually told from the point of view of the 'detective', keeping the explanation back from the reader for as long as possible.

- Lee Child, Harlan Coben, Anne Cleeves
- *Standing in Another Man's Grave* by Ian Rankin (Orion)
- The Mystery Writers of America website (https://mysterywriters. org) has a list of approved publishers and periodicals, and information about mystery and crime-fiction-related competitions, news and awards. There's a lively forum for members.
- Paranormal mystery, murder mystery, historical mystery

NARRATIVE NON-FICTION

In narrative non-fiction, factual events and topics are treated as though they were stories. For example, plot, setting and characters are fully realized in scenes, with a creative invention employed when factual details are not available. The narrative voice is usually not neutral (in contrast with, for example, journalism), but represents a character within the 'story' or a specific point of view about the events.

- Edmund de Waal, Katherine Boo, Duncan Barrett and Nuala Calvi
- *A Street Cat Named Bob: How One Man and His Cat Found Hope on the Streets* by James Bowen (Hodder)
- *Telling True Stories: Navigating the challenges of writing narrative non-fiction* by Matthew Ricketson (Allen & Unwin) considers the ways that novelistic technique can be brought to non-fiction subjects to communicate them effectively to a wider audience. Claire Gillman's book (see under Biography, above) has a chapter on 'Writing creative non-fiction'.
- Biographical fiction, travel writing, true crime

ROMANCE

There are three strong conventions within romantic fiction. First of all, a love story unfolds in a romantic way. Second, the love story is central; the book is about love rather than something else with a secondary love story. Finally, the story ends on a positive note with a Happy Ever After or Happy For Now.

- Nora Roberts, Nicholas Sparks, Stephanie Meyer
- *Me before You* by Jojo Moyes (Michael Joseph)
- The Romance Writers of America (www.rwa.org) is an active professional body. Its website includes fascinating information about the industry, including sales and bestseller statistics, information about readers and impressive author listings.
- Paranormal romance, gay and lesbian romance, Christian/ religious romance

SCIENCE FICTION

Science fiction is set in future or alternative worlds. Authors develop present-day scientific knowledge or theories beyond levels that are currently achievable, and then consider the implications of those developments. For example, the achievement of interstellar travel may facilitate encounters with alien species. Subgenres handle the development and explanation of the relevant scientific knowledge in different ways. In hard science fiction, for instance, technological developments are firmly rooted in scientific fact and explained in detail, whereas fantasy fiction deals with supernatural rather than natural phenomena.

- Margaret Atwood, Neal Stephenson, Ian M. Banks
- *Wool* by Hugh Howey (Arrow)
- See under Fantasy above. See also *Writing Fantasy & Science Fiction: How to Create Uut-of-this-world Novels and Short stories*, second edition, by Orson Scott Card (Writer's Digest), a very readable introduction to the genre by a successful writer. This book is largely a reissue of two older titles with some extra material.
- Apocalyptic, first contact, steampunk

THRILLER

In thrillers, the thrills are generated by giving the reader plenty to worry about. The story's hero is usually pitted against a significantly more powerful enemy, and faces considerable personal danger in opposing the enemy's plans. Thrillers use suspense techniques in the run-up to exciting action sequences. Storylines are often complex, involving red herrings, plot twists, hidden motivations and limited timeframes – heroes are driven hard and must use their ingenuity to win.

- John Grisham, Robert Ludlum, Lynda La Plante
- *Gone Girl* by Gillian Flynn (Phoenix)
- *Write a Bestselling Thriller* by Matthew Branton (Hodder Education) is a comprehensive introduction, particularly in relation to plot and characterization.
- Assassination, legal thriller, psychological thriller

YOUNG ADULT (YA)

Another age categorization, YA is generally considered to be books for readers from age 13 onwards. The genre focuses on adolescent characters facing teenagers' concerns: self-discovery and finding their own way in the world. Most other genres can have YA titles. YA books that find popularity with adult readers and subsequently become bestsellers are known as 'crossover' titles; these can be particularly lucrative for publishing houses.

- Suzanne Collins, Veronica Roth, Philip Pullman
- *The Fault in our Stars* by John Green (Penguin)
- The annual *Children's Writers' and Artists' Yearbook* (A & C Black) includes articles and information on writing for teenagers and the YA market.
- High school, YA romance, YA fantasy

OTHER GENRES

There are many other genres, generally less well known or popular than those listed above, and therefore less likely to spawn a bestseller. These include:

- Christian fiction – stories that reflect Christian values
- Western – set in the American Wild West
- sports fiction
- metaphysical and visionary fiction – fables and parables that address the problems of modern living and include an element of spirituality and often self-help
- graphic novel – illustrations are used to tell the story, a technique familiar from traditional comics.

Finally, a new classification that's proving very popular indeed is the New Adult category. This is an age classification, like YA and Children's, and it refers to stories about characters who are considered legally adult, starting from the late teens to mid 20s. All genres can be represented in this classification. Common themes are establishing independence, life after education and developing sexual self-awareness. *Fifty Shades of Grey* is the outstanding example of a book featuring a lead character in this age range.

Genre must-read

What books would you insist that a writer new to your genre should have read? Is there anything you ought to read?

Workshop: master your genre

To master your genre, make a list of ten best- or high-selling books that were first published up to one year ago in your genre and, preferably, in your subgenre. Don't include more than one book from a series. Do include at least two successful books that you wouldn't normally choose to read. Buy or borrow all the books on your list. There's a good chance that you'll already be familiar with some of the ten books. Read any that are new to you.

Now analyse each book:

Consider the physical aspects of the book.
- Cover – title, author's name, artwork, blurb
- Book length, chapter length, chapter titles
- Publisher and imprint

Consider the content.
- Settings – geographical, time period and timespan
- Characters – sex, age, background, aspirations
- Major plot events
- Writing style – sentence length, scene length, paragraph length, word length, tone (e.g. formal, popular)
- Pacing
- Anything else that's specific to the genre (e.g. use of technology, use of magic)

> What factors do the books have in common, and where do they differ? This exercise may be very difficult if your 'genre' is literary fiction.
>
> What does your analysis say about current trends within your (sub-)genre?

The workshop exercise asks you to look at the last year's bestsellers because conventions change. Writers must know their genre as it stands today. Readers are sophisticated; they will spot anachronisms. So while books from the distant past may have influenced you as a writer, there's no point in observing out-of-date conventions in a book that's looking for publication and success in today's market.

OTHER RESOURCES

The Writers' Digest website (www.writersdigest.com) has a library of articles including genre-specific advice.

Goodreads website (www.goodreads.com) can be searched by genre for recommendations for further reading, and identifies currently popular books within each genre.

Writing within genre

Genre can lend an appropriate structure to a book. For example, romance stories normally end with an HEA – the Happy Ever After – so the events of the story drive the characters to that point. It's much easier to write towards a fixed, known point in a story than to have to decide between the limitless possibilities of the blank page.

In romantic fiction, miss out the HEA, or the increasingly popular Happy For Now, and the author loses the goodwill of the reader. Lose the reader's goodwill, and they've lost future sales to that reader and to anyone who'll be influenced by her online review. Consistently bestselling authors are playing the long game, bringing their loyal readers along with them every time.

So is all genre writing the same? If you've completed the workshop exercise above on mastering your genre, you'll know the answer to that. Different writers have different takes on the genre. They show their mastery of the genre by playing up some elements and playing down others, and by introducing new elements. They have their own world-view, their own obsessions and their own voice. While there may be conventions and submission guidelines, formulaic work is unlikely ever to achieve bestseller status.

Publishing within genre

Publishers package, design and price books according to the genre within which they will sit. The style of cover is as important as the style of writing because it makes clear what the book's content will deliver. The content should deliver what it promises on the 'tin'.

A classic error in pitching is to present yourself to agents and publishers as flexible and writing across a number of genres. Agents often see letters from authors explaining 'I'm writing a YA series but also have a crime novel in development and I've written a non-fiction book too.' There are times when an author can cleverly combine elements from several genres to produce an exceptional bestseller, but at this stage it is too much all at once and will probably backfire on you. Instead of viewing you as the multi-talented writer you may be, they will feel confused about how they can help you and how you see your career developing. It's also unlikely that they will represent all three types of book, which increases the chance that your pitch will be rejected.

Genre tribes

Genre readers can be committed fans of their favourite writers and publishers, and now they can easily seek out fellow readers around the world to share the love. The Internet has not only facilitated communication between readers, but also between readers and writers, and between readers and publishers. Authors and publishing houses have access to instant feedback on their products and potential readers see the same comments and reviews.

Aspiring writers are advised to find out where their genre tribe hangs out online, and to hang out there themselves. Find out what the real fans are saying, what they love and what they hate about current publications, what genre conventions they'd like to see more of or never encounter again. Sophisticated and knowledgeable readers are a valuable resource. And as readers themselves, genre writers can become part of the debate and get involved in shaping the future of their category.

To find out what the best website is for your genre, visit related message boards and ask around. You will be able to find sites that allow writers to post new work and seek opinions from other readers. For some genres, these websites are sources of new writing for publishers collecting work for anthologies.

Genre websites also carry information about conferences for people who share common interests in the genre. At conferences, topical issues are discussed, research is presented, and opportunities abound to get to know others face to face. Conferences allow professionals to sell to one another (for example, specialist editors meet writers; writers meet agents and publishers) and to introduce new authors to the most committed, most connected readers. They are prime networking opportunities.

Networks of published genre authors can be remarkably welcoming and supportive; they have a vested interest in raising the profile and scope of their genre or subgenre and so, by co-promoting and guest blogging, they introduce their readers to fellow authors' books. And because of the connections and common interests within genre tribes, there's often more scope for self-publishing writers to bring their work to the attention of potential readers.

Exceptional books

Publishing professionals have an awareness of the tides of publishing trends and they know, from tracking book sales, when a trend has peaked. However, stories abound about publishers repeatedly rejecting the next big thing when it lands on their desks. Although every writer and publisher may dream of delivering a massive international hit, it's impossible to predict which books are going to be game changers.

Exceptional books are bestsellers par excellence. They may come from a specific genre, but they appeal to the more general reader and, therefore, to a much wider market. This can be achieved by playing down aspects of the genre that would be unpalatable for new readers, and by mixing in elements from other genres to add a fresh, new take to the story. The bestselling *Gone Girl* by Gillian Flynn (Phoenix) combined the suspense and conventions of the thriller with the domestic setting of an unravelling marriage, a familiar aspect of contemporary fiction; and its literary fiction techniques, such as the unreliable narrator, generated critical acclaim. There's nothing new in this: it's regarded as clichéd to describe concepts as '[one thing] meets [another]', such as '*Pride and Prejudice* meets James Bond'. However, the principle of refreshing one genre by introducing elements of another is sound.

Three outstanding series of books have played a significant part in reshaping the genre market in recent years: J.K. Rowling's *Harry Potter* series, Dan Brown's Robert Langdon series, and E.L. James's

Fifty Shades of Grey series. These three series all consist of big books that combine the conventions of several genres. This powerful genre mix provided the underlying structure for great storytelling.

All three series have been criticized for the quality of their writing, but this didn't stop them from selling in their millions. And the big sales brought attention from those who didn't like what they read, or read about: these series generated controversy, and this raised their profiles even further.

THE *HARRY POTTER* SERIES

The commercial success of the *Harry Potter* series grew markedly over the ten years between the publication of the first and last books in 1997 and 2007. J.K. Rowling blended two popular genres by joining the boarding school subgenre of children's fiction with the sword-and-sorcery subgenre of fantasy fiction. Adding to this mix, the books also have storylines that carry elements of crime, thriller, mystery, action and adventure, and even romance genres. The books became longer and more mature in tone as the series progressed, allowing Rowling to take child readers into their YA years, and capturing many adult fans along the way, making them perfect examples of crossover fiction - appealing to all age groups. The series led to a resurgence of the fantasy market.

THE *ROBERT LANGDON* SERIES

The Da Vinci Code, the second book in Dan Brown's series, was a runaway success in 2003. The book is a thriller with elements of murder mystery, detective fiction, action and adventure, a hefty dose of conspiracy theory, consideration of religious cults and a dash of the supernatural. Brown adds a touch of narrative non-fiction by claiming in the text that certain aspects of the story are true (these claims are contested).

THE *FIFTY SHADES OF GREY* SERIES

E.L. James originally wrote the *Fifty* books as fan fiction based on the two lead characters in Stephanie Meyer's *Twilight* series. The books combine romantic conventions (particularly in the characterization of the virginal young woman and the handsome, slightly older businessman) with erotic fiction conventions (the BDSM (bondage/discipline, dominance/submission and sadism/masochism) plotline) and contemporary fiction or commercial women's fiction conventions (the luxury settings, expensive gifts, flash cars and helicopters). Tempering the kinky sex content by mixing it with true love and capitalism made *Fifty Shades of Grey* the fastest selling paperback of all time, and introduced millions of readers worldwide to the erotic fiction genre.

Key idea

Exceptional books provide a shot of adrenalin to the market. They are followed by similar books, launched to take advantage of the new trend, and so the genre is revitalized, or a completely new subgenre is created.

Game changers

For good or ill, what books were the game changers in your genre? Exactly what made them different from the rest of the pack? And what conventions did they retain?

Workshop: genre bending

From your list of books in the workshop exercise above on mastering your genre, identify the three books within the same subgenre that you know best.

- Taking each in turn, consider how each author handles the following in comparison with the conventions of the subgenre: settings, characters, major plot events, writing style, pacing, anything else that's specific to the genre.
- Do the authors follow conventions exactly, or play down or eliminate certain conventions, or expand or make more of other conventions? Do they introduce aspects from other genres or subgenres? How effective are those decisions? For example, do you feel let down as a reader or do you appreciate the innovations? Is there anything you think they could have done differently?
- Now consider your own work in progress or recent writing within that subgenre in the same way. Have you met loyal readers' expectations? Have you played down aspects that would be too challenging for general readers? Have you played up more popular aspects?

- Look at each of the genres listed above in turn. What elements could you take from them to lift your work to a different level? For example, if you're writing a thriller, are there any aspects of YA fiction that could open out your story to a wider audience? You may want to bend your genre like this, or you may be more of a traditionalist.
- Which genre have you never read from? Buy a book from that genre and read it. What can you use from that genre in your own writing?
- If you were starting from scratch, what combination of genres would interest you as a writer?

Should a writer seeking a bestseller simply chase the hot trend? If it's in your subgenre, go for it. But be aware of the time lag in traditional publishing. A book may take a year or so to write, and a final draft may be submitted many months before it is printed and launched. Books arriving on the shelves now may have been commissioned a couple of years ago. Since then, things have moved on, and new trendsetters are being sought, commissioned and written all the time.

If it's not in your subgenre, do you have enough time to become fluent in the unwritten rules? Can you generate a passion for that genre that will come through in your writing? Readers can tell if writers are faking it.

The Bad _____ Award

Substitute your own genre for the blank in the title above, e.g. The Bad Thriller Award.

What constitutes bad writing in your genre? Make a list of major award categories.

Who would be the nominees for each category? Who would be this year's winners? Name and shame the authors who commit crimes against your genre.

It's unlikely that any of your guilty authors ever set out to win the Bad _____ Award. How can you guard against making the same mistakes?

Focus point

Genre classifications describe the contents of books. Genre helps readers to discover the next great story. For the publisher and bookseller, genre focuses marketing and sales efforts. For writers, genres provide structure to their writing and willing audiences. All parties know what to expect; there are fewer disappointments when readers hand over their hard-earned cash and invest their leisure time. It's a massive, international, multi-billion pound market.

It is certainly possible to build a genre book that, with luck at the publishing and marketing stages, could be a bestseller. From the exercises in this chapter, you'll have gained some ideas about the strength of your knowledge of your chosen genre, and about the ways in which your writing can be tweaked to meet and exceed genre expectations.

Where to next?

The next chapter looks at the writing knowledge and skills needed to execute your idea. You'll decide which idea to develop and you'll also make some other key writing decisions; and then you'll get ready to write.

3

Getting ready to write

This chapter covers some of the essential ingredients of bestsellers – things that the paying, reading public expects. And it mentions the one thing that, strangely, the reading public doesn't seem to mind too much about.

Putting it all together, creating a lengthy piece of writing out of your own thoughts is a thrilling challenge. I've separated out the elements here but, in the creative process, these elements can be addressed in any order, sometimes more than one at a time, and you can revisit them as your work progresses.

Everyone can learn to be a better writer. There's a lot to cover in this chapter, and as there are shelves of books available for every topic that we touch on, this chapter is just an introduction to the key points.

An original voice

Agents and publishers often say they are looking for an original, new voice. Some author's works are distinctively theirs. They have developed a tone and style of writing, often addressing a typical subject matter that makes their books instantly recognizable. Many bestsellers have achieved this: Dan Brown's novels are unmistakable, as are Helen Fielding's, Terry Pratchett's and Hilary Mantel's.

It's interesting to take apart a piece of a favourite author's writing, to analyse their voice and work out how they do it. Is it to do with the imagery they use, or with sentence structure? Is it about patterns of thought or their vocabulary? Have they mastered dialogue, using it in a distinctive way?

Beginners and more experienced writers alike can try a variety of genres and subjects to find out what best suits. When it is right, ideas start to flow and the writing begins to fall into place. However, copying the style and mannerisms adopted by established writers in their new genre won't help them develop an original voice.

Here are some tips for developing your unique voice:

- Start from the way you speak. Try to sound as natural on paper as you do in conversation. Don't pretend to be someone you're not – you'll make mistakes.
- Identify aspects of writing that you enjoy and that you'd like to do well, and consciously go about improving your skills in those areas.
- Analyse the techniques of the bestselling authors and learn from them.
- Avoid genre clichés in tone, style and vocabulary.
- Practise. The more you write, the more natural and effortless your voice will become. Be patient.

What to write

When people advise you to 'write about what you know', what they really mean is write as yourself, and don't force yourself to write something that feels unnatural just because you're trying to write for the market.

At this point, you should know which genre you are writing in and the conventions of that genre as well as be reading in that genre. It's not impossible but much more of an uphill climb to write in a genre with which you are entirely unfamiliar. Writing a bestseller has enough challenges without adding to the load.

Aim for a bestseller if you can do so authentically and convincingly. Write the book that you are best placed to write and that can be written only by you, now. It should be bursting out of you. You should be filled with enthusiasm about your idea and desperate to put it into practice. Aside from the writing, you need an idea you love enough to sustain you through the publishing and marketing process too.

Sometimes this happens for you immediately, only to flag later. For other authors it might not happen right away; instead, there's a slow build as the idea grows, but it does need to happen somewhere in the process. This variation is all perfectly natural; it is part of the writing process, so don't worry too much – we will cover this, along with concrete tips for managing it, throughout this book.

Let's take some time to maximize your chances of hitting upon a story you really care about. If you love your book there's a greater chance that readers will too.

What do you really care about?

Your idea could spring from a solution to a problem, something that annoys or amazes you, or from eavesdropping. Write down your answers to the following questions:

- What are the big themes and questions in your life, things that matter to you and perhaps have always mattered to you?
- What is it that intrigues you? How could you explore that in a novel?
- What would happen if your favourite literary character were alive today?
- Write down each and every one of your ideas, no matter how crazy or improbable.
- Now look at what you have written. What stands out from this as what really matters to you, enough to want to write about it over the course of a year?

Make sure you are committing to a project that stands a good chance of keeping your interest and energy levels up. It's your book and nobody else's, so you need to love it and be willing to pour that passion into telling your story.

Bestselling inspiration – how to find yours

 Anais Nïn

'My ideas usually come not at my desk writing but in the midst of living.'

A bestselling idea can start in so many different ways: a voice in your head, an opinion, a character or setting, a chance encounter, a great passion, a 'what if' or an 'if only'. The skill is in watching, listening and feeling so that when a great idea comes along, you'll be ready to catch hold of it and make something of it.

How you find your inspiration for the story you'll turn into a book is as individual as your novel will be. It can be an extraordinary event that throws up an idea or it could be something you notice in everyday life. You might already have an idea and are keen to start, or you might still be waiting for that light-bulb moment.

Author of *The Slap*, Christos Tsiolkas, has his mother to thank for the inspiration for his bestseller.

 Christos Tsiolkas, author

'While Mum was cooking up a storm in the kitchen there was a three-year-old boy getting in her way, ignoring her pleas for him to stop opening cupboards, banging pots and pans. At one point she gave him a very light tap on the bottom and he turned around, hands on his hips, and said to her: "No one has the right to touch my body without my permission."

It was not a dramatic or difficult moment – we were all laughing and Mum hugged the boy – but on the way home I kept thinking about the look of shock on the toddler's face and his mother's astonishment at his retort. I realized that by examining and writing about that mutual incomprehension I had the beginning of a novel.'

When inspiration hits like this there is nothing like it and the writing seems to pour out as if by magic, as Tsiolkas's experience bears out:

'I had been handed a gift. I started writing and it felt like flying; it felt as though I was writing a novel in brilliant daylight.'

DREAMTIME

For some writers, dreamtime is a vital component of the writing process – it's the time when you are not at your desk but still thinking about your writing. The beauty of doing other tasks while writing is that it gives your unconscious the chance to throw up an idea. Doing a boring task or even daydreaming becomes part of the writing process and this can work wonders for inspiration.

Neil Gaiman, author

'Inspiration comes from a bunch of places: desperation, deadlines … A lot of times ideas will turn up when you're doing something else. And, most of all, ideas come from confluence – they come from two things flowing together. They come, essentially, from daydreaming. Writers train themselves to notice when they've had an idea … writers don't have any more ideas than other people, it's just that they notice when an idea hits them. We [writers] don't really know where they come from and we are afraid they will go away.'

Neil Gaiman, author of bestselling book and film *Coraline*, is very modest but it's clear from looking at his output of short stories, novels, comic books, graphic novels, plays and films that he works incredibly hard. Hearing this from a successful writer is good news, because while it doesn't provide you with an easy step-by-step formula for writing a bestseller, it does mean that having a good idea and getting down to writing it is accessible and achievable for all.

We are endlessly fascinated with how writers and other creative people get their ideas. At any writers' event, that question is inevitably asked. Sometimes it's only by the unique combination or confluence of crazy ideas that we arrive at an idea that's truly unique. The next exercise may help: it is slightly outlandish but that's the point. If you are having trouble with which idea to go with, try flipping an ordinary idea or situation on its head.

Finding your inspiration: using 'what happens when'

Try Neil Gaiman's 'what happens when' exercise. 'We know what happens when a human is bitten by a werewolf but what happens when a wolf bites a goldfish?' (YouTube video, 'Where do you get your ideas from?', The Wheeler Centre, Sydney)

A bestselling example of 'what happens when' is Jane Fallon's *Getting Rid of Matthew*. There are numerous books about the protagonist striving to get her man but this is womens' fiction with a twist. The protagonist gets her man all right, but quickly realizes that it was a mistake and she doesn't want him, so she sets about reuniting him with his ex-wife as the simplest way of getting rid of him. It is the turning of a common quest on its head and coming up with a very different plotline that made this book stand out, enabling it to become a word-of-mouth bestseller.

(It no doubt gave the author's visibility a boost that she is Ricky Gervais' partner, but I purchased it on word-of-mouth recommendation and because of the strength of the concept and an assurance that it was written in a clever, page-turning way.)

Workshop: Sticky ideas

Once you have an idea of your own, how do you know whether it is good enough to craft into a compelling story? Let's have a play with your idea.

- Let the idea – and any characters that come from the idea – dance around inside your head for a few days to see if they become 'sticky', a description used by Marie Phillips, author of *Gods Behaving Badly*. Don't feel you have to write down your thoughts immediately; play around with them until they are ready to be told, demanding to be let out of your head and on to paper.
- Take time to notice what happens to your idea. Does it grow? Do more ideas, action, characters and plot development stick to the original idea? Take an hour now to sit down with the idea to see what happens when you make some notes about it.

- If it grows and continues to grow every time you spend time with the idea, then it's as good a sign as any that you might be on to a winner.
- Let your idea grow in your head; let it hang around with you – on the bus, at work, while you work. See what attaches to the idea. Is it growing? Do you get lost in it, to the point where you feel you are creating a world inhabited by people doing something out of the ordinary?
- Picture your character getting up in the morning, dressing, speaking. Imagine his or her opinions so that, as you write, you already have a strong sense of how they will react to any scene or action that you conjure up.
- If, on the other hand, it's not a sticky and you hit lots of dead ends, perhaps the idea won't grow or isn't ready yet and may not work for a book at the moment. Before you bin it altogether, though, remember that every idea arises for a reason, so try blogging or writing a short piece to see if anything further comes of it. Are you satisfied at the end of the blog that you've exhausted the idea, or do you still have more to say? Does the blog spark further ideas on the theme?
- If it is 'sticky' – still interesting to you – there's a good chance others might like it, too. Flesh out a one- or two-page outline of the idea. Put doubt aside. This is easier said than done, I know, but now is the time to give it a fair chance, unfettered by your inner critic.

Marie Phillips, author

'If one idea isn't sticking, try putting it together with another idea and see if they stick together. The Table of Less Valued Knights, my second novel, came from two different story ideas, neither of which fully came alive until I tried combining them.'

Throughout your inspiration phase, keep reading! Don't be afraid to look to other writers for inspiration – unless you find yourself in the habit of latching on to other authorial voices – though often looking at great writing produces a reaction. It sets off a spark. Remember that the books you read have been through many drafts, so it is important not to be put off by the seeming effortlessness of their writing and construction.

One of my favourite writers, Kate Grenville, author of *The Secret River,* says that the hardest thing about getting ideas 'is that little voice in your head that tells you all your ideas are no good.' She calls it 'the voice of doom'.

 ## Kate Grenville, author

'If you wait for it [the "voice of doom"] to go away, if you wait until you are happy with your ideas, you'll wait a lifetime and never get anything done. The thing to do is to go on writing in spite of the voice. It will fade and you will get your writing done.'

Having gone on to win the Orange Prize, Grenville knows what she is talking about.

 ## Start writing

If you still have doubts about the strength of your idea, try writing it as a short story; it may grow into a novel-length piece of work.

You could also try the process of free writing: Set your timer for an hour and just start writing and see what comes out; don't punctuate or think about what you're writing, just write.

The importance of story

A compelling story is where it all starts and ends. What is it, and why is it so important?

It all starts with the urge to write and the willingness to endure the bumps along the way. What pushes us on with steel and determination is a great idea for a story that you are burning to share, a story that you believe will resonate with others, too.

Story is everywhere, from the way we talk to our friends and children, in the lyrics of our favourite tunes, in ballet and opera, and it's there in a photograph, a painting, and more recently it has popped up in the branding of products. Even pulped fruit smoothies have a backstory; the success of brands such as Innocent could be put down to the story behind the brand. It's a cynical deployment of story, perhaps, but a successful one nevertheless, underlining the impact of a compelling narrative.

So why are we so obsessed with story? Why is it so important?

A good story, your story, is the thing that distinguishes your book from another. It is the heart of your work and what makes a person keep reading after the first page and want to keep on reading until the very end, at which point they are so engrossed that they are loath to step out of it and return to the real world. Your reader will keep on turning the pages if you make them care about your characters and how the story turns out. The reaction you want to elicit is 'Ooh, what happens next?'

The story needs to be clear and compelling enough to generate the kind of 'word-of-mouth sharing' that every bestseller needs. It is not always predictable, but when you get it right you can really get people talking. When Christos Tsiolkas's fourth novel, *The Slap*, was published, he achieved the result every novelist hopes for. He tapped into something universal that kicked off an amazing word-of-mouth buzz. For a while, everybody seemed to be talking about the same book. You felt left out of the conversation and compelled to buy a copy if you hadn't read it.

It really doesn't matter whether your book is idea-led as *The Slap* is, or character-led. What you need for a bestseller is one big story packed with meaning. It needn't be loud or brash or about extraordinary people. It could be an ordinary setting such as the country town in *Fargo*, where something out of the ordinary takes place. Or it could be an ordinary person doing an extraordinary thing, for instance pensioner Harold Fry who, without explanation, leaves his Devon home to post a letter to an ex-colleague, but walks past the postbox so he can deliver it by hand, hundreds of miles away in the North. We keep turning the pages to find out why he does it; and why it matters so much to him.

What is the journey that your story will take us on? Whose journey is it? What is their quest? What is it that really matters? What are they after? Is it love, honour, freedom or power and money? What is at stake? Are they running towards something or away from someone? Knowing the answers to these questions, and holding them carefully in your mind as you craft your tale, will help you tell a gripping story.

So, to sum up: a bestseller is based on a good idea, composed by an author who has sufficient writing skills to craft it into a good story. The oomph of that story helps do the hard work of letting readers know about your book by word of mouth and other forms of reader engagement. If you are looking for a neat formula that will guarantee you a bestseller, this is probably not what you want to hear. Focus instead on telling a good story; that's the first step on your route to a bestseller.

 ## Marie Phillips, author

'I think story is one of the hardest things to get right, and people often think (or desperately hope?) that they can do without it: they can't. The story doesn't have to be big, but it does need to move, even if only emotionally. Bestsellers are books in which you get lost utterly. They change your imaginative landscape so that you have to recommend them to everyone you know. It is impossible to imagine the world now without the writing of Lord of the Rings, Bridget Jones, *even* Fifty Shades. *There is only before and after.'*

Concept: being clear about your idea

What is concept-driven fiction and why does it have such strong appeal for agents, publishers and readers? There's no doubt that a great concept helps sell books. And in the current market it seems that a strong concept sells books more easily than fine writing.

HIGH CONCEPT

The term 'high concept' is more complicated. There are many different definitions around, and they don't always agree, but common themes are that a high concept is unique and can be summarized easily. Often, high concept relates not so much to the story itself as to the way the story is told.

 ## Key idea

When people in the publishing business say they want a high-concept novel, they mean that they're interested in ideas that can be captured in a title and perhaps a brief, pithy 'shoutline'. High concept is an idea that's crossed over from film but we now use it all the time in book publishing.

One example is the bestselling *One Day* by David Nicholls (Hodder, 2009), the story of a relationship told by revisiting the lovers on exactly the same day every year. Another is *Life After Life* by Kate Atkinson (Black Swan, 2014), which shows alternative parallel lives and deaths of one woman born in the early twentieth century. (The 1998 film *Sliding Doors,* starring Gwyneth Paltrow, is a similar high-concept idea, portraying the different courses one woman's life would take depending on the decisions she makes.)

Not all bestsellers need high concepts. There are plenty of high-selling books with 'low' concepts: you've heard similar stories before, and there's nothing unique about the way they are told. It can be difficult, however, to get a low-concept story across quickly in an enticing way; this will be familiar to anyone who has ever scrolled endlessly through on-demand film selections trying to find something worth watching.

High concept is not just about having a great idea: you also have to create something totally fresh and unique. It's an idea that you only have to tell someone about for it to immediately paint a picture in the listener's mind. A high-concept pitch (if it's working well) should do its job in an eye- or sound-bite – it should say everything there is to say about your idea and generate enthusiasm for your book. If the concept is strong enough, you'll find agents and editors willing to invest in your project and spend time editing your book to get it right. A high concept can be that much of a drawcard. Why? Because you make everyone's life easy. It's much less difficult to convince a publishing team to support a book if it's easy to explain – to the sales force, to booksellers and to readers. And it makes writing a compelling blurb a piece of cake.

Picture an editorial acquisitions meeting where the editor presents your book, seeking the support of the publishing team to make an offer for your book. At the table will be the accountant, the marketing director, the publicity director, the sales director, the digital person and the rights director, among others. If an editor can encapsulate the concept in a snappy one-liner, she can grab the attention and the support of everyone present. They'll get it – and your book's sales potential – immediately. The book is a no-brainer acquisition. What's more, the greater their confidence in your book and the easier they think it will be to sell to readers, the higher their anticipated sales forecast will be and the higher an advance they'll be able to offer you.

FINDING YOUR GREAT CONCEPT

The best concept for your book can be found, with a bit of work, in the subjects that fascinate you, that you need to work out for yourself, in the things that you'll keep writing about when the going is tough, in the one topic that you're certain the rest of the world needs to know more about.

How do you find your great concept? It might land in your imagination fully formed but, if not, it can certainly be built.

Write your one-sentence pitch

Writers who aspire to publication, and who are actively doing something about it, will find themselves, either online or in person, in the company of people who may be able to help. If someone asks you what your book is about, you need to have a good snappy answer.

So, what's your book about?

1. Write one sentence that summarizes the essentials by filling in the blanks: 'It's a [type of book] about a [character type], who [what she does] to [address the thing that's happened to turn her world upside down].'

2. Be sure to include any unique or unusual aspects. Rearrange the elements if needed.

3. Examples: 'It's a thriller about a police chief who fights to the death against the killer shark that's terrorizing his seaside community'; 'It's a fairytale about an unloved stepdaughter who receives magical gifts so that she can attend the royal ball.'

4. If you're dealing with a high concept, you may have to tweak the sentence structure until it adequately explains the big idea.

5. Once you've mastered the single sentence, try it out on some people. Are they interested in finding out more? In other words, does it promise a good story? Does it sound interesting to you?

6. If you're unhappy with your concept as it stands, make it better. Play with the character, plot, setting, or the way the story is told, challenging your first thoughts and changing details until you feel your interest return.

7. To practise this, incorporate your passion into the Cinderella story. If you're fascinated by prostitution in Victorian England, relocate it in time and milieu. If you're a tech nut, give Cinderella a lowly job at an Internet startup.

8   If you're still not happy with your concept, think about what it is you really want to write about! This is the time to invoke your passion. What do you need to write about, because no one else will do it justice? Build the topic that excites you into your concept.

Get the one-sentence pitch right and you may well save yourself time in the writing. If you know it works at this seed level and it is interesting to readers, then you can expand it using the three-act structure as a guide. Keep an eye on the plot and characters and, as it grows into a full-length novel, you increase your chances of keeping it readable.

Workshop: road-testing your bestselling idea

Since you are aiming for a commercial bestseller, it makes sense to test your idea on potential readers before you start to write. Imagine how it will boost your confidence to have a sense of its appeal before you get going, allowing you to tweak your idea to strengthen it and then lose yourself when you begin to write.

Try this with a writing buddy or mentor.

- Tell them about the top notes of your story, not the detail. Keep talking until you hear something that really grabs your attention.
- Listen out for something strong that stands out as the heart of the story that nobody else would tell in quite the same way. As you speak about your idea, you are likely to find yourself turning up some new ideas as your brain starts working in an entirely different way. There will always be something unique in your idea. It may be uncut and a little dull, yet showing promise. Keep working it until it begins to twinkle, right through to making it blindingly sparkly.
- Prime your listener to keep an ear out for the human and universal appeal of your story. It may reflect your experience or your unique view of something but when an idea really sings it's because it hits a familiar, very human note. It resonates with the listener and

reader. Your reader needn't have experienced the exact circumstances of your story themselves but the connection comes via the essential human elements of the story ... from the reactions, experiences and feelings of your characters.

- What makes a good story is also what makes a good speech. When you practise it, how does your audience react? Are they entertained or bored? Is there enough variation in your story to keep them interested? If you are reasonably good at speaking, try speaking your idea out loud, to see how it sounds.
- Are there elements of the unexpected or surprising, are there heartwarming or heartrending moments? Is your story informative, exploratory, revealing or instructive? Or is it one note?

Here are some questions that might help you in digging for your bestseller:

- Where do I take the reader?
- Where is my character when they pick up my book?
- What journey do I take them on?
- What do I want the reader to feel?
- What kind of experience am I promising (hinted at by the genre, title and cover) and what does my book deliver?
- If this were an event, how would it be billed?
- What would the top line be?
- What difference will it make to people's lives?
- How will it add to their understanding of people or the world?
- What subject matters enough to me that I want to write about it (and promote it) for the next two years?

 ## Summarize your idea

Write up your idea in summary form. Try to write it free-form, not too stiffly or trying too hard to get it perfect. Just write from the heart, in not too much detail; you just want to get to the simplest form of your idea, the very essence of it.

What makes a story commercial?

And what about the idea itself? In order for it to have mass, bestselling appeal, does the story have to be dumbed down?

Writing a book with mass appeal need not mean that it must be light or superficial. The proof of this is in the number of bestsellers of the past ten years that have tackled tough, and sometimes extremely sad, subject matter. They include *The Help, We Need to Talk about Kevin, The Curious Incident of the Dog in the Night-time* and *The Fault in Our Stars*.

In the past, commissioning editors often perceived these subjects as too tricky to publish. How and when did 'difficult' subjects such as disability and Alzheimer's and teenagers with cancer become the subject of bestsellers? It was when authors came along who could express the essential humanity in the story. If you write with humanity, authenticity, honesty, passion and engagement, you'll get a similar response to your writing from readers.

Further proof that a bestselling subject needn't be a 'popular' or soft one is Lisa Genova's, *Still Alice*, a book about a 50-year-old woman's desperate plan to cope with her rapid deterioration from Alzheimer's disease. It spent 41 weeks on the *New York Times* bestseller list, has won countless literary prizes and is a reading group favourite. There are over a million copies in print, translated into 25 languages.

There are three reasons why this story works commercially:

1 The way it is told

The story is unflinching and lacking in sentimentality but with a real human touch that allows us all to engage with the protagonist and her story. It was also written in a very accessible way.

2 Fit with the Zeitgeist

The chattering classes are aware of the rising number of cases of Alzheimer's and, with that, the likelihood that they have been or will be personally affected.

3 The author's expertise

Genova's background as a doctor of neuroscience adds another dimension to her writing: she travels the world, speaking about Alzheimer's disease, traumatic brain injury and autism.

You may not have a Ph.D. or career in your subject matter, but think about what drives you to write and what it is about your passions, interests and life that made you want to tell this story. You're devoting time and energy to this; why does it matter so much to you?

How well must I write?

If finding the perfect words to express what you want to say does not come easily to you, don't be alarmed. Writing is a craft and your style will evolve with time and practice. You don't have to come up with the modern-day equivalent of *War and Peace* to have a bestselling book – though you won't know what you're capable of until you get going. Many people say that bestsellers don't have to contain fine prose and that good enough writing will suffice.

In fact, many bestsellers, particularly runaway breakout bestsellers, are criticized for the poor quality of their writing, particularly the writing style. Yet the reading public buys these books in the millions. Does that mean that readers don't care about good writing, and that writers don't have to worry about it?

There's certainly a difference between excellent writing – the literary art created by the likes of Hilary Mantel – and the good enough writing that's acceptable in other genres. In the genres, good enough writing is all that's needed to get the story across, and it often delivers a faster read. It's only 'badly written' in comparison with literary excellence or it might just not be to your taste. (And anyone who seriously thinks that published genre bestsellers are badly written should spend time reading some of the unedited writing on the Internet, as well as some self-published work. It's eye opening.) As readers, we can forget how difficult it is to master the craft.

There's been a general rise in standards in fiction and non-fiction. Literary genre books, such as *Frog Music* by Emma Donoghue (Picador, 2014), are popular. It's a literary historical murder-mystery novel, based on a true crime.

 Key idea

In the end, it's up to you whether you decide that you have enough desire and talent to become an excellent writer, or whether you want to be a good enough writer and spend more of your time and effort on other aspects of your story. There's room for both in the bestseller charts.

WHAT DOES IT TAKE TO WRITE A WORD-OF-MOUTH BESTSELLER?

Andrew Crofts is one of the world's finest ghostwriters. Throughout his bestseller *The Ghost* Robert Harris quotes Andrew's seminal book *Ghostwriting*. He is particularly passionate about the sorts of books that have created a new audience, such as genre fiction, celebrity biographies and misery memoir.

When I asked him what it takes to write a word-of-mouth bestseller, he replied: 'Good storytelling, not fine writing.' As to why there are certain bestsellers, like Dan Brown and E.L. James, that people love to hate, he told me that it was probably because they are so successful despite not being the best writers out there.

You don't have to write a literary classic to have a potential bestseller, but you *do* need to have a great story at the heart of your book. It is that essential storytelling factor that may encourage an agent to take your book on, even if it isn't polished. If your writing is good but lacks a decent idea, they will probably ask you to get back in touch when you have another idea. If the story is strong and offers something that's not been told before, but the book needs structural or editorial work, they may be more inclined to take a punt on you.

If good storytelling is your weakness, then that is what you need to work on and where you need to get help.

Andrew Crofts, ghostwriter

'*Books that generate strong word of mouth stand a better chance than many of becoming bestsellers. That is, books that generate dinner-party conversation of the sort that feeds into our base fears about our lives, relationships, sex, work, success and our children. It's the kind of book the middle classes can talk about over coffee.*'

Andrew says that a good test of whether you have a good story is whether or not it stands up to the 'dinner party test'. By this he means that, when you have an opportunity to tell people about your book, you manage to get and keep their interest through the telling.

The dinner party test

Check out your book's word-of-mouth rating with this exercise.

Work out your one-sentence pitch and keep working on it until it's perfect. Forget detail; just focus on the essence. Try it out at your next dinner party or event. Pay attention to the reaction you get, rather than on how well or not you pitched.

Responses are generally split into two sorts:

1 'Oh, but why does he do that?'

2 'Ooh, and happens then?'

Can you see the difference? The first person is not caught up in your story. They're confused; what you've told them doesn't make sense. The second person wants to know more, and if you get that response there's a good chance your pitch is working. If, while you are talking, more people join the conversation then you know you are really on to something.

 ## Focus point

This chapter looked at the key decisions to make and the commitment needed to attempt a bestseller. You now know how to find inspiration and develop a clear sense of your story, the most important aspect of writing a bestseller. You know what makes a story commercial and what it takes to write a word-of-mouth bestseller. Even if your writing style isn't perfect, as long as you write with humanity, authenticity, honesty, passion and engagement, you'll get a similar response to your writing from readers.

Where to next?

Once you know that your idea has legs, you can move on to the practicalities of planning and plotting your book. Then, with no more delays, it will be time to start writing.

PART TWO
Write

4

How to approach your writing

The first part of the creative process is gathering ideas and finding inspiration, perhaps reading around a subject that unconsciously becomes research. At the early stages, you may not be certain that you have a story to tell. You may have just an idea, or an image, or a snippet of overheard conversation. At this point your role is first to notice ideas and then to start to put things together: that postcard from Paris combined with a line from a Beatles song; the rainbow effect of petrol on tarmac combined with the smell of that weird house nearby with newspapers over the windows. Eventually, a combination of elements generates a spark and you'll start to find relevant material everywhere you look.

Some writers dive from this straight into writing and go for it. Others take a step back, building the structure first rather than diving in.

Developing a structure

You may find that you are inspired to get straight on with the writing and that, when the creative fire eventually burns out, you have a complete manuscript. Nevertheless, it's impossible to come up with a coherent book-length manuscript without developing some sort of structure at a certain point in the writing, and knowing what you need to do next. Some people work out the structure in advance before they get down to the business of writing; others write first and develop the structure later. Either way is valid. All that matters is that the structure works and that the manuscript is finished. If your method yields both of these results, you don't need to change a thing.

Neither of these positions is more creative than the other. Writers who plan first and write later are applying their creativity to the big picture of the whole story and then to the act and scene level. Sentence-level creativity comes with the first draft. Writers who write first and plan later are applying their creativity at the sentence level now, to see where that takes them, and will look at the scene, act and story levels when the first draft has been written. Some writers do a combination of the two: a bit of planning and a bit of white-hot writing when it bubbles up.

A benefit of planning before writing is that the writer always knows what she needs to do next. This means that the best use can be made of short bursts of writing time. Having a planned structure means that the writer can see where plot elements are not working and fix them before they become written and (emotionally) more difficult to change; it's tough having to rewrite or, worse, discard whole passages, scenes, acts, subplots, or even stories. Anecdotal evidence from writers who've tried both methods suggests that another benefit of planning ahead is that the writing process, from first idea to final draft, tends to be faster.

 Key idea

Some people need a clear vision of how their book will take shape from start to finish before they start to write. Others feel stifled by a plan, needing only an idea or a character in order to get under way and begin to write.

PLANNING TIPS

When you are thinking about how to plan, ask for recommendations from writer friends who have a similar writing and planning style to yours. You might want to make notes in a notebook, or use your wall as a planner if you have space above your desk. I have painted a square of blackboard paint under a print on my wall. When I'm planning I lift the print off the wall and chalk away. I can hide it once I'm done for the day.

Choosing the right equipment and props

- If you are a visual person, make a mood board.
- If you are quite organized, try index cards (see the workshop exercise later in the chapter).
- If you like to work in a linear fashion, try a flow chart.
- If you're more of a free-flowing type, try a mind map™.
- Check out software too. Writer's tools like Scrivener offer free trial periods and tutorials to help with planning, outlining and draft revisions.

If you prefer to plan but find most styles of planning don't work for you, try a mind map™ (invented by Tony Buzan). Put your idea at the centre. This is the hook, the one big idea, the bones; now clothe it with flesh and substance. Here are just a few questions to get you started:

- How does it feel?
- Whose story it is? Which character is at the centre of the story?
- Which character comes through the strongest?
- Where is it set?
- What voice comes through?
- Do you have a sense of what the beginning, middle and end of your story might be?

If a burning idea is enough to kick-start your novel, you can write your synopsis or outline and start writing to see where it takes you. If you stall or lose heart, then go back to planning. If you keep firing on all cylinders, then carry on. The synopsis is there to remind you of the overall story and plot. Revise it as your story evolves or changes during the writing.

KEY DECISIONS

Whether you make them consciously or unconsciously, every book you write requires a number of key decisions. There'll be times when your plot or your characters effortlessly drive these decisions. At other times, you'll need to think each decision through, perhaps going through a process of trial and error before arriving at your final decision. It's also likely that you'll reverse some of these decisions in a later draft; that's all part of writing. What's important for now is to make decisions so you can start.

You need to make decisions about:

- which idea you commit to working up to a novel
- whether to plan your book in detail or write a synopsis and leap in
- your writing schedule – when, where and for how long?
- research – is it needed before you start or can you check and fill in the facts later?
- the genre you will be writing in
- your plot
- characters – whose story is it and why?
- whose point of view it is
- setting – where and why?
- timeframe – what timeframe does the novel span?

How to make a start

This chapter is about removing barriers to writing, especially as you've set yourself the high ambition of achieving a bestseller. Whether you are a new writer or a seasoned one who hasn't yet got the results you want, it really helps to make a full commitment to your writing by taking the following steps.

1 Test the idea

The first thing to do is to test the strength of the idea. Use the sticky ideas exercise from the previous chapter as your tester to see whether the idea will grow up to be a book. Think about it, mull it over, make notes, start to write to see what emerges for the idea or character. It feels good to make a start and move away from that frightening blank page.

2 Write your synopsis or outline

Now knuckle down to writing a synopsis, outline and structure, with a rough sense of beginning, middle and end. This gives you the sense of a container into which you can pour your thoughts. You feel you've ticked the planning box and you are now comfortable to put it aside and carry on writing. It's like a fallback position. You know the outline is there if you need it. Go back occasionally to compare it to what you've written but don't allow it to wholly dictate what you will or won't write.

3 Keep asking questions

Consult your synopsis or outline whenever you need to check what is behind all this. Ask, what am I really trying to say and am I saying it? Keep asking whose story it is and what it is really all about. If you don't do this, you'll find that the editing process turns into a nightmare of wading through acres of material that doesn't pull its weight. The other useful thing about this approach is that, because the synopsis has been used as a working document, it should be a fairly good representation of what you have on the page in your book. This might seem obvious, but it is surprising how often there is a mismatch between what an author says their book is about in the synopsis and what is actually there on the page in the manuscript. Using your synopsis as a record of what you are writing lessens the chance of this happening.

4 Write every day

A different kind of planning also needs to be mastered: the ability to plan and manage time. Few writers have the luxury of unlimited time to write, and even those who do often find it difficult to get the work done when there's always the chance of starting properly tomorrow. Get into the habit of writing every day, even if you don't feel like it. Make a pledge or commitment to yourself – in writing.

Figure out the logistics of 'when and where' works for you and make it a regular thing. If you take the work out of always having to decide when and where to sit down to it, you will lessen any resistance or doubt you might feel. You're simply doing it at an agreed time and for an agreed period each day, each week – whatever it is you decide to commit to.

How many hours will you commit to writing? Will it be:
- for an hour before everyone else gets up?
- on your commute?
- in your lunch hour?
- part time?
- full time?

If you have a tendency to procrastinate, get yourself an accountability partner or creative buddy – someone who will contact you on a regular basis to check your word count and how you have moved on with your story, and set a time and a goal for when they check in with you again.

Key idea

By writing every day, you are treating your creative work as you would do a paying job – you turn up and do what has to be done. By writing every day, the narrative remains fresh in the forefront of your mind and you'll be ready to start work at a moment's notice. And your subconscious will work on story problems when you're not writing.

5 Have a deadline and set goals

Deadlines provide great structure to the writer's year. If you don't have a publisher's deadline, aim for a submission deadline for a writing competition, or a personal deadline such as completing a book before hitting a certain age. When the deadline is tight, a good plan is essential. For a writer who doesn't plan first, it can be difficult to estimate how much work and time is needed before the manuscript is ready for submission.

To ensure that you get your first draft written, you need to find and set a realistic writing pace and commit to writing goals, such as 10 minutes or 30 minutes, or 300 or 1,000 words, a day. Find your pace and work out how long it will take to achieve your daily goal. Your word count will add up; it will build slowly until you are in the thousands and tens of thousands until you have finished.

Commit to your writing goals

The following steps will help you commit to your writing goals:

1. Figure out how many words per day and how long it will take you to achieve a first draft.
2. Put your word and date goals in your diary and set alerts.
3. Put deadlines into your smartphone or computer so that you get reminders.
4. Set reminders for when it is time to write and do it even if you don't feel like it. If you don't, you'll never know what might have come out in that session.

5   Set the word count on your draft and measure your progress.

6   Put it up on your wall or in your diary.

7   Tell your friends and family what you're doing and be clear that this is Do Not Disturb time.

Now write out your plan.

- I will sit down for **this number** of hours per day/week to write.
- I will write at **this time** each day/week.
- I will complete my first draft on **this date**.

Talli Roland, author

'Every writer works differently, but for me the most invaluable piece of advice on setting writing targets came from Stephen King's On Writing. *King writes every day (including Christmas!) and he sets himself a daily word target: in his case, 2,000 words a day. Sometimes the 2,000 words take him an hour or so, sometimes the whole day, but he always gets them finished. I liked the thought of having a measurable target, so I decided to follow suit. It's definitely a struggle some days, but at least when 4 p.m. rolls around I know I've accomplished something.'*

Author Talli Roland writes romantic fiction. Her debut novel, *The Hating Game*, was short-listed for Best Romantic Read at the UK's Festival of Romance; her second, *Watching Willow Watts*, was selected as an Amazon Customer Favourite. Her novels have reached the bestselling charts in Britain and the United States.

6 Dare to be imperfect

Writing isn't as hard as you might think, once you're in the right space and place. The trickiest thing is actually showing up: sitting down to do it in the first place, and then keeping at it, especially when it comes to the hard graft of taking stock of what you've got in the editing and redrafting process. Productive writers have strategies and tricks to cope with both.

If you are incredibly motivated and can work to a strict schedule, then write yourself a tight plan. If you aren't naturally that way inclined, then figure out what will work for you.

With the first full-length book I wrote, I completed it in 12 weeks. I did this by writing a chapter per week, pushing on, even when the chapter was far from perfect and sometimes downright awful. If I'd redrafted and waited to get Chapter 1 perfect, I might still be working on that first chapter now.

As I have stressed, if you want to write a bestseller, you must treat writing like a job. If you want to write a book purely for pleasure or are working through a 'things to do before I die' list, even then you have a deadline, pun intended. If you really, truly want a finished book in your hand and be working towards pushing it to bestseller status, then you need to work and work at it. If your goal is to find an agent and publisher, it's worth knowing that they will only invest in authors who they believe are in it for the long haul: those who have a long-term future as a writer. Obviously you don't need to worry about the agent and publisher if you are planning to self-publish but, if you want a bestseller, then all the evidence from successful self-publishing shows that you must apply the same rigour to yourself and your work for the long term.

The technical aspects of writing

A lot of writing is done without full awareness of how we do what we are doing. Whether you plan or not, at some point in the writing process it will be useful to have an awareness of certain technical aspects of writing. When something isn't quite gelling in your writing, it can be because one or more of these elements needs tweaking:

- the plotting
- the characters
- the setting
- the pacing.

We will cover all of these below.

If you feel you have a strong idea and prefer a more 'suck it and see' approach, you don't necessarily need to find out how to write before you can start writing. Start writing and figure out what your weaknesses are, get feedback on your writing, and come back to this chapter to seek help in the problem-solving section here to address the weaknesses in your work.

TIGHT PLOTTING

Plotting your book is a key part of planning. Plot is the causal chain of events in a story. When writers plan their work, they are generally deciding what events should be shown in the narrative, and in what order.

The three-act structure

The standard plot shape is the three-act structure. This has been observed since Ancient Greek times and, with variations throughout the years, is still effective. The three-act structure can be found in all genres and all narrative forms. It works equally well for short and long fiction, and for narrative non-fiction. For example, the title of *Eat, Pray, Love: One Woman's Search for Everything* by Elizabeth Gilbert (Bloomsbury Publishing, 2007) declares its three-part structure. It also cleverly encapsulates the concept in the title. No surprises that this book turned out to be a word-of-mouth bestseller.

Most published books follow either the three-act structure or a variant of it – there's not much wrong with beginning, middle and end. Beginning writers should aim to fully understand the three-act structure as a fundamental aspect of the writer's craft.

At its simplest, the three-act structure works as follows:

Act I – The beginning, or orientation

The characters and situation are introduced and a story problem invites the lead character to act, raising a question in the reader's mind (for example, will the lead succeed in … ?) The challenge here is to give enough background information to help the reader understand what is going on without slowing down the story or boring the reader.

Act II – The middle, or complication

The lead character faces difficulties in addressing the problem and we see how they respond. Provide enough tension here to keep the reader engaged with, and interested in whether the character will succeed or fail. This is where you must keep the reader turning the pages.

Act III – The end, or resolution

In accordance with what he has learned in Acts I and II, the lead character either resolves or fails to resolve the problem. Either the loose ends are completely tied up or there is a resolution of sorts, perhaps for now, and the way is left clear for another book in the series.

The end can include a surprising twist or turn, a reveal that causes us to reframe what we thought we knew about the characters and the truth of their narrative. This is a pulling together or resolution of all the different threads and character storylines.

Other structures

Some stories demand non-standard plot structures. For example, if the story unfolds in a non-linear way, with jumps in the timeframe, a standard beginning, middle and end structure may not be possible. Non-standard, non-linear plots can generate high-concept books, such as David Mitchell's layers of narrative in *Cloud Atlas* (Sceptre, 2004). If you would like to try something fancier than the standard three-act structure, then task yourself with studying the structure of a few of your favourite books. And spend more time and attention on the planning phase so that you'll nail the trickier structure you're attempting.

There are many books available on plotting, and plenty of advice on the Internet, too:

- Chris Sykes's *How to Craft a Great Story* (Hodder Education, 2013) is an excellent introduction to structure, plot and the creative decisions that writers have to make.
- Christopher Vogler's *The Writer's Journey* (Michael Weise Production, 2007) is a modern classic that looks at plot development in relation to mythic structures, particularly the hero's journey.
- Christopher Booker's *The Seven Basic Plots: Why We Tell Stories* (Continuum International Publishing Group, 2005) is a fascinating study of different story types.
- The Writer's Digest website (www.writersdigest.com) has articles on aspects of plot, or search online for images that illustrate plot structure – you will find links to the better-known theories.

Workshop: index card plotting

A quick way to develop a plot is to use index cards. Smaller cards work well, or cards cut in half.

1 Thinking of your great concept, how many scenes do you think your story will need? If it's your first full-length book and you have no idea how to answer this, aim for 80 scenes in the first instance – you'll soon find out whether that's too many or too few. You'll need at least twice as many cards as the number of scenes.

2 Now, with that great concept in mind, brainstorm all the scenes and story events that you think may appear in your story, writing an idea on each card.

3 Don't criticize or edit anything – get it all down and you can sort it out later.

4 Write as quickly as you can, scribbling on each index card one event or scene, or a line of dialogue, or even just a point you need to make.

5 Start anywhere in the story and keep going until you completely run out of ideas. Your cards might say, 'Mathilde's birthday party where Cara reveals her secret', or 'Something about Lucas's mother coming to stay?' or 'Bob and Brian fight to the death' – whatever's in your story. This is part of your creative process. Don't worry about rules - you can't get this wrong!

6 Now look at what you've got on the cards. See if you can find the first and last scene of your story. If not, just identify the earliest and latest for now.

7 Are there events that have to happen in a certain order for your story to make sense? For example, perhaps the murder takes place, then the body is found, then a lead proves vital, then the suspect is arrested. Place the cards in the right order as far as possible. They may be next to each other, or you may need them to be spaced out. Write new cards for anything you forgot to include.

8 Are some of the cards too small to be scenes or events on their own? Marry them up with other scenes, or recognize them as placeholders for that missing scene for the time being.

9 Conflict is the driver behind all stories. On every card, identify at least one source of conflict. You may have to rewrite some cards to introduce conflict.

10 Can you identify which cards need to be in Act I, the beginning? Include anything that's introducing the characters or the situation, or that's kicking off the story's main problem.

11 Now see which cards should be in Act III, the end. What events feel like part of shutting down the story, tying up loose ends, the fight to the (possibly metaphorical) death, the answering of the story's main question?

12 Do the rest of the cards fit into Act II, the middle? This act is all about things getting progressively worse for the lead character, and is usually the bulk of the book where the story proper plays out. Act II gets half of the total number of scenes in the book. Act I and Act II get

a quarter each. So, if you have 80 scenes, there are 20 in each of Act I and Act III, and Act II has 40.

13 Working on the floor or a large table, put your cards in order, allocating each a place that feels right. Go with your gut instinct on this – you've been exposed to story structure all your life.

14 Get rid of 'doubles'. Put random elements that don't fit into this story to one side; they may be perfect for your next book.

15 Do you need to add empty cards into the order as placeholders for scenes that you haven't created yet?

16 Does this progression of scenes and events make sense? This is unlikely to be your final order of scenes. It's the plan for now and it can be changed.

17 If possible, pin the cards up where you can see them and revisit the order when you can. If you don't have the space, gather them together in the correct order.

18 Keep spare cards and a pen with you at all times. Your subconscious will be working on this and you need to be able to capture the ideas as they come to you. Add the new scenes in as appropriate.

19 Read through your cards in order. What do you think of your plot so far?

One of the key aspects of plot is causality. Because a character does one thing, another thing happens. When this chain of causality is broken, holes appear in the plot and the reader doesn't have enough information to understand the progression in the story.

If there are too many scenes that are not part of that chain of causality, plots can become ill defined and flabby. The story's power is dispersed. Certainly there's scope for subplots in a story, but they should be well-structured plots in themselves, with their own beginnings, middles and ends. They should also link with the main story, either reinforcing or contradicting it.

Find a plot

If you're struggling to come up with a plot of your own, you can fall back on the standard plotline for your genre. Some writers are drawn to certain genres by the perceived ease of plotting. For example, most detective stories have easily identifiable story events and steps, and the structure of many romance stories is a variant on boy meets girl, boy loses girl, boy wins back girl.

- Look at how a recent bestseller has structured the plot. Can you learn from this? Of course, you shouldn't copy the plot exactly, but you should be able to use it as a jumping-off point for your own story, changing the characters, the setting, the milieu, for example.
- Consider using a plot from a different genre – it might be more difficult to adapt to your story, but it may suggest alternative story lines.
- Can you resurrect the plot from a classic? Shakespeare did this, and others have re-imagined his plots in turn.
- If you're completely drawing a blank, pick a fairy story. Still not sure? Use Cinderella.

Keep shaping and working on your plot until you feel it's ready to be written.

DEVELOPING STRONG CHARACTERS

How do we create strong characters? Some writers build dossiers with details of characters' lives, past and present. They may interview their characters to see how they'll respond to questions, or observe them in difficult situations. Their goal is to get to know the characters as well as possible before the story starts so that the characters' actions and reactions are plausible. Interaction between characters generates the plot.

Other writers build characters specifically to meet the demands of the plot. Many stories feature a lead who changes both on the outside, perhaps by learning a new skill, and on the inside, by changing their attitude. The writer knows the skill and mindset that are missing at the start, so designs a character that would embody these deficiencies. For example, if the character has to learn to be brave, he will start out risk averse; if he has to be able to shoot the antagonist in the final scene, he should start out a pacifist who has never held a gun. How would you characterize a risk-averse pacifist? What does he or she look like? What does he or she do for a living? And so the demands of the plot provide the seeds of character.

Strong characters are those that we think of as real people (or conscious entities, depending on the genre). We know that real people have their good sides and their bad sides, their strengths and weaknesses, their virtues and flaws. We know that real people have habitual ways of doing things, and have a default mindset that might be caring, or aggressive, or lazy, or witty, or all of the above. They have quirks and secrets, scars from the past and ambitions for the future. We know the things that we love about other people, and the things that we hate. All these things that we know about real people are what we want to know about characters. And we expect the writer to know, and to tell us these things at the right time, not too soon that it spoils the chance for a reveal, and not too late so that we are confused or feel that a vital piece of information is missing.

 Key idea

There are hundreds of books and resources that address creating characters, and hundreds of chapters about character in general writing reference books. It may take you a while to find a theory or practice that works for you. In the meantime, learn writing techniques from an author you admire.

Characters and plot

You've seen in the section on plotting above that the three-act structure relates to things that happen to the characters, and that the story progresses in relation to action taken by the characters, which necessitates further action in turn. It's impossible to talk about plot without talking about character at the same time; events are only important if they affect the story's characters.

Each storyline – whether it's the main storyline or a subplot – has a main character. The lead character of the book is generally the one who acts in response to the problem in the main storyline, who faces the difficulties, and who tries to restore equilibrium at the end of the day. In most books, this lead character will also be the main point-of-view character. That means that the main storyline is seen through the lead character's eyes. The reality of the story world is presented to us according to the details that the point-of-view character notices, and we know what this character is thinking and feeling. In contemporary writing, we tend not to have access to another character's thoughts in the same scene.

The point-of-view character is normally presented to us as first person ('I slept') or third person singular ('She slept'), depending on how close to the character the writer wants us to be. Second and third person plural are not often used.

Characters and roles

Characters have roles to play in the story. The lead is the one who acts to answer the story question. The antagonist is the lead's enemy, the person who stands in opposition to the lead's plans. In books without an identified antagonist, the role can be shared by a number of characters working against the lead in different ways at different times, even if they appear to be on the lead's side. It's a good idea to keep the number of named characters as small as possible, so see whether you can get characters to fulfil more than one role in the story. For example, the love interest may inadvertently betray the lead to his enemy.

Strong characters on the page

From your recent reading of a book you admire, which character is the most memorable? Take your time to find out how the author has created this memorable character on the page.

- Find the first mention of the character.
- What are you told? Is it a physical description, or an aspect of personality?
- How does the author reveal that information? Is it in the character's own thoughts, or reported by another character, or implied? Does the author do this well? If so, make note of the technique.
- Read the book again, looking specifically for the things that made the character memorable. Mark up the page, make notes, analyse. Is the character consistent, and is this a good thing in the story? Or are there contradictions and, if so, why do these occur? Copy out pages of the text if it helps in your analysis.
- What have you learned about how this strong character was conveyed to the reader?
- Look at your own work in progress. Find the first mention of your main character on the page. Is there a new technique you can now apply, or can you tighten your writing?
- Are there any changes you'd like to make to your character, or to the way your character is revealed?

You can use this technique to learn any aspect of the writers' craft.

You might find it useful to fill in a character questionnaire. For a free download, see www.dev.stewartferris.com

THE RIGHT SETTING

'Setting' refers not only to the geography of the story world, but to the social structures and industries; the culture, institutions and morals; the time period and the passing of time; and the public and private spaces inhabited by different social groups in general, and by characters in particular.

While familiar settings need less explanation, settings in some genres require more detailed description to establish a fully realized, four-dimensional stage for the story. Think of the imagination and extrapolation that go into world building in science fiction or fantasy writing, or the research needed for accuracy in historical fiction.

At one end of the spectrum, stories benefit from a crucible setting – a defined space that no one leaves when the going gets tough, so they stay and see the story out. An example would be the small town of Pagford in *The Casual Vacancy* by J.K. Rowling (Sphere, 2013). At the other end of the spectrum, an event in a character's life has implications that reach out beyond the domestic and the immediate locality to the whole world, or beyond. For example, in the recently reissued *Ender's Game* by Orson Scott Card (Orbit, 2011), we're taken quickly from a medical procedure on a gifted child to interplanetary warfare.

Genre writers, in particular those keen to explore and extend boundaries, might consider whether to create a setting that's true to type in the genre or one that's against type.

Alternative settings

- Identify the scene in your novel where everything changes for the lead character. This is likely to be close to the start of Act I. What's the setting for that scene?
- Have you ever seen the same setting used for that kind of scene? For example, shiny office buildings have been the go-to setting for millionaire businessmen to meet willing ingénues in recent years.
- If you've seen that setting before, list at least a dozen alternatives. Can you create a setting that would be quirky or threatening, silly, disgusting, intimidating, or one where the characters couldn't speak? What's the filthiest place that it could be set in, the cleanest, the most relaxing or the most exhausting? What would be the very worst place for this particular scene to occur? What is the most

unexpected, unlikely and bizarre setting that readers of your genre would expect for this scene? Why not set it there?
- Whichever setting you use, make sure you use it again whenever possible, changing either some aspect of the setting or some aspect of the character to show that the events of the story have made a difference.

CONTROLLED PACING

Pacing refers to the reader's experience of the passage of time in a story. There are times when you'll want the story's events to pick up speed, and times when you'll want to slow things right down. Immersed in the story, readers are not likely to notice pacing unless it goes wrong, when events move too slowly to be interesting or too quickly to be understood.

The techniques used to slow down pace or to pick up pace are the mirror images of each other:

To speed things up:
- summarize
- use short words, sentences, paragraphs, events, scenes and chapters
- describe sections of action
- delay an outcome
- use dialogue.

To slow things down:
- dramatize
- use long words, sentences, paragraphs, events, scenes and chapters
- add descriptive passages
- explain an outcome
- describe thoughts.

Writers need to be able to use both speeding-up and slowing-down techniques in different parts of the book; neither relentlessly fast nor slow will work for an entire book.

Summarize/dramatize

Summarizing lets the writer move time quickly over the boring bits, the parts of the story that don't have a major impact on the character but that need to be mentioned for logic's sake or to orient the reader in time. For example, making tea, a day at work, a war or a decade can be summarized if needed. For instance there is absolutely no need for the reader to witness your protagonist waking in the morning unless it is absolutely necessary to the plot.

Too many books begin with a yawning, stretching, tousle-haired character, squinting at the alarm clock and wishing they hadn't drunk quite so much the previous evening. The exceptions are, for example, if you are setting the scene for them to discover a bump on their head, to realize they have amnesia or turn to discover a corpse in the bed next to them.

Dramatizing events, breaking them into scenes through which the reader moves with the characters, second by second, slows the passage of time to real-life pace. These are the parts of the story where something changes, where events have impact, and the reader wants the details.

Short/long

If an event isn't summarized away entirely, the writer manipulates the amount of page space and hence reading time by writing short or long. This is effective at all levels of text, from the word to the book as a whole. In the build-up to an important scene, the preceding scenes may become progressively shorter, with short paragraphs, sentences and words, picking up the pace as the reader rushes to the pay-off. But the important scene is long and detailed, giving the reader time to get the most from the unfolding drama.

Action/description

Pure action sections, where physical action and reaction follow hot on each others' tails, for example in a fight scene, show that things are moving so quickly that the point-of-view character has no time to report their thoughts or feelings, never mind anything about the setting that's not drawn into the action. Don't confuse the reader by allowing the character to be reflective. It will slow down the action and spoil the scene.

By contrast, if your character has time to look around and describe what they see, it's obvious that there's nothing pressing for their attention; the pressure is off. After an action-packed scene, it may be a welcome rest for the reader.

Outcome delayed/outcome explained

Jump-cuts shuttle us from one incomplete scene into another scene entirely and back again. Cliffhangers make us wait until the next scene or chapter to find out how the escape is made. Delayed outcomes in general can have us reading frantically through the intervening text to find out what on earth happened. But if the outcome is allowed to play out within the scene at a steady pace, with scene endings and chapter endings coinciding, we reach a natural break and potentially a pause in our reading, confident that we know all we need to know for now.

Dialogue/thoughts

Readers can rip through a rapid exchange of dialogue, particularly if it uses short lines and creates a lot of white space on the page. They love it. But overdo it and the book will feel lightweight. In contrast, a densely packed page can slow the reader right down, while the point-of-view character considers what's happened, what it all means, what might happen next, and what she should do. Depending on the genre, such dense pages can be used every so often, as long as the writer is careful not to stall the story.

The bestselling *Twilight* by Stephanie Meyer (Little, Brown and Company, 2005) provides a masterclass in controlling pacing. The story speeds along when Edward and Bella are apart but, in every scene with the lovers together, the pace slows right down, allowing the characters and readers time to savour the developing romance.

Finally, readers keep turning pages because they're worried. They want to find out what's going to happen to the characters, and whether or not it will turn out all right. For a book to be a page-turner, the writer must worry the reader by piling on the conflict. Look for ways of introducing clashes between characters, from polite disagreement among allies to an enemy's murderous assault. Start the clock ticking so that the lead has little time to address the story problem, then shorten the time available and make the pressure rise. Think about what it is that makes you keep reading when you should be doing something else and use that technique.

Your first draft

If you have arrived here, you are ready to write your first draft. Whether you're a feet-first non-planner or you've planned and tightly plotted, it's time to get down to work. Writing a bestseller isn't going to be easy. In fact, writing anything the length of a book isn't easy – that's why there are so many unfinished and unpublished manuscripts clogging up bottom drawers. Some days, assembling a decent paragraph is much more difficult than it ought to be. But, if you're going to write a bestseller, you have to start somewhere, some time. That might as well be here and now.

Key idea

Waiting for the light of genius to fall upon you before starting to write won't yield results. And thinking and talking about your book will only get you so far. You need enthusiasm, skill and the willingness to work hard and get the words out on paper.

As shown in Chapter 4, some writers love the creative freedom of getting the first draft down on paper, and some prefer to edit as they go along rather than leaving it until the rewriting stage. Both approaches are valid and down to personal choice. Most writers will edit to some extent as they go along. The key is to get the balance right. Make progress through your book, rather than obsessively revising and redrafting earlier sections that don't quite look right. Unless you keep writing, you are never going to get enough practice to improve the craft. And craft does improve with thoughtful practice.

If you struggle to complete projects, the best way for you to proceed is to get the first draft done as quickly as possible. Don't try to edit at the same time, just push on with the story and get it all down. The longer it takes to get a full first draft in place, the more likely you are to become bored with the project or distracted by the next great concept. Once the first draft is finished, follow a structured plan of revision and creating further drafts. So don't worry about redrafting or evaluating. That'll be done later. Just push on through the writing and leave evaluation and editing until you get to the end of your first draft.

Just do it!

Sharpen your pencils, straighten your desk, do all your filing and bake a cake by all means, but do start when you say you will. If you break off to do some research, or go online to check 'just one more thing', then you will be making the number one mistake many creative people make, which is to put walls in your way, allowing distractions to prevent you from getting into flow.

Start your book anywhere you like. You don't have to start at the beginning of your book. Choose a scene that fires you up and begin there. (If you planned out your scenes on index cards or other methods described earlier, it becomes easier to identify a scene you are burning to write.) Some writers find that it can be tough to start there, getting hung up on the opening line. Your perfect opening line – the one you finish up with in your final draft – will come out somewhere in the process. When we reach Chapter 6 on evaluation we will revisit your opening, so leave any concerns about it aside for now.

Just start and keep going for the allotted time – do as artists' do and make a mark on the page. Any mark, any word will do, just do it and don't stop until your timer goes off.

Steven Pressfield's book *The War of Art* has provided a much-needed impetus for many a writer. As he says: 'Start before you're ready. Don't prepare, begin.'

So enough preparation, now make a start: Bash out a first draft. Get your words out of your head and on to the page. Good luck!

Focus point

Some of the important elements of writing a bestseller are:

- a good concept
- an original voice
- writing that's somewhere between good enough and excellent
- tight plotting
- strong characters
- the right setting
- controlled pacing.

Not every bestseller does everything on this list brilliantly. A famous name can generate sales even when there are problems with the execution. A skilfully constructed plot can detract from deficiencies in character building. But an unknown writer who masters these essential elements has more chance of success than one who does not.

Where to next?

The next chapter looks at common problems that might have arisen when you started to write your first draft. It offers advice and practical help should you become stuck.

5

Problem solving

Sometimes, in the course of writing our first draft, we find that we are flagging or that we need help with specific problems that crop up. We may find that we need to strengthen certain skills or fill in gaps in our technical knowledge, or we may have problems that have little to do with writing but a lot to do with mindset, focus and priority.

A tendency to overthink is both the beauty of, and the trouble with, being creative. The same rich and wild imagination that enables us to create an enchanting piece of writing can also trip us up. We need to know how to overcome these hitches and redraft consciously, making full use of feedback, and then polish our book and know when it is good enough to send out.

This chapter looks at some of the most common problems and how to fix them.

We're very good at imagining all sorts of reasons why we shouldn't write our book, why our novel won't work and why people won't like it. We might have the following reasons:

- We are perfectionists.
- Our expectations are too high.
- We believe we can't do it.

We don't want to curtail our imagination that can serve us so well. Just do as Steven Pressfield suggests, and tell the voice, 'OK, I hear you – you may be right – but I'm going to give this a go anyway.'

Many things may impede the success of your book, so let's look at some of the most common problems and how to fix them. You may have had feedback or know yourself what your weak points are. First come technical or craft problems, often termed 'writer's block', then mindset or human challenges.

Writers' block

This has to top the list as the most commonly cited problem. Many writers would say that this arises because of technical difficulties and not being skilled enough to know how to solve them, or from simply drying up creatively. I believe this problem has less to do with writing and more to do with mindset but as it is such a major issue it stays top of the list. Writing is a big undertaking, in time, energy, skill and willpower; sometimes it scares us and the fear paralyses us. The only thing to do is to keep on writing through it. Show up at the time you've allotted to your writing and do it even when you don't feel like it. You will see the results. It won't be perfectly written every time, but in the long term you'll have a finished, polished book to show for your efforts.

If you are blocked because you can't find a way to resolve a particular problem with your book, step away and come back to it. You may find that when you leave it alone the answer comes to you. Novelist Tim Winton has three desks and when he has a problem with one project he gets up and moves to another. If you think it is a mindset issue, then find a meditation on banishing negative thoughts and building your confidence. I promise you – based on personal and professional experience – that if you keep writing through it, your block will eventually fade and go away.

PLOTTING PROBLEMS

You may identify a weakness in your plot at the beginning, the middle or the end of your story. You might have a boring, slow start, a lack of conflict in the middle, or a protagonist who is not involved enough in the unfolding of the action. Whatever the problem, you need to check that your plot is working by going over the whole chain of events, scene by scene.

Tighten the plot

A useful method for identifying the essential plotline of your story is to start at the very end and work your way backwards through the scenes to the very start.

1 Starting with the last scene, identify the immediate cause of that scene. This cause should be found in the second-last scene. Now, looking at the second-last scene, what was the immediate cause of that?

2 If some of your scenes aren't part of the chain of cause and effect, they may be parts of subplots. Trace the subplot from end to beginning just as you are doing with the main plot, but be aware that subplots don't need every single scene played out.

3 If you come across scenes that are neither part of the causal chain of the main storyline nor part of a subplot, consider whether they are necessary. Can you cut the scene? You may need to relocate pieces of information to other scenes.

4 If you come across a plot hole, where the causality has broken down, create scenes to fill the gap in the story.

5 What's the story's timeline, from the earliest event to the latest? Can you shorten the timeline? Thinking radically, what's the minimum time you'd need for the story to take place? Do you have good reasons for not sticking to this shortest possible timeline?

TOO MANY IDEAS

You can't stop writing and you can't stop thinking up new ideas. You have the opposite of writer's block. You have so many ideas you can't choose or commit to just one.

Focus on one and see it through to the end. Writing as fast as you are able to is essential if you have loads of ideas clamouring for your attention. When it is done, not only should you promise yourself a reward but you should also send it off for someone else to critique for you, leaving you free to leap to another project until that book comes back.

WRITING TOO SLOWLY

If you write steadily enough but can't stop yourself going back over what you've done, you'll spend so much time redrafting that you get in the way of the free and creative flow of your story. Our top tip at London Writers' Club is to write your first draft with your heart, your second with your head. Just let it all out in the first draft and get to the end.

The best tip for writing faster is not to edit when you are writing. Don't look at your screen when writing: type now, edit later.

 Key idea

Don't edit while you are writing. Type now; edit later.

PREMISE OR THEME NOT STRONG ENOUGH

Go back to your original idea. Why was it important to you then? Did something change or did you forget to hold on to this? Does your writing buddy understand and care about the theme of your book? If not, ask them what would make it interesting to them. In the pub or over dinner, raise the topic (you don't have to say it is your book): 'I heard a story about a man who …' Ask people what they think about the story. Do they believe it? Ask whether it is interesting to them and what aspects of it interest them most. Tell more of the story and note which bits they most respond to. If a discussion or (result!) debate ensues, you know you are on to something.

To start you off, think of *The Slap* and how people might discuss that. What would you do if someone hit your child at a barbecue? Or from the other side, how would it be if you were at a barbecue and you got so angry with someone else's child that you slapped them? What might happen next?

TOO MUCH DESCRIPTION

Take a marker pen and highlight all descriptive passages and scenes. Then read through only to address this problem. Ignore everything else. Are these descriptions necessary? Delete any that slow down your plot. For example, if your heroine's life is in immediate danger she would not have time to reflect on her surroundings. If, on the other hand, Hannibal Lecter's serial killing buddy has her held captive, she has all the time in the world to notice every crack and crevice in her surroundings and every sensation she is feeling.

LACK OF CONCEPT

High concept can sell (see Chapter 2). If it is missing, you can inject it at the redrafting stage.

OTHER PROBLEMS

Here are some other problems that others might have identified in feedback or in a rejection letter, and what to do about them.

- **Weak voice**

  Try free writing without worrying about the results. Write as you speak; do not censor the voice that emerges. Listen to it and let it grow in its expression and embodiment.

- **Unbelievable characters**

  Ask for specific feedback. You need to know exactly what it is that doesn't work about them. There are good (free) character questionnaires available online. As you flesh out details about your character, your answers will help you to strengthen their credibility.

- **Loose ends**

  Track them down from the beginning of the thread and cut them out or tie them up. Every thread or storyline needs its own beginning, middle and resolution.

- **Plenty of action but no real story**

  Go back to your synopsis. Identify the beginning, middle and end to your story. It may be that your story is there but the pacing is wrong and is obscuring the story. If the pacing is too fast, the reader won't get the chance to take in important elements of the story. See how to slow it down in Chapter 4. Comb your manuscript for places where the action doesn't advance your story or character development, and cut it.

- **Nothing new or different**

  Take some time away from writing and do something different. Recent neurological research has indicated that it is only when we do something out of the ordinary, and bizarrely, particularly if it is something that we find unappealing, that we create new neural pathways. This might be worth a try, to provide the fresh new perspective you need.

- **The ideas of others rehashed**

  First, identify the aspects of your book that are unique to you. Focus on those and build on them. Find settings, characters and aspects of the plot that are 'borrowed' and flip them. Move your story to another time or even another planet. Change your woman into a man. Radically alter the outcome. Try anything that starts you writing more creatively.

- **Inconsistencies and grammatical mistakes**
  Remember that every book needs professional help with editing and proofreading. Do budget to have your book professionally edited. It will vastly improve the readability and quality of your book.

Mindset or human problems

You might have a whole list of reasons why your book isn't finished but if you want to be a successful writer you must sit down and write at the time you committed to in your writing commitment earlier. If you really want that bestseller, you will find the time. Don't blame anything or anybody else and take off the blinkers if you are the one who is reluctant to commit to paper.

If it never feels like the right time, and there is always something other than writing to do, by all means do a quick tidy of your desk and have the right pen to hand, but do crack on.

If all else fails, and life gets in the way, commit to a shorter, more manageable daily amount of time. Use a kitchen timer or a focus-booster app and do a 20-minute micro-block of writing. When you finish, write yourself a quick note of what needs doing next time you write, so you'll start faster and work with more focus.

 Chuck Close, artist

'*The advice I like to give young artists is not to wait around for inspiration. Inspiration is for amateurs; the rest of us just show up and get to work. If you wait around for the clouds to part and a bolt of lightning to strike you in the brain, you are not going to make an awful lot of work. All the best ideas come out of the process; they come out of the work itself.*'

NOT FINISHING

If you find it hard to get through to a finished first draft, take your brain off the job. Put aside any doubts or thoughts about what you are writing and just write. Just blast out the words, to the end of a first draft. Write without censorship or editing; suspend your judgement until you have got to a first draft of your book.

Knowing that you can, and will, change your book in the revision process helps free your mind of doubts and fears that the book isn't good enough. If you are a serial non-finisher, then you first need to take out all your projects and make a note of what each project needs. Decide which project you will work on to completion. Make a writing commitment with clear goals and dates for this particular project (see Chapter 4). Find the inspiration and help that suits you best: go to a writing club, a reading evening or find an editor or mentor, but do get this project finished.

Trickery

Don't let the thought of writing weigh too heavily. Writing this section, after a long week of work and with three weeks of school holidays looming, I was plagued with thoughts that the book would never be finished, so I tricked myself into writing for just 20 minutes more while my children were occupied. An hour later I had another 1,500 words and a smile on my face.

SHINY NEW PROJECT SYNDROME

This one can have some crossover with not finishing projects, above. If you are a perpetual starter who enjoys the initial buzz that comes with a new project but fizzle out before it's finished (and already have the next idea begging for attention), try instead to focus on one project at a time and see it through to the end. Before abandoning a project, be clear about whether it is for the chop, or whether you are simply bored and resisting the effort of getting over the inevitable rough patches of the writing process. Just because it is hard or you hit a dead end, doesn't mean it isn't working. If in doubt about the staying power of the idea, go back and redo the sticky ideas exercise in Chapter 3.

It is great to have plenty of ideas, because a bestselling strategy includes writing more than one book, but be disciplined and try to tackle them one at a time. Or have a key project and a fallback one that you can turn to if you get stuck on book one.

LACK OF DISCIPLINE

Sometimes it is good to face the pain sooner rather than later. You can avoid the pain of getting up an hour earlier to write, but that pain will set in in a year's time when you look back and bemoan the fact that that another year has passed and you have failed to complete your book. Try a little pain tomorrow – get up an hour earlier to write – and you'll avoid the bigger one in a years' time.

Another aspect of lack of discipline is to focus too much on the finish line before you've even started. While it can really spur you on to visualize having an agent and a publisher and your book on sale, too many writers who haven't actually started writing their book spend time thinking about how to get a publishing deal. It's great to have the end game in sight, but first you must get deep down and dirty in the writing process. Get a sense of what your project really is and a clear idea of who your reader is first, before focusing on agents and publishers. You won't know who'll be the best type of agent and publisher for you until you've written your book.

Forgetting to start with a good container (see Chapter 4) can also reflect a lack of discipline. An outline is like a container: it provides some guidance and boundaries as you write – you can lose yourself inside the container when you're writing. When you set some limits and write freely inside the container, magical things can happen. You're not restricted by the container, though; you can change its shape or even change the container.

TOO MUCH DETAIL

Don't let the detail obscure your story or allow it to slow your book at the start. How many pages does it take you to arrive at the first event in your novel? Sometimes the first third of a book can be just filling in the protagonist's backstory with nothing eventful happening. Cut away if this is true of your book.

Often, in a first draft, we write a lot of detail to help ourselves to write the book, to fully picture the setting, the characters and their motivations. We do this to become familiar enough with the world we've created, to make conjuring up the story livelier and easier. You don't need to reveal all of this to the reader. Be selective about what you tell them and set the rest as an aide for your memory. Get into the habit of writing a few pages (or more) of detail before you start to write. There you can fully flesh out, and play with, characters, setting, plot and anything else that helps you fully imagine and inhabit your novel.

Trim away most of the detail, keeping only the words that move the plot forward. Save the trimmings in a separate document entitled 'Character/plot/backstory'. It will be there for you to access when you need it.

Every writer has a different way of creating, processing and executing their ideas, but this approach works whatever your style.

When you're fixed on an idea or subject on which you feel strongly enough to write a book, it can feel overwhelming, and perfection and procrastination can dog you. It is hard to find your voice and tap into your passion for your idea when you are paralysed with doubt. If you get stuck, stalled or are finding it hard to know where and how to begin, this exercise should get you moving again.

Getting it out when you are stuck

Whichever stage you are blocked at, I urge you to push your way through:

- Tell someone you're blocked.
- Write about it.
- Write down how you'll feel when you complete your book. Then write or imagine yourself in five years' time and how you'll feel if you still haven't given writing your book your best shot.
- Set yourself daily or weekly targets.
- Make yourself accountable to somebody else, by attending a creative writing workshop, for example.
- Get a writing coach or editor or find yourself a writing buddy to help you set and stick to your goals.
- Don't wait for the ideal moment or a whole or even half day. Stick to your agreed writing commitment.

Focus point

Much of writer's block is about fear of failure. If you are having trouble getting on with it, sit down and set the timer for 45 minutes so you'll be 'tied' to the book and to the seat for that length of time. You'll probably find that, once you've started, you'll be fired up and lose that sense of there being anything between the brain and the page; and the words will seem to type themselves.

Have a rant, bash away on the keyboard or in longhand with your favourite pen, and keep on writing, without quality control, until you find your voice, your unique way of telling a story. It may be that there is just one good line or paragraph in pages and pages of writing. That is enough for now.

Keep going and your passion for the theme of your book will give it the wow factor which will help you find your voice. As John Steinbeck says: 'And now that you don't have to be perfect you can be good.'

If you need a visual aid, Elizabeth Gilbert, author of *Eat, Pray, Love*, has an inspiring TED Talk on fear waiting for genius to show up. It's a fascinating talk about the extremes of failure and success in writing and how similar they both felt to her!

Where to next?

This chapter has been about letting your writing flow: to focus on your goal of writing the best possible book you can and then commit to regular desk time to write and see what emerges. Now that you have your first draft and you've ironed out some of the problems you encountered along the way, it's time to move on to evaluating what you've written.

6

Evaluating and redrafting

Once you have finished your complete first draft, you're well on your way to writing a novel and you're ready to evaluate what you've written. You've squeezed out your creative juices, come up with a theme and a storyline and some decent characters, and sprinkled in some dialogue that helps us understand what they're up to and why. This is the bit where you squeeze a bit harder to get it right.

Now's your chance to get face to face with what you've produced; to look closely and critically at what you've created and to understand what still needs doing to it, in order to go forward with it. We will look at how to road test what you have with some exercises and show you how to ask for and use feedback.

Your first draft is complete!

The first thing to do, on completion of a full first draft, is to celebrate and take a break. Not everyone gets to this stage of writing a book, and getting to this stage is essential if an author wants to have a product to sell. However, don't be tempted to take too much time off from the project: it's easy to lose momentum.

The second thing is to look for what is right with your first draft. What are you most proud of? What stands out to you as unique and different? What do you like most about what you've written?

THE CRITIQUE

Next, get into critique mode. Look at the following aspects of your work in turn:

1 **Concept**

 Does your great concept still explain the story, or does it need to be tweaked following changes you made in the writing?

2 **Tone**

 Look carefully at the tone of your work. Read it aloud. How does it sound? Are you happy with it? If not, be honest; were you writing as yourself or were you trying to sound like someone else? Take out any prose that sounds forced or unnatural.

3 **Story**

 Now read the whole manuscript from start to finish, not editing anything but getting a sense of the whole story. Does it follow logically? Do the acts have the right proportions? Do events have the right weight? Does the pacing work? Do scenes have to be in a different order, or added, or deleted? Make rough notes of the things that need to be changed at the story level.

THE REVISION

Once you have gone through the manuscript, check your notes. If they make sense in the context of the whole story, go ahead and revise, making sure that the timeline works and the chain of causality is intact. The amount of work that needs to be done at this stage depends on how much planning was done before writing.

- Once the structure is in place, revise individual scenes. Print them out one at a time in case changes in one particular scene demand rewrites at other places in the story. Make those rewrites as you go along. Read the scenes aloud; note where it's difficult to follow and whether there are any mistakes. Rewrite the scene as required.

- Aim for the very best writing that you can manage, free of mistakes in spelling, punctuation and grammar, and with the structure as you want it to be. This may take several cycles of redrafting. You may be able to reduce the number of drafts with more experience.

- Once your manuscript is as good as you can make it, put it aside for as long as you can manage. Come back to it with fresh eyes, as though you were reading a stranger's work. Reread it and make any more changes.

When you have a second draft that you are satisfied with, this is the time to find out what others think.

Learning your craft

If you're intent on writing a bestseller, you've probably worked hard to make yourself aware of some of the things that need fixing in the manuscript and identifying your own weak spots as a writer. What do you need to do to increase your knowledge and skills in these areas?

If your first draft is a long way from where you'd like it to be, don't lose heart. Your writing skills will develop if you keep at it, and you can and will improve as a writer. Every time you write, your writing should evolve a little more. When you're redrafting, you notice something that could be improved that you didn't see last time. You work the words harder. It's not easy and, again, there is an element of feeling the pain but you've got your sights set on a bestseller, so buckle up. If you really are stuck, get help.

How good we can expect to become at writing is debatable. Writing is a craft that benefits from hard graft but just as, while anyone can learn the piano but may not progress to the level of a concert pianist, not everyone can write superbly. Author and creative writing professor at Kingston University, Hanif Kureishi, whose debut novel *The Buddha of Suburbia* won the Whitbread first novel prize, caused a stir at the Independent Bath Literature festival by declaring that storytelling can't be taught in a course. At the very least, though, we can learn enough skills to put down our story and make it readable and seek help to identify and resolve our weaknesses.

Hanif Kureishi says:

> '*A lot of my students just can't tell a story. They can write sentences but they don't know how to make a story go from there all the way through to the end without people dying of boredom in between. It's a difficult thing to do and it's a great skill to have. Can you teach that? I don't think you can.*
>
> *It's the story that really helps you. They worry about the writing and the prose and you think: F— the prose, no one's going to read your book for the writing, all they want to do is find out what happens in the story next ...*'

The good news is that, even if your story is weak or a commercial hook is absent altogether, these important elements may be injected into your book, even at a late stage in the writing and, as Kureishi says, working with the right mentor can be a great way to hone your skills. Your skills will continue to develop over a lifetime of writing.

As a writer, you learn on the job, whether you study a course or not, and the learning never stops. Whether a course is right for you or not, or whether it will teach you what really matters, comes down to your learning preferences and what you do outside the course to develop and hone your writing and storytelling abilities.

If you know that you are more confident and capable with some technical know-how, then investigate courses to see what would best suit you. There is a wider choice of writing and publishing courses than ever before, from short courses with the *Guardian*, online courses with the big publishing houses, through to university degrees and MAs.

 Key idea

It's the power of our story more than how we write it that will help us create a successful book.

Identifying and playing to your strengths

By the end of your first draft, you should strive to have a clearer picture of your strengths and weaknesses. Now is the time to establish what they are and make use of your insights in subsequent drafts.

Run through these and think about what you do best.

1 **Power of observation** Do you notice things that others don't? Are you aware of small details? Are you often told that you are observant? This is a great skill to have for recall and for all genres of writing.

2 **Listening** Are you a keen listener? Do you hear more than others and remember it for longer? Perhaps give this skill to one of your characters. How might it help them in their journey?

3 **Power of perception** Do you pick up on non-verbal clues, that which lies behind what people say? Use this in your work; perhaps it lends itself to quiet novels, or a mystery or detective novel.

4 **Steeltrap mind** Do you only have to hear, read or experience something once to remember it? This gives you the ability to dredge something up when it is useful. This strength is useful for research, for writing descriptive scenes and for writing complicated plotlines.

5 **Eye for detail** Can you vividly recall and recreate something you've seen? This strength is fantastic for writing investigative, detective, crime and legal thrillers. It's also good for literary fiction or books with an unusual setting.

6 **Very visual** This strength is useful for describing your setting, especially for books that rely on a strong sense of the locale, especially in far-away or unfamiliar locations. It's also a good skill to have if you are writing a travel memoir or any other fiction that transports the reader to another place.

Now think about your strengths as identified above and assess whether they are a good match for the genre you are writing in. Do you have a talent that could be put to good use in another genre? How can you tap into these strengths to boost your writing?

Your evaluation checklist

By now you should have worked on the problems that arose in writing your first draft and have improved your book by ironing out flaws and weaknesses in your book. Madeleine Milburn is a London agent with a good reputation for finding and launching new writers. Here are her tips for writing bestselling fiction. They make a comprehensive checklist to read against your first draft.

- **Character** – a strong character is the most important part of making your novel a bestseller. People don't usually remember the plot of a book or a film but we always remember strong characters. Think Harry Potter, Sherlock Holmes, Inspector Morse, James Bond, Hamlet. These are all brilliant and highly memorable characters. Make the reader empathize with your main character. We want to be able to relate to them.

- **Pitch** – keep it simple. If you can't pitch your book in one sentence, it may be that the plot is too complex or complicated. The most satisfying plots are straightforward: linear, with a beginning, middle and end.
- **Pace** – keep your chapters short, as this automatically adds pace to writing. Put hooks and cliffhangers on the end of each chapter to force the reader to read on. You want to make your book impossible to put down. Keep your sentences concise and keep descriptive paragraphs on the short side.
- **Concept** – think of a strong and original concept. Agents can use this to pitch to publishers, and publishers can use this to pitch to retailers, and readers can use this to pitch to friends. The best publicity for books is word of mouth.
- **Dialogue** – use as much dialogue as possible as this brings your story alive and really speeds up the pace of your novel. The reader doesn't want to read huge paragraphs of description unless you are writing a very literary novel.
- **Location** – try using locations that everyone can relate to. Big cities like New York and London are attractive and great for genre fiction. If you do use more obscure settings, make sure your readers can relate to your themes.
- **Research** – do research what you are writing about but use your knowledge sparingly. The reader will be more interested in details about your characters rather than detailed descriptions about what you know. You don't want parts of your novel to sound like an account.
- **Read** – if you are writing genre fiction then read the most popular books in that genre. You need to know what your readers want and expect. You need to know your competition!

  - If you are writing a crime or thriller, read the bestselling crime authors such as Harlan Coben, Lee Child, James Patterson, John Grisham and Patricia Cornwall.
  - If you are writing psychological suspense, read the bestselling suspense authors: S.J. Watson, Nicci French, Tana French and Sophie Hannah.
  - If you are writing women's fiction, read Sophie Kinsella, Jill Mansell, Lisa Jewell, Kathryn Stockett, Marian Keyes, Tara Hyland, Jane Costello and Jojo Moyes.

- If you are writing blockbusters, read Jackie Collins, Jilly Cooper, Tasmina Perry, Victoria Fox, J.J. Salem and Tilly Bagshaw.
- If you are writing accessible literary fiction, the kind of reading club books that people love to discuss, read books by authors such as David Nicholls, Maggie O'Farrell, Markus Zusak, John Boyne, Kate Atkinson and Carolyn Jess-Cooke. Richard and Judy picks are usually accessible literary novels.
- If you are writing erotica, read *Fifty Shades of Grey* by E.L. James!
- If you are writing Young Adult fiction, read the most popular books aimed at that age group, for instance Stephanie Meyer (though no more vampires!), Suzanne Collins, C.J. Daugherty and S.B. Hayes.

Read the opening chapters of bestselling books and then read your own opening chapters out loud. Does every sentence grip you? You need your readers to be mesmerized by your voice, unable to put your book down.

The key to success: what your book is about

Knowing what your book is really about is absolutely key to your success. Of course you know what your book is about, you may think, but you still need to make absolutely sure that you have focused on your original aim and that you are delivering on that aim.

You might imagine that Hollywood script doctor Mark W. Travis would have a no-fail neat formula to solve any problem in a film script, enabling the movie to go on to be a box office success. Assuming that his method was to step in with quick-fix technical screenwriting advice, his method came as a surprise. His success in fixing movies is based on honing the original story, checking the writer's intent and delivering on that intent.

KNOWING YOUR STORY

There is only the story. A good story can do so many things – persuade, wrap us in lovely prose, give us words that move us, entertain us, make us laugh. What we achieve with our story is as personal as why we write it in the first place. For the purposes of redrafting it's crucial to know what you wanted to say and whether you have achieved it. Have you told the story you set out to tell? Yes, I am repeating this message because it is a bestseller essential.

When mentoring writers, I read their writing only after we've discussed their story. First they describe their story, just the top line, to explain what happens, leaving out any detail. Rather than fine detail, the important thing is to know what it is about this story that will allow the reader to truly get at it, at a very deep level. That's not to say that the story itself need be profound, but that it is immediately understandable in the way that both *King Lear* and *Red Riding Hood* are.

The writing itself is much easier once the writer is clear about their story, as the prose itself is working to tell the story. All readers really want to know is – what's the story; that's what we most want when we pick up a book; if the writing is beautiful too, that's a bonus.

Key idea

Don't get bogged down trying too hard to write beautiful prose if it doesn't come naturally to you. Don't spend too much time agonizing over what the market wants, either. Just sit with your idea and give it a chance to grow and ensure it has the characteristics of a compelling, easily repeatable story so that when the time comes readers can easily tell others about it, too.

WHOSE STORY IS IT?

'What is your story?' sessions can be illuminating. The next question is 'Whose story is it?' Sometimes the author realizes that the story lies not with the character that they set out to write about but with another. They might say it is Miles's story that they are telling and reflect that in the synopsis but, when looking more closely at the story, realize that it is Fred whose voice is coming through more strongly and whose story is demanding to be told. It's critical to know whose story it is.

Often, the heart of the story isn't where we think it is, but buried with too many characters, heavy description, pointless actions, and scenes that fail to pull their weight in the scheme of the overall story.

Watch out for the detail trap, both in the writing and in evaluating your book. When asked what their book is about, writers can go into great detail explaining their characters' quirks, how they look, what they think, where they go and what they do, but these things don't constitute a story, they are just details, however personally important they are. Fill in the blanks: 'At its very centre, my book is about …'

Key idea

The one thing that can dramatically increase your chances of a bestseller is knowing your story inside out.

Workshop: the essentials of your story

Pretend your book is a Hans Christian Andersen tale and write it up very simply in two or three pages.

- Start your book with 'Once upon a time', introduce us to the main character and their world on page 1 and their arch enemy (whether a human or an obstacle) by page 2, move swiftly to what the arch enemy threatens to do to the protagonist, and the race against time that ensues. Tell us how it ends – is it happily, sadly or resolved?
- Think about the journey you took your main character on. What did they go through? How are they transformed? Is there a moral to the story? If so, what is it?
- Trim away any details that distract from the story, so you are left with the nub of the tale and ask yourself whether it ticks all the items in the checklist above.

Test your story to improve your draft

Here is a useful checklist to ensure that your next draft will have the attributes of a bestselling story. You should aim to tick all these boxes. Keep the list close by as you write, as it may take several drafts to achieve this.

Does your book:

- have broad enough appeal for readers and is it told in a human way that we can all understand, regardless of your theme or subject?
- set out a story and tell it in such a way that we care about the main character and the outcome?
- tell a story that's interesting enough to sustain our interest over a whole book?

- have the right amount of background information for us to understand and care about what is happening?
- give us a clear idea of what is at stake for the main character and the challenge/s they face?
- have scenes that pull their weight because you know the function and purpose of each scene?
- read tightly without flab or dead scenes that slow up the story?
- give the reader a reason to want to turn the page, i.e. is there enough happening with the right amount of tension?
- entertain, move or excite the reader enough that they are eager to tell their friends and family about it?

Many people – even writers – have seen more movies than they've read books and therefore our idea of how a story works and how it should unfold is often very visual, so it's useful to look at how story works in this familiar medium. I interviewed Mark W. Travis, a script doctor who is called on to rescue movies that aren't working, often mid-shoot.

With a hunch that it's not that much different to what makes a good book, I asked him what makes a movie special.

Mark W. Travis, Hollywood script doctor

'A *universality of the story that makes us feel emotionally involved. A writer needs to make us spellbound, invited and allowed in, emotionally involved with the story and the characters and what is unfolding. It may be counter-intuitive but the more personal a story is, the more universal it is.*

Deep down inside we have the urge, the need to share something, to communicate with others; whether that's one, one hundred or thousands of people. One of the most powerful forms of communication is storytelling. When story is autobiographical it is at its strongest.

We can't get very far through the day without telling a story. We are often not aware of it because we do it all the time. As storytellers, we are potentially more powerful than most rabbis and priests. People give themselves over to us for a period of time, whether it is a movie or a book. We are trusted. This is a big responsibility – having the reader in your grasp – what do you want to do with this responsibility? What is the story that you want to tell?

If you are writing solely to make money, it probably won't be very good. The wrong impulse is driving it. Write something that is meaningful to you. Write it as well as you can imagine. Make it deep, profound and rich. Most times we see right through any formula. Making a great movie or book is less about formula and more about vulnerability, fully expressing whatever the emotion is. Danny Boyle, director of Slumdog Millionaire and the London 2012 Olympics opening ceremony) is someone who does this well.'

Strong opening lines

A strong opening paragraph can grip a bookshop or online browser and encourage them to purchase your book. It can also double as a great hook for your promotional material and book blurb. One of the most memorable opening pages for me, due to its clear voice and pure chill factor, is *The Lovely Bones* (Picador). It is guaranteed to send a shudder down the spine of any reader.

Alice Sebold, *The Lovely Bones*

'My name was Salmon, like the fish; first name, Susie. I was fourteen when I was murdered on December 6, 1973. In newspaper photos of missing girls from the seventies, most looked like me: white girls with mousy brown hair. This was before kids of all races and genders started appearing on milk cartons or in the daily mail. It was still back when people believed things like that didn't happen.'

We are utterly with the author, transfixed from the first line. The bar is set high and the impetus is there to keep this gripping standard going. As well as having a great opener, this is a good example of a high-concept novel because the unique point of view provides such an attention-grabbing, easily explainable proposition.

Revisit your own first chapter opener and check to see how compelling it is. Send out your work to trusted readers and ask them, 'Would this opening make you trust me enough to spend your time reading this book?'

If you come up with an opening paragraph anywhere near as good as Sebold's (I'm still trying) and follow it up with delivering a story that stays strong and true to that promise, then you'll have it, you'll be on to a winner. If you start writing with the strongest thought you have (regardless of whether it remains your opening line after editing), that line will not only keep readers engaged but as the author it will keep your mind focused and allow you to tap into a strong, clear and focused voice for the entire book.

There are many different ways in which writers access their best ideas. Perhaps Sebold was munching on her cereal, not yet fully awake, reading the side of the milk carton and wondering, 'What if you were the missing girl on the side of the carton, and what if instead of giving voice to her distraught parent or her murderer, you told the story from the point of view of the murdered girl from the grave?'

Your favourite opening lines

If you're stuck, take a break to ponder how your favourite books begin and the impression and mood created from the outset. Think of the most impressive openers you've encountered and find out how the author got their idea, by reading interviews, the author's website or their Amazon author page, or build your own fantasy of how they might have got the idea as I did.

Taking and using feedback

In the process of writing a bestseller, writers have to be able to take criticism and rejection. It's a fact of professional writing life. The only way to learn how to take criticism is to be exposed to it. It's easier said than done, but definitely achievable.

When you have a draft of your manuscript that's as good as you can make it on your own, print out a good copy for your first reader(s). It would be disrespectful to the people who are giving time to your project to circulate writing that's not as good as you can make it. Choose your first readers wisely – two or three at most – and brief them well. Let them know what you want from them and what they should look out for.

Workshop: testing the emotional strength of your book

Mark W. Travis suggests the following exercise for road testing a book. You can apply it to your whole book or just pick out the parts that don't seem to work as well as you want:

'Test the emotional impact of each scene by noting how you feel when you read it.

- First, read your book through, scene-by-scene, writing down your own feelings for each scene. How do they feel to you as an observer?
- Are you clear about what you want your story to do to the reader? Do you want to entertain, thrill, frighten or move them?

When you are clear, find a test reader and ask them how they felt during and after reading each scene of your book.

- How successful were you in achieving your goal?
- How did you rate?

Your aim is to get the audience to connect with the emotional flow that you intended the book to have. If you didn't hit the spot, how can you rewrite it to produce the feeling you wanted to create?'

If you have successfully got the reader in your grasp, that's great. You want them held firmly yet gently enough so that they'll willingly stay with you throughout your book. And then, once they've read it, you want them to shout from the rooftops how great your book is.

Make sure that your test readers have enough experience of the genre to understand what you're trying to do, and to comment fairly. Ask them to mark parts of the manuscript that were problematic: the sections they skimmed over, or had to reread, or couldn't understand. They may be able to suggest solutions. Their suggestions might be valid. However, you need to look at the sections that caused them problems for yourself, and to try to work out what went wrong and how to fix it.

In your local area or online, there will be writing groups and classes. Get to know your fellow writers. One or two of them might be excellent first readers for your work, and you can return the favour for them. This is helpful in itself but a bonus is that you'll see another writer's work in an early stage rather than always seeing polished, finished books.

For general workshop sessions, you may have to share your work before you've reached the end of your first draft. Be aware that this may affect your confidence. Some say this is all part of the process and getting used to sharing your work will help you toughen up, which can be true, but if you really feel it will hinder rather than help your writing, it may be an idea to leave sharing your writing until you have completed the first draft stage.

If you listen carefully to your first readers, you'll have more changes to make. When you have another good draft, you may want a professional opinion. There are growing numbers of manuscript consultants and editors who can advise on developing your work. Try to get a personal recommendation, and make sure you understand the scope of their work, their fees, and their timetable before signing up.

 Key idea

When you receive feedback, listen to it all and make notes. Don't reject comments, don't get defensive and try to explain – you want to know exactly where this reader thinks the problems with your manuscript lie. You don't need to agree or disagree but can decide later whether their points are valid and how you're going to address them.

Redrafting

The reader is important to you and your book sales, so it makes sense to know your reader and what they like, so you can start to think about how you can generate word of mouth for your book. Why now, you might think; surely that is the dirty business of marketing and you don't want to sully the creation phase with thoughts of the market? We consider the reader here in the redraft process because if you redraft your book without knowing why you are redrafting you could well end up with different words, though not necessarily better ones, which may not help you scale the heights needed to produce a bestselling book.

First, ask yourself: What do I have here and what am I really saying in this book? Getting back to why we tell stories in the first place, you could say that we tell stories in order to entertain, educate, communicate or simply to express ourselves. What is your purpose with this book? If you didn't know when you started writing, you should be closer to knowing now.

The number of redrafts you do will vary but you will need at least one or two, or as many as it takes to do all the things to it that you know need to be done.

FINDING YOUR 'HOOK'

When asked what their book is about, many debut novelists summarize the plot (the action of the story), when they are really being asked to describe the theme of their novel. Knowing and being able to express this can, in turn, lead to understanding what the hook of your novel is – in other words, what will hook readers into the story and make them want to find out what happens, and turn those pages you have so lovingly and painstakingly imagined and crafted.

In a workshop or pitch setting, I relentlessly question authors on this. I work with writers who can turn out well-written novels, with interesting characters, in settings I want to know more about. But it isn't enough. What is often missing is that elusive hook. It's the hook or concept that makes you able to distill it into a sentence that readily makes the book interest an agent, and then the agent can easily convey that to a publisher, who is able to smoothly pitch to and get the publishing team on board, make it easier for a cover designer to grasp the idea and turn that into an powerful cover. And then the bookseller or Amazon reviewer can enthusiastically recommend your book and the reader can grasp the concept the moment they pick up your book.

Key idea

Come up with a killer concept and you make your own life easier as well as those of anyone else involved in the process of turning your book into a bestseller. If you don't really know what your book is about, your reader won't either. Produce an unfocused book and you'll get in the way of the reader enjoying and championing your book. If you want to whip up good word of mouth, you have to earn it, so you must sort out this aspect of your work.

THE USP OF YOUR WORK

The question needing to be answered in your redrafting process is: Why would anyone want to publish this book? What is it about this book that makes it special or unique? Every author needs to answer those questions, more so than ever in today's overcrowded publishing market.

Publishing is incredibly competitive and publishers are incredibly hot on needing a reason to publish a book beyond a nice idea and good writing. As we have seen, the current market demands a strong concept or hook to draw readers in. (Later on, when pitching, you'll see why these questions are posed in this section.) In order to take your book on, agents and publishers also need to feel your book is a story that must be told or that the voice is so unique that it must be heard. The difficulty is that they see a multitude of goodish books – and good isn't enough to get published.

Give publishers a compelling reason to publish your book beyond well written or just good enough. Is there anything you could do to strengthen the book, to give it a more specific and defined angle? Go back and revisit your opening chapter to double-check that you have this covered. Check your genre fit too.

Here's an example of two key things to check for and inject at redraft stage if you were writing a thriller.

Opening paragraph

Your opener should be a perfect match for your genre. Write a gripping opening, consistent with your genre, that grabs the reader's attention with immediate action: you need to connect with the reader straight away and show them what you are writing. Draw us into the plot immediately and keep us with the main protagonist from the outset. We need some scene setting and description, but don't overdo the descriptions or the reader will feel bogged down and the book will have a slow start.

Look at other thrillers and read their first paragraphs – they will draw you in immediately (this is very different to, say, romance, where you want to be slowly led into the book, or a literary book which can start just about anywhere).

Plot development

Remember that 'less is more' with thrillers – you must use each event in the story almost as a cinematic scene and each one must serve to add to the plot. This might not be obvious at first to the reader – especially if the scene is a flashback/forward – but will become obvious as they continue to read.

Luana Lewis, author

'The term "psychological thriller" is fashionable in the current market. At the heart of the psychological suspense novel is the way in which some form of trauma or abuse (usually in early childhood) impacts on and warps the development of empathy and twists and pervert human relationships.'

ADVICE FROM AN EXPERT

For 14 years Rebecca Carter was an editor at Random House, where her acquisitions ranged from literary to more genre-led fiction, novels light and dark, for old and young, set everywhere from Afghanistan to Acton, and non-fiction in the areas of history, travel, food and nature writing, political and cultural polemic, often mixed together and with a strong emphasis on story. Now an agent, she is building a list that reflects and broadens these preoccupations. She has some useful advice for authors who are redrafting but fear they may simply be changing words and are unsure whether their work is improving.

Rebecca Carter, agent, Janklow & Nesbit

'There is a danger for authors that they get stuck on trying to get sentences perfect because it is so difficult for a writer to get perspective on the whole. It's like being the swimmer in the swimming pool churning through the water, concentrating on technique, but not being able to see whether you're going in a straight line. This is when it's useful to get the feedback of a reader who can tell you what it's like to experience the book for the first time. However, I would stress that simply getting a friend or acquaintance to read your book, doesn't necessarily help. They might identify the bits they liked and the bits that bored them, but they won't necessarily be able to put their finger on exactly what the problems are and how to fix them.

This is where an experienced editor comes in. An editor knows all the tricks of the trade – how changing the point of view of a scene might help, or rewriting a third-person book in the first person, or cutting or adding a whole element of the plot. If you don't have a handy editor to hand, letting your book sit for six months, not reading it at all, might help you get more perspective on the whole. People often say to me that, coming back to a novel after time away, makes them feel as if it was written by someone else. It also gives them the energy to be more interventionist rather than just tinkering. It's so hard to "kill your darlings", but sometimes it's essential. I really love Sandra Newman's handbook How Not to Write a Novel. *She is so funny about all the things that writers do wrong that, if a writer has made the same mistake, it leaps out a mile.'*

Editing

Once you have redrafted your book, you are ready for an editor. Good editing can make a silk purse out of a sow's ear, transforming your book into something much more attractive and appealing to agents, publishers and readers.

 Rebecca Carter, agent, Janklow & Nesbit

'*The number of drafts a book goes through during the editing process varies enormously from book to book. It can be ten or even more with the agent and then – if publishing via the conventional route – be edited some more by the publisher. Certain problems are often so intrinsic to a book's conception and its plot that they are impossible to eradicate, however much editing is done.*

I worked for about a year on a brilliant debut novel to smooth out the rather unconvincing melodrama of the ending, where a murder took place. It was a novel in which all the other events were about the protagonist's everyday life and relationships, and then suddenly her mother is murdered. We did at least three drafts and managed to make everything as convincing as we could. But reviewers – who really liked the book – still picked up on the melodrama of the murder.

However, editing definitely had a transformative effect on the book. It was in a very rough state when I acquired it. The author was a musician who was trying to capture the urban life and street language of her crowd. The dialogue was brilliantly slangy, but often went on for too long. The plotting was too complicated and not correctly paced. And the relationships between the brilliantly vivid characters unfolded in a slightly rambling fashion. Luckily my boss at the time let me acquire the novel because I said I would work with the author to fix these things. I thought it was important that a fresh voice like this be heard – otherwise there are whole realms of experience that stay out of the world of "literary fiction". Editing changed it from being a novel written in the heat of personal experience into something highly enjoyable for a reader.'

THE EDITORIAL PROCESS

In an increasingly competitive market, many writers hire their own editor or use an editorial consultancy before pitching their book. Self-publishers need to hire their own editor.

There are three stages to the editorial process, whether you self-publish or work with a publishing house:

1 structural edit

2 line or copyedit

3 proofread.

1 The structural edit

A structural edit looks at the big picture: the overall structure, the flow and how well the story is told. Does the writing need improving, perhaps, in the expression, tone or prose used? Often, structural problems will be resolved as part of the redrafting process but it is nevertheless important to have at least one fresh pair of eyes on your manuscript when you have completed it. If you have an agent or a book deal with a publishing house, they will usually do some structural work on your book; however, it does need to read well and should be in the best possible shape before you deliver it to them.

Once you have the manuscript sorted out and have done your final draft based on structural edits, it goes to a copyeditor.

2 The copyedit

A copyeditor will read your manuscript line by line, checking for sense and grammar, querying and checking anything she is unsure of. She will also mark up headings and style for the next stage, which is text design. If you are self-publishing, it is your job to brief the copyeditor, letting them know what to look out for, anything you are especially worried about, weaknesses and so on, and then let them get on with it.

Most editors and proofreaders work using tracking on screen. If self-publishing, you are in control of this process. It is useful for you to see the changes made (so that you can approve the changes and also learn from the process), so ask for a clean edited copy with all changes taken in and a copy showing the tracked changes for reference. If you have a publisher, ask them what you can expect in the editing process and when you might be needed to check proofs as often you are asked to turn them around quite quickly.

Your book also needs preliminary content (front matter) and endmatter, which is what goes at the front and the back of a book. You'll be familiar with it: you see it every time you pick up a book, but you probably don't usually take much notice of it. These are the sorts of pages you will need to include with your manuscript:

- Front matter
    - acknowledgements
    - copyright page (self-publishers only)
    - contents page
    - dedication
- Endmatter:
    - sales material/contact details
    - further information/resources, if necessary
    - references, if necessary

Pick up several books of the same genre as yours and follow their approach, adapting it to suit your book.

The book is now ready for text design, by which I mean formatting it to make it look like a book rather than a typescript. Provide the designer with examples of text that you like and tell him what you like about it.

3 The proofread

Once the book is edited and the changes agreed, and the text has been designed, a clean set of proofs is produced. The proofreader and author independently proofread the manuscript. The proofreader (or indie author) then amalgamates the changes from both sets of proofs into one set of proofs. Any changes are then sent to the text designer, who charges according to the number of changes needed.

A final set of proofs is then produced. It *should* be perfect!

Who will edit?

Writers often ask whether it will be the agent or the publisher that will do most of the editing. This depends on two things: how polished your writing is; and the individual approach of your agent and publisher. Recent trends have seen a shift in responsibility for editing from the publisher to the agent.

> ## Rebecca Carter, agent at Janklow & Nesbit
>
>
>
> 'It is too broad a generalization to say that editors in publishing companies don't edit any more. Many of them work extremely hard to edit books, often outside working hours. However, it is also true that the need for those editors to take on more of a marketing and sales role – in convincing their colleagues to take on a project in the first place, then in writing excellent copy, making sure the cover is right, having marketing and publicity ideas, talking to journalists, etc. – means they have less time for editing. Agents are often picking up the pieces in this respect and doing additional editing for their authors.
>
> What is more, because editing takes time away from all the crucial jobs mentioned above, publishing companies are less willing to take on projects that need a lot of editorial work. As convincing retailers to stock and market a book becomes ever harder, publishers want books they can run with immediately and make a big splash with. If a project disappears into the "being edited" shadows for a while, it can lose impact in-house, which then impacts on the way publishers present it out of house.'

Keep going or give up?

Most writers write because they 'have to'. They write not knowing whether their book will ever be read by anyone other than their mother, let alone be published. This determination and courage is what makes publishing such an amazing industry.

In a workshop setting, I always encounter at least one writer who has been working away on a book for years, and yet they are unflinching when gently told their idea isn't working. This doesn't mean they need abandon their project; there is always a reason why they chose a particular storyline or subject, so the first course of action is to delve deeply into that. By reconnecting with the original intention, there can be a way to make a story work. Sometimes, though, this feedback is received with relief and taken as a kind of 'permission' to put the project aside, something they've been wanting to do but were felt unable to because it would be too much like admitting weakness or failure.

If you really feel that an idea has reached a dead end, put it aside and have a break or start on a new or fallback idea. Think back to Marie Philips, whose second book wasn't working until she blended it with another idea to come up with a book that not only won her editor's approval but also is uniquely hers.

But what if your book really isn't working? Carole Blake has a story about surprising a roomful of writers at LBF with a straight-from-the-hip answer to an unpublished writer.

Carole Blake, agent, Blake Friedmann

'At a "how to get published" day-long seminar before a London Book Fair some years ago, a man in the 200-strong audience had described in great detail how he had faithfully followed the instructions in my book for preparing his submission letter, his partial manuscript, etc., and had had it rejected by more than 40 publishers and agents. He said he was completely puzzled as to what he was doing wrong. He obviously came from the school of thought that says if you follow the rules you will automatically get published. I replied: "There is one thing you may have overlooked. You may not be a very good writer." The room became a vacuum as everyone inhaled at once. It wasn't my most tactful moment, but some people seem to have such self-belief, unfortunately unleavened by any powers of self-criticism.'

Sometimes we need this; it's tough love. Perhaps Carole did that author a favour: he may have sought objective advice on his manuscript, and if he found she was right, redoubled his efforts to improve his writing and make the book better. If, on the other hand, the writing was good but the pitch poor, he may have been spurred on, changing tack in his efforts to find a publisher.

7

Literary agents: the gatekeepers

Literary agents provide a direct route to publishers. They know the publishing industry; they are in regular contact with many editors. They know their tastes, their pet likes and dislikes and what they are looking for.

When you pitch via an agent, your work gets priority over the 'slush pile' where unsolicited manuscripts lay waiting to be read. (And these days many publishers do not accept unagented work at all.) Editors trust agents to send them only good-quality work, which makes them more eager to receive their submissions and read them quickly. There's more of a sense of urgency around an agented book because publishers know that it may well be being read simultaneously by rival publishers.

This chapter explains the role of literary agents in publishing; what they are looking for in an author; what turns them off; and how to impress them. It also covers what they are good for and how they can help your career.

What are agents good for?

Before you go to the trouble of finding an agent, you need to know whether it will be worth the effort. The advice to new writers has always been that if they are to have any hope of getting a book deal and having a successful career in publishing, they need an agent. But is this still true in the days of social media and the explosion of independent authors doing it for themselves?

The answer is that if you want to pursue the traditional publishing route then you'll find it easier with an agent. Having an agent has always been the best way of finding a publisher. Let's have a look at what agents do on behalf of the authors they represent. I act as literary agent to non-fiction writers but I am also a writer who believes in a flexible, adaptable approach to publishing, as every writer is different and will find their own route to publishing their books.

The role of an agent

Working with an agent is not just about a single book deal; it's a long-term relationship. An agent will:

1 look after your writing career
2 take a 360-degree approach – looking at all the ways in which your book could become a launch-pad to other things
3 provide editorial comment and help
4 be a sympathetic sounding board
5 look after money matters, including negotiating and chasing invoices
6 keep an eye on the publication process from submission to publication, marketing and beyond
7 make your book more likely to be read by publishers in the first place, as agents are a level of quality control
8 help you get a higher advance
9 be able to negotiate a more favourable share of rights income
10 be more likely to get foreign rights deals
11 look out for film and TV opportunities or use a sub-agent who specializes in this
12 be on your side; you won't be doing it alone.

What to expect from an agent

Writers are often unclear about what to expect from an agent and they can have unrealistic expectations. It's not easy to find an agent and it may feel that they are holding you back from finding a publisher. There is a reason for their choosiness: they are in business and work on commission, only getting paid once they sell your novel. And, like you, they want to work on projects they are passionate about. Often, they can spend up to a year editing and helping you before the novel is ready to pitch to publishers. So, while they are elusive to begin with, when you get one, they are completely on your side.

What an agent will *not* do is morph into a third parent, always agree with you, magically make your book a bestseller while you stay at home and write, or absolve you from any responsibility for promoting your book and engaging with readers. If you are a good writer but not so great at business or self-promotion, then you need to either improve your skills in this area *or* forget the idea of self-publishing and instead refocus and increase your efforts to find an agent and publisher. You'll still have to do a lot of your own promotion, but with an agent and publisher you'll have someone on board who will act as your champion in these things.

Choosing an agent

The process of researching and choosing an agent should begin before you start to pitch. The agents we invite to speak at London Writers' Club tend to be young (or young at heart) and hungry – just like our authors. When choosing an agent, go for someone you feel you could be friends with; the relationship with your agent will be long and close. Do your research to find an agent who has experience selling your genre.

You do need an agent and publisher who understand and are right for you, so make your choice wisely. If it turns out to be a wrong choice you can move agents, and publisher, though it isn't a decision to take lightly, and (under most contractual agreements) the original agent and publisher will retain rights to their share of income from the books you worked on with them.

Ed Wilson, agent at Johnson & Alcock

'You can find out about agents via the Internet; you can find your match pretty much anywhere – big corporate agents, middle-sized agents or one-man bands. Johnson & Alcock are in the middle somewhere. The size of the deals they do doesn't mean that one agent is better than another. Some agents do lots of small deals – with children's picture books, for example, which usually attract a maximum of £5,000 advances – compared with agents who do the prime, big deals where they can get six-figure advances.

When deciding who to approach, who you'd like to work with, don't just go for the most visible agents. Work out what you want. Do you want to deal with someone's assistant (as may be the case with the more high-profile agents) or do you want them on the end of the phone when you call? As well as the deals they've done, look at author care – look in the acknowledgements of their author's books. If they don't thank their agent, that's a bad sign.

An author's relationship with their agent is going to be the most important in their career. The days when an author would find an editor for the whole of their career are long gone, and the point of solidity, the point of continuity, is now more often the agent.

At some point in your career you're going to be rejected, whether that be by agent, publisher or, if not at those stages, then later, with a poor review. The sooner you are, the sooner you'll toughen up and get ready for the business.

When an agent takes your submission off the pile (whether real or virtual) and begins to read, they'll quickly make up their mind about whether you've got something, often as early as the first page. Your challenge is to encourage them to keep reading. When faced with a stack of 50 manuscripts, an agent knows that they will reject most, if not all, of them, so of course it makes sense for them to get to the most likely *outcome, rejection, as quickly as possible and get to the good ones – the potential bestsellers – faster.*

When it comes to submitting your work, the most important message I have is that it's a job; take it seriously.

Because writing is a creative endeavour, people often think that it deserves less scrutiny than the rest of working life. However, you're not sending out your book on the off chance that someone might quite like the look of it: you are applying for a job, to be part of a stable of commercial creatures, thoroughbreds who need to go out and sell books.

Being an author requires you to sell yourself as an author. Your first step, that you have to take seriously, is pitching to an agent. You must treat that task with professionalism, so don't send out your covering letter or email with a typo. When an email first comes in to me, you have approximately a minute to grab my attention in your pitch letter. Agents are inundated with people sending them their manuscripts; we receive 50 to 100 per week, sometimes a lot more. We only take 15 per year from the slush pile; that's a 0.2–0.5-per-cent hit rate. Agents always say they don't look at submissions the minute they come in, but the reality is we are always on the lookout for the next bestseller, we have that tingling sense, so we do have a quick peek at the email when it first comes in.

Whether or not an agent takes you on depends on the quality of your work, but you have to be tenacious (without being annoying) to get it read in the first place. I do believe that people with talent do get there in the end, but you really have to want it.'

What do agents look for?

When an agent starts reading your manuscript, there are some key things they look for:

- **A compelling voice**
  Of more than 100 literary agents who have shared their wisdom at London Writers' Club Live, every single one of them said that a clear, strong and compelling voice is what excites them. It is what makes them want to take a punt on a debut author. The best way to describe this is that it sounds like a clear, consistent *character* who insists on coming through as though

from another place. It doesn't sound like any other voice they've heard.

- **Longevity and a wealth of ideas**
  Agents – and publishers – want writers who can demonstrate that they're not a one-trick pony. They are after authors who aren't limited by writing entirely from their own experience – a well of material that can quickly dry up. At first glance, this may look like another form of gatekeeping and it is, in a way, but it also has benefits for your career and for making your writing life easier and more professional. Remember, everyone involved in a book deal is investing in you as a writer, not just in the book currently under discussion or submission.

  In terms of your career, thinking about your next book and getting on with it while pitching book one takes some of the pressure off writing book two. Many authors find it tough to write book two when they are under the pressure of promoting book one, and may suffer from performance anxiety if book one is particularly successful. (See Elizabeth Gilbert's TED talk on 'Success, failure and the drive to keep creating', where she describes her extreme success as feeling the same, and just as uncomfortable, as having her writing rejected.)

- **A unique idea or a fresh spin on an old story**
  Check again that you have hit on something that no one else has covered and worked on in the way that you have. Of course, we know that hardly anything is new and original, so it is in the packaging, the concept, choice of words and the execution that we make something different and give people a reason to buy.

  Historical novelist Philippa Gregory's books are a good example. Few would have thought there was anything new to say on the subject of the Tudors, but she proved that a fresh angle was possible. Her best-known novel, *The Other Boleyn Girl*, was made into a TV drama and a major film and the mass-market edition of *The Kingmaker's Daughter* sold 19,871 copies in seven days in March 2013.

- **Big concepts**
  The Slap is a good example of this type of book. It has been published in 28 countries and sold over 1.2 million copies worldwide, including an astonishing 300,000 in Australia. It won several awards, including the Commonwealth Writers' Prize, and was made into an ABC television series in 2011.

What to avoid

Here are some key reasons why authors don't get a book deal:

1 **You don't send your work out.**

 How is any agent going to represent you if you don't submit your work? You're suffering either from perfectionism or from the 'waiting to be discovered' fantasy. This isn't about writing but about mindset. I know from firsthand experience that it can be tough, but put aside your negative thoughts and focus on the work itself and send it out when it is 'good enough'. Seth Godin, entrepreneur and author of 17 books, including *Lynchpin*, describes putting a product out into the world as 'shipping'. It is essential to making things happen. Go to the audit exercise in Chapter 5 and start to make shipping a part of your writing habit.

2 **You don't finish.**

 You'll never know whether your book could have made the bestseller charts if you don't finish it. If you suffer from this, visualize yourself in a year's time: do you really want to be in the same place you are now with some good ideas half developed but nothing finished or on submission? Writing and polishing are wonderful things but not finishing prevents you from shipping and means that your great idea will come to naught. See the audit exercise below.

3 **You don't act on feedback.**

 There's no point asking for feedback if you don't take it on board. A fresh pair of eyes is invaluable and can quickly highlight problems with your manuscript that it might otherwise have taken you many months to uncover.

4 **You pitch prematurely.**

 You're not ready, or your manuscript isn't ready. Never ever send a first draft; an experienced reader can spot them a mile off. If you don't believe me, save your first draft in a separate document rather than overwriting it and compare it with your final draft. If you ask an experienced author how many drafts they wrote before publishing, they will probably say five to ten or more. You don't have to radically rewrite each time; sometimes a new draft is just 5–10 per cent of new material.

5 **You send out a generic pitch letter to all the agents you pitch to.**

 You must tailor your letter to each agent you submit to. You are effectively asking them to go into business with you, so approach it with the care and attention it deserves. Say why you are sending it to them specifically; it makes it more personal if you say why you thought they might be the right person to represent your book.

6 **Your book isn't good enough to be published.**
Ouch! This is the most painful one of all to face and is surprisingly absent from much advice to authors. If it is true, accepting the fact and working with it may benefit your work and career enormously. We've all heard of successful writers receiving multiple rejections before being published and we know it is a subjective business so, while your book might be good, it might not be right for an agent at this time. Your book may be good but not good enough to compete with other, better books. What you need is a clear sense of what you need to improve in order to be published or whether it does need to be abandoned.

 Key idea

Before concluding that the book just doesn't work, get an objective critique. You need to know what is wrong with it, what needs fixing and whether they think it can be fixed. Seek the advice of a mentor or professional editor if budget permits, or do a swap with a trusted writing buddy, as it is likely that agents will be too busy to give detailed feedback.

7 **Your pitch package lets you down.**
- You've sent out a first draft.
- Your letter is too long and doesn't get to the point.
- Your synopsis fails to sell your story adequately.
- You haven't done your homework – for example, you get the agent's name wrong.

All these things will be covered in the next chapter about pitching, so this won't happen to you.

8 **You send it to the wrong agent/s.**
Nothing is more frustrating than talking to a much-rejected author and realizing that most of their rejections were because they sent the manuscript to an agent who doesn't represent their particular genre (or they sent fiction to someone who represents only non-fiction). Even when an agent says, 'This is good but it's just not for me', this means that they too are the wrong agent. You need to find out who will be a good fit for your book, so do your research.

9 **Current trends are against you.**
You are writing in a saturated or overcrowded market. Many editors turn down books that are actually pretty good because there are too many similar books on the market. Your options are to keep trying despite the feedback you've been given or hold on to the project and bide your time. Fashions change; there are cycles in publishing. Take it out every now and then to see how you can inject some new magic to take it from good to amazing.

Writing audit

This exercise will help you decide what and when to pitch. Be businesslike about it and then settle down to make some creative magic.

1   Take all your unfinished projects out and skim-read them.
2   Which do you have the most enthusiasm for?
3   Choose this one to work on this time; tuck the others away until next time you do an audit.
4   Compile an action list: what do you need to do to finish it?
5   Break it down: set yourself a series of steps and targets with mini-deadlines, the final one being your pitch date.
6   Set a regular time for committing to this project.
7   Set an external deadline: book an event or find a tough writing buddy to help you keep to it.
8   Start work.

Find your voice

Many agents say that they're not convinced by a book unless they can hear the author speaking aloud to them, as if they are in the same room. They're referring to the voice that comes through in the writing. To check whether your book has this bestselling emotive quality, try this:

1   Scribble down in a list or free-form what it is that you want your reader to feel when they read your book.
2   Speak your words aloud. How do you feel?
3   Have you given yourself goose bumps, made yourself laugh, made yourself cry? Whatever the appropriate emotion for your book and its genre, ensure that it is delivering what you would like your reader to feel. For instance, if your thriller

makes people feel weepy rather than enthralled and eager to turn the pages, then perhaps you're writing in the wrong genre.

4   When asking a writing buddy or friend for feedback, ask them how they felt when they were reading it. Then tell them how you wanted them to feel. Is it a match? If not, what went wrong? If there is a mismatch, what can you do to resolve this?

What you can learn from rejection

It's inevitable that even the best writers will face a few rejections, so how can you mentally prepare for the knock-backs that may come your way? In theory, following the 'tick list' that you should know by now – *write the first draft, write a killer proposal and a great query letter and send it out to a dozen agents* – will result in at least one agent offering you representation but, unless you are extremely lucky, the reality is very different and rejection is more likely.

There is a silver lining in rejection letters, however, because they often have something to teach us. Sometimes rejections come from agents that are simply a wrong match for your writing (and you) rather than because of any failures in your writing. Read the rejection carefully and take on board any feedback. Change your mindset so that you stop feeling victimized by the process. Treat the letters as constructive criticism and thank the agent for their time; you might get some further advice and recommendations in return.

 ## Kirsty Mclachlan, agent at David Godwin Associates

'Submitting to an agent can be tough – if you've asked for feedback and subjected it to thorough evaluation and know your book is good, don't get put off by nos; just think of them as "not great matches". Be inspired by Kathryn Stockett's The Help – as a first novel, it was rejected by nearly 50 literary agents but has now sold more than a million hardcover copies, thanks to word of mouth alone, mainly via book clubs and blogging.'

Be creative and include other ways to find agents and where agents can find you, not forgetting that they need writers as much as writers need them. Try festivals, author clubs like London Writers' Club, competitions, pitching events and the London Book Fair, to name just a few. The Bookseller is the publishing industry's weekly magazine and is a great source of information, facts and even gossip about the publishing industry. You'll certainly find out what different agents and publishers are commissioning and working on.

When an agent is interested

Once an agent says they like your work and asks to see the full manuscript, what happens next? They will probably suggest some changes, which you make. You resubmit to them and you're waiting to hear what they think. A week, then a month passes and you still haven't heard anything.

Do you have an agent or not? This in-between middle thing is quite common. The agent is keen, as they've said, and they've suggested changes necessary in their view to make the work attractive to publishers, if they haven't asked you to sign an author agreement yet they probably think the book won't succeed without these changes and they are still considering whether the book can be made to work. Sometimes this phase can take some time. If you are in any doubt about where you stand with an agent, just ask, politely: 'Where do we go from here? Is there anything further you need from me?'

Once an agent is satisfied that they have a good chance of selling your book, and feel that they can work with you and has taken you on, they will then start the task of placing your book with a publisher. This is where they use their knowledge of publishers and their editors to find the right fit for your novel.

Focus point

1 If you feel passionate about your work, don't give up.
2 Do your research when looking for the right agent.
3 Get out from behind your desk and find other ways to meet agents.
4 Take feedback seriously, use it to improve your work and your pitch.

5 Do check that your book has legs. The type of rejection you
   get should alert you to the quality of your book and whether
   it is a question of taste and fitting into an agent's (and
   publisher's) list or if there are faults in your writing and idea.

Where to next?

*Now that you know what an agent does and what he or she needs
from an author, the next chapter tells you how to pitch your book to
give it the best chance of being placed with an agent.*

8

Preparing your pitch

Pitching is the aspect of publishing that attracts the most questions whenever an agent speaks to a roomful of writers. Agents have a huge volume of reading to do, week in, week out. They are short of time and have to read fast to get through the stack of manuscripts they are faced with. They may not always be able to give every writer feedback, but they are incredibly generous with their free time when it comes to going out and networking and meeting authors, so do go out to meet agents when and wherever you can.

Now that you know more about what an agent does, you will have a sense of whether the agent–author relationship would benefit you and your career. You have also learned some of the reasons why you might receive a rejection. Armed with that information, you have reached the stage of being ready to pitch your book.

Every agent who speaks at London Writers' Club Live events gives members their personal email address and encourages authors to submit when ready. This is a huge benefit of writing networks and the number one reason why you should be getting out to writers' events and festivals to meet agents. (And other writers are often very generous with advice and help, too.)

Madeleine Milburn, agent

'When submitting, be as articulate and professional as possible in your introductory email. This should start with a short paragraph introducing the work you are submitting – the genre and the intended readership. A short, compelling blurb should follow. When writing your blurb, imagine you are talking to the literary agent in person about your book. Pitch your book in an enticing way that will make us want to read it immediately. Tell us a bit about yourself that is relevant to the book you are submitting. Your pitch should be as strong as a blurb on the back of a bestselling book. Remember, a blurb "sells" your story whereas a synopsis "tells" your story.

Towards the end of the letter it is useful to include a sentence or two about the next book you are working on. It is important for us to see that your next book would appeal to the same readers.'

Preparing your pitch package

Getting your pitch package right won't guarantee that you'll get an agent, a book deal or end up with a bestselling book on your hands. But what it *will* prevent is falling at the very first hurdle. Here is the London Writers' Club's step-by-step guide to preparing your synopsis and pitch package for fiction.

Your pitch package should include the following elements:

1 Synopsis
2 Submission letter
3 Title page
4 Author background and promotional hook
5 Market potential and competitive or similar works
6 Chapter synopses
7 Sample chapters

THE SYNOPSIS

The synopsis acts as an overview of a book. It should tell the story in a clear way, without selling it, and take up a page or two, no more. You may want to include information here about the market for your book and the competition (but don't just list the competition; tell the agent how your book differs from the competition). Tell the agent what makes your book stand out.

A synopsis is not a retelling of your book but a stand-alone tool – and it will help the agent decide whether they want to see more of your book. The sample chapters (see below) will show your writing style but the synopsis is the outline of your narrative.

Some helpful tips to bear in mind when you are writing your synopsis are:

- Trim it down by taking out all adjectives and adverbs, unless really vital.
- Don't include secondary characters or plots.
- Tell someone about your book – by talking through the synopsis and trying to make someone understand the story, you will hit all the right points.
- Take a look at the backs of other books – TV listings and film blurbs – and how they all manage to refine a story right down to the bare skeleton.

Writing the synopsis

A good list of questions to ask yourself when writing a synopsis is as follows:

- What is the story about?
- Who are the main characters?
- What do these characters want?
- Why do they want it?
- What stands in their way of getting it?
- What is the theme of the novel?
- What is the novel about?

Don't leave any cliffhangers; you must include the whole story. Tell it in the present tense.

Then read your synopsis aloud to get a sense of how the words flow. It must make sense – when an agent's time is short, they will not have the time or inclination to ask you to explain it.

THE SUBMISSION LETTER

Although they are always looking for the next big thing, agents are also incredibly busy, working on their current list of titles. They have only a small amount of time in which to read submissions. The submission letter will therefore be your crucial shop window – it must entice, intrigue and grab the agent's attention. Don't bore the agent with too many details; the letter should be concise and simple, professional and to the point.

The sample pages show 'how' you can write and the synopsis says 'what' you are writing, so the letter needs to be an 'information pack' with a paragraph about the book that will draw the agent's attention to the other pages.

Here is a checklist of what to include in the letter:

1 **The reason you're writing to them**

   What do you actually want the agent to do? Are you asking for feedback, for advice or for the agent to represent you? Many letters do not do this and though the assumption is made that they are looking for representation, it's a bit odd not to make it clear.

2 **The title of your book**

   It's possible to win over an agent at this point, so much so that they'll be excited and won't need to read anything else in your pitch but will go straight to the writing sample.

3 **A brief summary of your book**

   This is your very brief elevator pitch – keep it to three or four sentences at most. Remember that the sample pages will give an idea of the style of your writing, and so the letter needs to be brief and to the point when summarizing the story and the concept of the book. Once you have polished your synopsis, look at it carefully to see whether you can condense it down to three or four sentences – look at blurbs on the backs of books to see how to use similar language to entice the reader (the agent). This paragraph should contain the 'hook' – your sales point.

4 **Market position of the book**

   Who is your audience? Who are your readers? If you have approached an agent because they represent an author you admire or because you feel your work is similar or inspired by them, it's worth making that connection. It also shows that you have done your homework and have targeted the agent well. This doesn't mean saying, 'Read it now or miss out on the next Dan Brown'. Make it about the agent, so say, 'As agent to Dan Brown, you might be interested in my work in the same genre.'

5 Information about you, the author

Include a paragraph about why you were able to write this particular book. Keep the details relevant and say why you decided to write it, how you can personally market it and how your background can help sell it. Say whether you have written before and let your personality shine through. I was recently told that a book was 'written in anger', which was compelling and fascinating. Show that you know your subject well and that you are qualified to write about it.

6 Thanks and request for advice

End the letter by thanking the agent for their time; reading the pitch package alone will take some time, and if they agree to read the full manuscript it will take them four or five hours, plus an hour or so to digest the material and then respond to you. Ask them for some advice as well – they might just point you in the right direction even if they decide to say no to representing you.

Workshop: submission letters

The following list of things to watch for will help you prepare for and anticipate any objections and, ultimately, the reasons why the agent may reject your book.

- Firstly, check the length of your letter. An agent only has a short window of time to read submissions – often it's early in the morning or late in the evening. Pare down your letter so that it includes only the most vital elements. There are times – and every agent differs – when email submissions are requested. Emails are, by their very nature, short and to the point. Agents want to know what your book is about – a bit about you – and to be convinced to read further.

- Start the letter in the conventional way – 'Dear ...', and state why you have chosen to send the proposal to them (for example, do they represent a writer you admire or a writer similar to you?). Say what you are attaching/enclosing.

- The second paragraph should be a short and snappy few sentences about the underlining concept of your book. Think about your subtitle and make it memorable; it needs to really add something to the title. It can be used to explain the title more, to add something more to the title's meaning but should still be interesting and easy to say/ good to look at on a page and, essentially, not too long.

- The letter should fit on one side of A4 and be three or four simple paragraphs. Take out the padding and just keep it to the point.
- State what your intention is in writing your book – again, keep to just one or two sentences.
- A paragraph about you! This information is especially vital to a non-fiction proposal. Why are you the expert? Why can you tell this story? Why are you the only person who can write this book? If you have relevant experience, do ensure that the agent knows this from the outset; otherwise they will wonder why you are writing this book; why anyone would want to read a book on this subject by this person.
- Agents need to know why this book is relevant now. Do what you can to make your book feel part of the Zeitgeist.
- State clearly your final word count, as you should only be pitching when you have a completed manuscript. I've lost count of the number of authors who've told me, 'the agent asked to see more of my work but I didn't have any more, I then was in a panic to get it finished which hindered rather than helped my writing.'

TITLE PAGE

Once you have worked on your title and subtitle, give your proposal a title page. If you have chosen the right title, this will really help to imprint it in the agent's mind. It also reinforces the use of the title as a marketing tool.

Set your title in a large, bold font in the middle of the page. At the bottom of this page, put your copyright line (just © and then your name and the year you completed the current material), your postal address, email address and your website if you have one. This looks professional and efficient and it also means that, if the letter goes missing, the agent still has the vital details.

 Key idea

It cannot be emphasized enough how important a good title is. Say your title out loud – does it work? Can you imagine telling others about it, booksellers ordering copies over the phone, or people typing it into an Internet search? Does it have a five-star quality? If not, work on it until it's absolutely right.

AUTHOR BACKGROUND AND PROMOTIONAL HOOK

This will be an expansion of the short paragraph in your letter. Frequently, authors send out a proposal and neglect to mention that they have a compelling background reason for writing their book, which may present an excellent promotional opportunity for the agent and publisher.

For instance, I mentored a YA author whose novel is set in a gypsy world. She wrote a decent synopsis and pitch letter, but it was only when she was asked why she wrote the book and how she knew so much about gypsies that she mentioned that her schoolteacher mother worked with gypsy children. And so she grew up hearing their stories at the kitchen table. Not mentioning this would have been a missed opportunity that could have enabled the agent to see a good hook for PR.

Break down your 'About the author' into paragraphs in your proposal, and always use and work your backstory:

1 Be clear about your compelling reason for writing your book.

2 Make sure you put that reason across effectively.

> ## Key idea
>
>
>
> If you haven't done so already, work on your backstory. It needn't be wildly exciting; it just needs to be relevant – in some way linked to your novel.

MARKET POTENTIAL AND COMPETITIVE WORKS

Think about the demographics and statistics of potential readers. Who do you see as the readers? Who are your core readers? What will they learn? Again, think about the timing of your book – it should be both relevant to today and have a timeless quality. Find other books that might compete – how does your book differ? Which books would you compare your book to? How does your book further complement or expand the genre?

CHAPTER SYNOPSIS

Just as you wrote your synopsis of the whole book, you need to write one for each chapter. This should give the agent a sense of the tone of your book, more details about the content and how the narrative arc will work – how you have moved your book's storyline forward.

THE SAMPLE PAGES

This is the real meat of the proposal. It's often the bit that the agent will leap to – over the rest of the proposal – to find out exactly what your writing is like and its tone and style.

OTHER CONSIDERATIONS
Prologues

Writers frequently use prologues without really understanding why they are doing so. A prologue is only successful if it really adds something important to the book. What is the purpose of your prologue – what do you want it to do? Often, prologues introduce the theme of the book by using a flashback. In a prologue, characters are introduced and it should act as a little 'scene' with those characters. To compare it to a film, a prologue will be like the bit at the beginning, before the titles and the start of the real body of the film. If done badly, it can just delay the start of the story and confuse or even put off readers. Often prologues are written in an entirely different voice and style to the rest of the novel, which can give the wrong impression to an agent.

Doomed pitching (and how to avoid it)

Remember that at each agency there are many different agents with different interests and tastes. Don't bring on more rejections by pitching to the wrong agent, or pitching in such a way that you won't stand a chance.

 ## Charlie Brotherstone, agent at A.M. Heath

'My client list is quite eclectic – my non-fiction client list is largely made up of politics and sport writers and my fiction client list is a mix of commercial fiction, psychological suspense and more literary fiction. There are four main agents at A.M. Heath, all with very specific tastes and lists, so it's vital with us, and when writing to any agent, to personalize your letter and state why you are writing to a particular agent. It's harder than ever to get published, so think long and hard about why your book stands out.

I enjoy working with authors editorially, even though some books can take a year from the point when I offer to represent an author to when the book is ready to submit to publishers.'

Here are Charlie Brotherstone's four no-nos of submission letters:

1 Typos and spelling errors

2 Aggressive letters or those with a sense of entitlement or a 'you must publish this book' type claim

3 Letters addressed to the agency as a whole or to many agents

4 Premature pitching – sending out first drafts or books that are clearly not ready to be submitted.

Charlie says that what agents are looking for, what makes a bestseller, is that 'sweet spot': that is, accessible novels. These are the books we want to discuss and communicate about with each other. They are great book club books, perfect for discussion because they are often issue led and have big concepts. They emphasize an uncomfortable situation.

Your pitching checklist

Ask yourself these ten questions before you pitch:

1 Is my book ready to send out?

2 Have I redrafted and edited to the best of my ability?

3 Can I describe my book in one snappy line?

4 Have I got the right title?

5 Do I have *and can I provide* a compelling reason for why this book should be published now?

6 Am I clear about what is at stake for the key character/s?

7 Is what is at stake important enough for the reader to care about it?

8 Have I created a strong enough set-up that the reader will care about what happens in my story and to my characters?

9 Am I clear about my backstory and do I use it effectively?

10 What do I bring that is new to the world – is it a unique idea, a fresh spin on an old story or a familiar idea turned on its head?

The three-sentence pitch

Imagine that you have just bumped into an agent – at a dinner party (it does happen) or at the school gates – or an editor is introduced to you via a friend in the pub. What happens? Do you bore them senseless with too many details about your book, tying yourself in knots, and blow your chance of actually 'selling' your book – or do you pitch them your three-sentence pitch?

Having a three-sentence pitch (TSP) is essential for word of mouth but also for your promotional material. Your TSP will become your friend, so make sure you know exactly what it is, work at it, hone it and repeat it. It will be the pitch you include in a submission letter/email and it will be the way you describe your book to friends and colleagues. Ensure that it is bright, bold and memorable.

 Key idea

Every book is about one of two things – either a stranger enters the room or the protagonist goes on a journey. We need to know what makes your book different, so your pitch must say more than 'it's about love and friendship', which is the subject matter. Take it further until you have something as powerful as 'love conquers all' – but less clichéd.

FIVE STEPS TO A WINNING TSP

1 **Do some research.**

Look at some examples of how things are pitched. Look at film trailers and book blurbs, and read TV listings to see how programmes are described. Take down your five favourite books from your shelves and practise writing TSPs for those books.

2 **Know your book.**

This may sound obvious, but you really do need to know the underlying themes and what you are saying about your themes. If your book is about love, what are you saying about love? What is your take on it? And who is the main character? What is their journey? What are the beginning, middle and end of the book? What is the framework you have used to hang your story on – the timeline and location? Really know these details well and you can use these to build a great pitch.

3 **Tell the story.**

Your TSP is a description of what actually happens – it is the plot, the story, the narrative arc. Don't use up valuable pitching time or space by telling the agent, your book is about love and friendship. Tell the story. So begin with the main character: 'it's when x', faces the conflict/obstacle, 'it's when x faces y' and then the 'journey', 'it's when x faces y and goes from A to B'. The journey can be a physical or an interior journey.

4 **Work out the 'what ifs'.**

Build a pitch around the 'ifs' in your book – or in other words – the questions in your book. A book – fiction or non-fiction – should always ask questions and should set a premise up at the start. So for example: 'What if a girl had two imaginary friends and one day, the friends went missing?' (Pobby and Dingan written by Ben Rice), work out the 'what ifs' in your book.

5 **Add a twist.**

Finally, sprinkle some gold dust on the pitch by adding a bit of a twist, a bit of uniqueness and 'you-ness'. What is the tone of your book? What's unusual about the main character? How did you write it? Why did you write it? Is it frightening or funny? Which genre is it in?

Write a three-sentence pitch

Prepare your own three-sentence pitch. You won't necessarily get it right straight away as it is different writing skill needing practice, so experiment with a few different ways of doing it. You may write a page or even two when you first try this, but slowly and surely you'll whittle it down to three sentences. Keep refining it and it will evolve into something strong and useful.

Focus point

The truth is that there are no guarantees, nor is there a hard-and fast-rule or format that will get you a commission. Some authors have had offers based on few sentences scrawled on a napkin while others have produced the perfect proposal and still received rejections. Nevertheless it is always best to produce a solid proposal, based on all the advice in this chapter, and show an agent that:

- you can write the book
- your backstory demonstrates that you're 'qualified' to write the book
- your book is worth investing in
- you are professional and businesslike and will work hard with the agent to ensure your own success.

- you have more than one idea and are committed to a writing career.
- you are flexible and will listen to and respond to feedback.
- you will work hard to promote your book.

Where to next?

The next chapter is about publishing your book and the key decisions you need to make to get your book successfully to market, whether that is via conventional routes or via the newer forms of publishing that have opened up.

PART FOUR
Publish

9

Trade publishing

Literary agents can do much for a writer's career and, although they are the conventional route to publication, they are far from the only option available. There is a wide array of publishing choices now open to writers, which include conventional, or traditional, trade publishing of books and ebooks, as well as digital-only publishing.

In this and the next chapter we will explore what you can expect from the different routes to publishing and their pros and cons. And there is a checklist of the essential tools you'll need if you decide to self-publish, with suggestions for how to get further help. Finally, we will look at hybrid and other unusual and exceptional authors.

You and your publishing career

It may seem late in the game to ask this, but it is important for this stage of thinking about your bestseller. Why are you writing a book and what do you want to do with your book?

These are the kinds of answers that typically arise:

- To make money
- For fame
- To have a writing career
- To give to friends and family
- To see what I am capable of
- To tell a story I'm passionate about
- For the love of writing.

You might think that the first two reasons are the ones that will motivate you and give you the best possible chance of achieving a bestseller. They're not. Despite the abundance of bestselling success stories, the majority of authors are unlikely to make their fame and fortune writing a book. Only a very small number of authors dominate the market in the UK and elsewhere and, while you can and should keep on striving to be in that top rung of authors, you need a clever strategy to enable you to write and publish good books, while building an audience for your books.

Not only do fame and fortune elude all but the mega-selling super-authors but there are also many more authors failing to make a living from their books than those who succeed. Both indie and published authors face the disappointment of depressingly low book sales. Typical earnings of professional authors aged 25–34 were just £5,000 per annum, according to a survey by the Authors' Licensing and Collecting Society. They found that '60 per cent of people calling themselves "professional authors" said they required a second source of income to pay their bills.'

Look closely at a bestselling author's career path, and you'll see a lot of hard work and determination. Of course the money is important as it keeps them fed and allows them to keep writing, but it was largely their passion and belief in their writing that sustained them through long days and nights of writing and rewriting a book they were never sure anyone but their mother would read. What you might also notice is that their path was rarely straight and true: usually it was meandering, packed with trial and error and studded with highs and lows.

Since you are reading this book, it's fair to assume that you are passionate and serious about writing and that you want a writing career rather than a one-off book. In this case, there is a good chance that you will persevere with your writing, a key requirement for success. You'll need to be agile, open to experimentation, and prepared for rejection and failure while still remaining hopeful. If, however, you are writing a one-off book out of a determination to tell a story for friends and family and you would also like it to be a bestselling success, this chapter is for you too. Many writers set out to write 'just one book' and love it so much that they carry on writing.

If that sounds like a tall order, and lonely and hopeless to boot, you might find it easier to bear if you get out (or online) and meet other writers. It really does help to meet other people willing to do the work, to keep writing come what may, to persevere at their writing. They are your peers and they can offer encouragement and support. The enormously successful indie author Hugh Howie knows that his sales have benefited from taking an active part in writing communities and he firmly believes that we should regard other authors not as our competition but as our community.

> ## Key idea
>
> To help you on your way to a bestseller, it is important to consider all the publishing options available to writers. The options are wider and more accessible than ever before; write a good book and make the most of what the technology allows and you will edge closer to a bestseller.

The state of publishing today

In recent years, trade publishing has been through enormous upheaval, largely as a result of the loss of print sales to digital formats and because of the radical shift from bookshop to online sales. The publishing industry is experiencing a shifting balance of power between authors, publishers and booksellers, and technological changes have altered that balance for good.

As ebooks and self-publishing gained a strong toehold in the bestseller lists, publishers initially seemed to want only to retain their dominance, but recently appear to have become aware that they need to pay more attention to the most essential cog in publishing: the writer. There have been some moves to prove their increased awareness but many authors argue that they still have a long way to go – for instance, pointing out that they don't receive their fair share of ebook royalties and that they are not paid often enough.

In an effort to recoup the revenue they've lost that previously came from print, many publishers have now established digital-only imprints, where they publish titles that, as the name suggests, are published digitally only. Many authors ask whether this is sufficient innovation and whether, if they can reach their readers directly via online retailers, they really need publishers. Can't authors sidestep publishers and sell directly to the reader? The answer is yes; it is possible and it can also be more profitable, which is why so many authors are doing it.

All authors must make their own decision about the route to take and there are advantages and disadvantages on both sides. For example, two big-name indie authors who've enjoyed the most success via self-publishing acknowledge the value of trade publishers, both verbally and in action, by continuing to work with them in their publishing.

 ## Sylvia Day, author

'I don't think publishers have any advantage whatsoever for ebooks. They're at a huge disadvantage. They overcharge. They have complicated distribution agreements, which limit them for offering ebooks in certain areas. I honestly cannot say that it would be a wise decision for an author to sell a digital edition to a publisher unless they have different terms in the contract to limit the disadvantages.

'On the print side, publishers have a tremendous advantage. The print marketplace has not accepted self-published books. They don't like books that are not returnable. They still go out in the system as a print-on-demand book. Distribution for self-published authors for print is abysmal.'

(Interview by Jeremy Greenfield of Digital Book World.com. http://www.digitalbookworld.com/2013/hybrid-author-sylvia-day-the-world-cannot-survive-without-the-publishing-industry/)

What to expect in trade publishing

Trade publishing is dominated by the Big Five: Hachette, HarperCollins, Macmillan, Penguin Random House and Simon & Schuster. There is a tendency to want to be published by one of these five, but there are many good medium-sized and small publishers and it is worth looking at them all. The quickest and easiest way to find your way around the publishing houses is to look at who publishes the books you read and the books in your genre. You might be surprised at how many bestsellers are published by smaller publishers. J.K. Rowling, for instance, is published by the independent publisher Bloomsbury.

Trade or conventional publishers pay an advance and royalties in return for an exclusive license to a range of rights agreed and set out in a contract. They pay all the costs and do all the work involved in editing, producing, printing and distributing your book and also put their resources behind promoting and marketing your book.

For many authors, it can be a wonderful experience to be taken into a publishing house and given plenty of care and attention, but for others it turns out to be frustrating and disappointing. The attention you receive and how many resources are allocated to your book depends on a number of factors. Well-known or established authors not only receive more attention but they also attract a greater marketing spend. And if the publisher has fought against other publishers to acquire a title and paid a high advance for it, they'll work harder to make that book a success. The debut author, who arguably needs more support and resources than the established author, tends to get much less.

While this might be unfair and inconvenient for the debut author, for the publisher this makes perfect economic sense. The more they have paid in advance, significantly more for a big-name author, the more pressure they are under, and the harder they work, to recoup their investment. Though some authors have bitter tales to tell about their publishing experience, in theory the publisher is on your side. You're in business together: they've invested in your book and will do everything they can to sell copies. The more books they sell the larger their profit – and yours – though, as we will see in the next chapter on self-publishing, many indie authors argue that the author's share of the profits is not big enough.

As we saw in Chapter 7, the first rung on the ladder to finding a trade publisher is the agent. Your agent will draw up a list of publishers to whom he will submit your book, sending your book only to the publishers they know to be a good fit for your book. Their experience of the industry, their role as a filter of projects and their long working relationships with publishers ensure that the publisher will take the submission seriously enough to read and consider it. You first need the agent and then a publisher to fall in love with your book. Get this right and they will be your champions throughout your career. Both will advise and help you to develop your author brand.

The submission process

Your agent, having accepted you (see Chapter 7), will typically choose a number of trade publishers to submit your book to. When a publisher looks at the work of a debut novelist, they are sizing it up to establish whether or not it will sell and whether it will sell in sufficient numbers to justify investing in your book. They take a risk when they pay out an advance and they want to be pretty sure they'll get their money back plus a healthy profit. They are trying to establish whether you are worth that risk.

If you don't have an agent and want to pitch directly to publishers, do so armed with the knowledge that research has shown that less than 1 per cent of unsolicited manuscripts find a publisher. If you are determined, keep an eye out for small presses who will accept unagented submissions. The bigger publishing houses don't normally take unsolicited manuscripts but they may sometimes have windows of time in which they will accept manuscripts without an agent. Check the relevant websites – most have clear guidelines regarding submissions.

 ## Kirsty Mclachlan, agent at David Godwin Associates

'When an agent sends a book out into the world, it is a very similar situation to when an author sends their book to a publisher. We do our homework, research what each editor is looking for, hopefully chat to the editor first, and then tailor each submission email to the editor in question. It's a very personal business and it pays to work on that. Then we play the waiting game, which varies enormously in length. I've received an offer literally overnight and another time it took six months for an editor to read a book and then offer. There are no set rules.

There are some typical outcomes when a publisher is interested in your book. When a publisher is keen, they can either offer straight away or ask to see the author. The author is increasingly part of the publishing process, so the publisher wants to see whether they can speak about their book in an engaging and eloquent way. You don't have to be a stand-up comedian or a trained actor; it's more about the passion you have for your book and how you convey that. It's important for you to meet the editor so that you get a chance to see whether you will be a good fit. Marketing people, publicity, digital and rights people may also attend the meeting, so you'll get a sense of the whole team.

If you are lucky enough to get a few publishers showing interest, then your agent will set up meetings with each of them. After the meetings, the agent will ask the publishers to come back with their offer by a 'hear-back' date. If they decide to run an auction, they will take the highest offer after the first round and then go back to all the other publishers and ask them if they'd like to increase their offer. However, this offer is not just about the level of advance: there are other elements at play such as the editor's vision for the publishing of the book and the rights. At some stage the agent will ask for best overall offers, which means the very best deal including all the elements – contractual and otherwise.

The agent will then discuss all the offers with the author and they will make a decision together. The agent should be fairly transparent when the auction is running but they shouldn't reveal who the publishers are (to one another). And they should keep the author up to date with all developments.'

Key idea

Take care not to have your head turned by the wooing strategies of some publishers, who might offer you cakes, chocolates, presents, books, and a crowd of keen people at all meetings. The most important thing to do is to put aside all that and listen to what the editor says. Making a connection with your editor is vital to a good working relationship further down the line.

Some editors may want to meet an author even if they're not convinced about the particular book they've been pitched, so it is a good idea to have a second or even a third book idea up your sleeve, if possible. If a publisher does not want a book being pitched but they still like the author's writing, they may perhaps commission another book that the author has in the pipeline.

One note of caution: stick to the same genre with your projects. Agents and publishers are wary of authors who want to straddle a number of genres simultaneously, particularly when they are starting out. It is tough enough to get a debut author started and established in one genre, let alone several at once. Once you have proved yourself, they may become willing and able to look at your career more flexibly, although, for obvious reasons, they'll want you to continue to write in your successful genre. The usual pace for bestselling genre fiction is to release one book per year, so you really need to love your chosen genre, given how much of your life will be spent writing it. (The trend in bestselling self-publishing is to produce more, writing and publishing two books per year, so bear that in mind when choosing trade or self-publishing.)

The acquisitions process

What do you have to do, in your proposal and in person, to make a publisher confident enough in your book to want to publish it? What you must do is show a publisher that you have written a book worth investing in.

When a publisher assesses a book to decide whether or not to take it on, they look at trends in the market, at competing authors and at the authors they already publish in the same genre (see the acquisition overview sheet in the Appendices). They also weigh up the marketability of the author and the work. If you know that your genre is hot, find out what the numbers are and include the sales figures in your proposal. In developing your idea, keep in mind that the more unique your book, the easier it is for a publisher to promote it, so they may be more willing to help build your author platform.

A publisher needs to see an author demonstrate that they know who their audience is and where they are to be found, and that they are willing to take steps to build that audience. Some books get lucky and stumble across their audience, but that can't be relied upon.

A publisher won't take an author on, no matter how good or well written a book is, if they think there is any doubt that they and their work can attract an audience. They prefer to choose authors – whether previously published or not – who have a platform already or who have demonstrated their ability to build an audience. They will look at the size of your audience for blogs, podcasts, Twitter and Facebook as well as your database of fans and readers. This explains why successful bloggers have often been an attractive option for publishers, although even this is no guarantee of success for a book. For instance, the hugely successful, and hilarious, US blog 'Shit my Dad Says' didn't quite translate in the UK when published as a book, although it was huge in the US.

Publishers recognize and respect authors who treat their writing as a business. If you take it seriously and demonstrate that in all your dealings with agents and publishers, it will be noticed. Think carefully about when you can realistically deliver a finished and polished manuscript and deliver what you promised when you say you will. Don't take the risk that the publisher will have had second thoughts about your book. If a book is languishing on the publishing schedule because it takes too long to edit, the people in your publishing house may get tired of looking at it. It becomes dull and overlooked.

You also don't want anyone else to have crept into your space. I've not seen two identical books, but if the subject is 'Zeitgeisty' enough to make it exciting, commercial and bringing with it a sense of 'this needs to be published now', there's an increased chance that someone else will have a similar idea. It doesn't have to be exactly the same as your idea to be a spoiler. Similar can be enough to put off your publisher and make them look for a way out of publishing your book.

MEETING THE PUBLISHER

When a commissioning editor tells you they are interested, they will take your book to an editorial or acquisitions meeting. At this meeting will be quite a number of people in-house whom your book has to impress. You may not be aware of them or meet them all, as it is the editor who wants to acquire your book who has to do the convincing on your behalf. The strength of their pitch relies upon the strength of your story and your pitch.

Who are the people involved and what are they looking for?

- The **Publishing** or **Editorial Director** needs to be sure the book is a good fit for the list and will make money.
- The **Publicity Director** is looking for a promotable author with a good backstory.
- The **Marketing Director** wants to know whether the author understands their audience and the marketplace and that they are able to build an audience.
- The **Sales Director** weighs up the strength of the idea and how broad the appeal is, to predict how many copies they believe will sell.
- Special **salespeople** decide whether the book might appeal to non-traditional outlets, such as museums, art galleries and book catalogues such as *The Book People*.
- The **Rights Director** thinks about which foreign publishers they can sell your book to. They'll look at how well your idea will

travel, considering whether it will work other English language territories and in translation.

- The **accountant** runs out a profit and loss calculation for your book, based on the confidence of marketing and publicity and the predicted sales and rights figures given to him by the above people. The amount of advance offered to the author is calculated on the 'health' of these figures.

If they decide they want to publish your book, sometimes you'll meet the editor you'll work with at this point, or you may meet a team of people. Your agent will tell you what to expect, but always prepare in advance of meeting an interested publisher. Take time to look at what they publish; observe what they do well and perhaps what they do less well so that you know what they can and can't do for you.

The most likely people you'd meet with the editor are the marketing and PR people, who will be quietly checking out how easy you'll be to promote, running through a checklist in their head. They will be probing to find out everything from your backstory, who you can get endorsements from, whether you would be convincing when interviewed, through to what hooks there are for PR, and the audiences you can reach that they can't.

 Key idea

Have your backstory ready for your first meeting with a publisher. Ensure that it is relevant to your book and that it has a 'hook'. Recall the spark in you, the personal reason why you wrote this story at this time. Was it something in the news or a chance remark that set you thinking? Did a memory come back to you? How you got the idea is interesting to people and starts the ball rolling for conversations that create enthusiasm for your book first in this meeting and ultimately for promotional material and interviews.

Many debut authors fixate on the book launch, on literary reviews and on getting books into the bookshops. These are lovely things but they aren't what that sells the most books, so don't be surprised if the publisher doesn't spend a lot of time discussing them. The publishers will do whatever they think best for your book and so what they want to hear from you at this stage is potential audiences and opportunities for sales that are unique to you. They want to hear about the communities you belong to, your social media followings and anything else that you know will help to sell books in reasonable numbers.

The book deal

A book deal offer isn't just about the money; there are non-financial issues such as whether the author likes and trusts the editor and publishing house and can envisage a long and happy career with them.

RECEIVING AN OFFER

If you are working without an agent and you receive an offer, you will need to negotiate the amount and other terms of the contract yourself. It is wise to get help with this as the contracts often run to 30 pages or more and will bind you for many years. There are freelance contract advisors who can help and the Society of Authors offers free contract vetting advice to their members. Carole Blake's book *From Pitch to Publication* explains the entire process in detail, including the negotiating and contract phase.

THE ADVANCE

The publisher is not paying you for the work itself but is advancing you an amount of money against the future royalties they believe you will earn through book sales. The advance is usually paid in three stages: on contract signature; on delivery and acceptance of the manuscript; and on publication of your book.

Given that the advance is an investment, it is a mark of the publishing house's confidence in their prediction of what they think your book will earn for all involved.

Key idea

Your job is to increase the quality of your book, and the perceived worth of your book prior to pitching, in order to maximize their confidence in it and the size of their offer. The most obvious way to do this – and, yes, this advice is repeated throughout this book – is by writing a good book and building your platform and profile.

PUBLICITY AND MARKETING

How much a publisher does for you is variable, as we saw earlier. The more a publisher spends to acquire a book, the more they will allocate to the PR and marketing budget to maximize sales and recoup their investment.

Don't choose a trade publisher thinking that they will take care of all the marketing for you; they won't. There is no guarantee of exactly what they will do for you. The PR is mostly focused up to and around your book's publication date rather than being an ongoing push. Most authors will receive a little attention prior to publication and perhaps for a month or two after your publication date and then the marketing people will move on to other books.

 ## Carole Blake, agent, Blake Friedmann

'Few publishers are prepared to tie themselves to marketing obligations in a contract. Instead, I make them pay handsomely so that they have to work hard to earn it back, and I maintain close contact with the publishing team (everyone who works on Peter James's books, for instance) at the publishing house, so that I know on a day-to-day basis what they are planning to do, how they are planning to do it and when they are planning to do it. Peter copies me in on every bit of correspondence with his publishers around the world, so that I am current on everything and can step in quickly if something looks like it's not shaping up right.

Macmillan make detailed marketing presentations to us several times a year well in advance of publication dates so that we are always involved in their plans. I work like this with all my clients.'

From pitching to publication

If successful, the process from pitching to publisher to final published book could look something like this:

1 Agent sends synopsis, covering letter and chapter samples to select publishers.

2 Publisher is interested; asks to see more of the book and/or wants to meet.

3 Publisher is still interested and wants to take it to an acquisitions meeting.

4 Publisher makes an offer.

5 Agent and publisher negotiate and agree on advance and royalties, subject to contract. Contract is issued; finer points are negotiated; contract is signed.

6 Signature on contract is paid (second payment is made on delivery and acceptance of completed manuscript, third and final on publication).

7 Delivery date is agreed.

8 Book is delivered – editor will do a structural edit and discuss revisions with you.

9 Copyeditor is briefed – you will look at any changes and discuss any queries.

10 Final MS goes to text designer.

11 Proofs are produced, for final, letter-by-letter, word-by-word reading by you and a professional proofreader.

12 All corrections are taken in and off it goes to the printer.

13 Usually at least a month prior to publication, copies are in the warehouse.

14 Advance copies are sent to you.

15 Your book is published.

The digital revolution

Dan Franklin, Digital Marketing Director, Penguin Random House UK

'The future of books is authors.'

Having felt the pain of watching indie publishers take a lead on digital, particularly in genres such as romance and science fiction, trade publishers are working hard to adapt and innovate. They are now paying much more attention to digital, with digital-only imprints springing up everywhere. They are also being forced to take more account of authors' needs and wants. Here are some recent publisher initiatives, it is important to be aware of these initiatives as they can help you to grow your book income and achieve your goal of a bestseller. It remains to be seen whether trade publishers will be as effective as indie communities but they show willing and a belief in the power of community, and are making a good start.

- Penguin Random House UK has launched 'My Independent Bookshop', a new reader recommendation platform allowing book lovers to set up a virtual bookshop, share their favourite reads and discover, recommend and review books online.
- Pan Macmillan launched a women's lifestyle website, 'The Window Seat', with book content as well as culture and entertainment news; they have also launched a new women's fiction book club.
- HarperCollins ran a Romance Festival online over a whole weekend, involving a wide range of authors, publishers and agents who got involved in discussions, Q & A, competitions and readings.

THE FUTURE OF TRADE PUBLISHING

The future of trade publishing is anyone's guess. While digital has claimed a permanent place, it seems that print isn't dead, though further change is inevitable and wanting to maintain the status quo at any cost doesn't help anyone, least of all authors.

 Carole Blake, agent, Blake Friedmann

'Change brings opportunity. I like what I see around me: today's marketplace makes it easier than ever for writers to get close to their readers. Things like social media and online marketing are all for the good. But if you're asking me to predict the future: no way! I just try to seize the opportunities as they occur, for me and for my authors.'

The pros and cons of trade publishing

The advantages of trade publishing are as follows:

- **Professional editing**
  Whether it is your agent or your publisher, or both, who edit your book, editing is a big plus point of trade publishing. Editing includes everything from structuring your book – how it flows and how it opens and ends – to correcting grammatical

and factual errors. With fewer publishing houses and less time for editing in house, there are many more freelance editors, so it is possible to access professional editing as an indie publisher, but at your own expense.

- **Status and prestige**
  Some people believe that being publishing by a trade publisher has much more kudos attached to it than self-publishing. They argue that, given the level of gatekeeping, editing and investment involved, there is a stamp of approval aspect to being trade published.

- **Advances**
  What trade publishing does provide for is for the author to have an income while they are writing. A self-publisher must work without an advance and must either keep costs low or fund their publishing from other sources.

- **Freedom**
  Many authors value the freedom to write that having a trade publisher allows them. You can get on with your writing while others carry on with the editing, designing, publishing and business side of taking your work out into the world.

The drawbacks of trade publishing are as follows:

- **Slow timescale**
  One of the key criticisms of trade publishing is that the process is too long, from pitching to an agent, then agent to publisher, and often there is more than a year's wait until publication. And if your genre is hot and no one can be sure when it will peak, you run the risk of the market having moved on by the time your book is published.

- **Infrequent payments**
  A huge bugbear is the wait to be paid. Royalty statements, and payments, are only sent out twice annually and even then some income is retained against possible future returns from bookshops. This contrasts with self-publishing, where you receive income monthly and many online platforms have dashboards where authors can see sales in real time. Those who want to see the system changed argue that with accurate point-of-sale information available, there's no reason why trade publishers can't change their twice-yearly accounting, since they know exactly how many copies have been sold.

- **Low payments**
  It often shocks new authors when they find out how little they will be paid per copy sold. Most books are sold to retailers at

a high discount and so the royalty is calculated on the price received rather than published price, but let's say your royalty is 10 per cent of published price and you get the maximum royalty possible. For a paperback costing £10, the most you could possibly earn is £1 per copy. With the discounts given to bookshops and online retailers, it is much more likely that you'd see 50p or less per copy. And, that is before the agent takes their commission of 15 per cent. So a lot of copies need to be sold to earn a good living via conventional publishing.

Key idea

Without opening up a can of worms about the resale of artistic works or about a charity's right to this income, it is a fact that Oxfam and the other charity bookshops, which charge around £2 for a paperback, can make more profit per copy from each book than an author does through trade publishing!

Physical versus digital

Trade publishing is criticized for its assumption that authors will continue to pursue the traditional route to get a publishing deal. As we will see in the next chapter, some high-profile indie authors are refusing publishing deals and/or negotiating more favourable terms than ever before, arguing that the trade needs to work harder to keep attracting bestselling authors and to make deals more financially attractive, or authors will increasingly choose alternative routes to market. Some pundits point out that a further benefit of increased digital sales is to reduce potential lost sales that result from the resale of physical books or the sharing of physical books. This is a fast-evolving part of publishing, so do keep refreshing your knowledge so you are informed and up to date.

The print run

You may wonder whether having a publishing deal means that you are more likely to achieve a bestselling book. Will your book be in a bookshop? How many books will a publisher print?

The large publishing houses print in bulk, and as a rule you won't have any say in the initial print run, unless you are running a big event or have a direct deal where you need a fixed number of copies large enough to encourage the publisher to increase the print run. Your publisher pre-sells your book to the big chains and independent bookshops and lists on Amazon, so they base their first print run on those pre-orders, plus a bit more. They are very careful not to over-order, so don't be surprised if the initial print-run figure seems very low to you.

Why try to influence the print run? Because in theory, the more books that are in circulation, the greater the potential for sales and the closer you will get to a bestseller. And if you are working hard to promote your book and you succeed in creating a swell in demand, there's less risk that a successful PR campaign will be in vain because your book is out of stock and waiting several weeks for a reprint. Often, the potential buyer will forget about it and find another book to buy in the meantime.

Increasing the print run

Here are some ways of increasing the print run for your book.

- Arrange an event where your book is included 'free' in the ticket price, pricing the ticket accordingly. You will have agreed on the amount of author discount from the publisher at contract stage, so right away you can start to make money.

- Be nimble in your thinking: do you have a story, a setting or character that relates to a museum, a society, a club or a tourist attraction? Approach them to see if you can do a promotional event and secure book orders at the same time.

- Look for and secure speaking engagements for around the time your book is available. You may have been asked in the past to speak at events, often with no payment but, once you have a book to sell, you can make the event profitable for yourself. Ask the organizers to promote your book in exchange for you speaking.

- With a book in hand, every time you speak you now have a moneymaking opportunity happening. Your publisher will happily organize the delivery of books to be sold at an event and may also agree to produce promotional materials, such as a flier, for you.

Cover price

Pricing and discounting is of great importance for authors as it has an impact on the potential for making a bestselling income. When you are trade published, these decisions are not yours to make.

In the early days of digital, many publishers priced their ebooks similarly to their print books, even though with ebooks the setup and distribution costs are lower.

The reasoning seemed to be that, if print and digital books were similarly priced, that might provide an enticement to keep buying physical books.

If we self-publish, the argument goes, we can set the prices for our books. This argument overlooks the fact that self-published books sit alongside – sometimes indistinguishable from – trade books and so do compete and must compete on price. Set your price too cheap and people might wonder why; too expensive and you won't be able to compete.

The cover

It is generally agreed that book covers help sell books. Only if you are self-publishing do you have total control of the choice of cover; if you are publishing with a trade publisher, you don't. The publishing house will take care of the cover design, but you can ensure that you have some input by providing a one-pager with your ideas, attaching any covers that you particularly like. (And unless you have a cover designer universally acknowledged to be brilliant, don't attempt to send in a cover design; it rarely works in an author's favour.)

When you are publishing with a trade publisher, you'll probably have a marketing and cover clause in a contract like this one:

> 'The publishers shall have entire control over the following matters in relation to the work: publication date; production; materials; manufacture; design; binding; jacket; inlay and embellishments (if any); the manner and extent of any advertising; the number and distribution of any free copies and the price; format and terms of sale.'

If everyone is clear about the genre you are writing in and you all agree who your audience is, this should reduce any misunderstandings. Nevertheless, the choice of covers and titles can be a huge bone of contention between authors and publishers, which – if not handled sensitively – can result in bad feeling on one or both sides. So it pays to ensure, tactfully, that you will have some say in the cover design and not be completely overruled.

Donald Winchester, literary agent at Watson, Little

'If the cover isn't right, there are ways to persuade the publisher to alter or even replace it with another – even though many publishing contracts do not permit the author the power of cover approval – but it's important to approach the situation carefully. The author and agent should approach the publisher with a united and considered front, showing a concerted attempt to engage with the logic of the initial draft cover. An instinctual "I don't like it" won't work! Neither, in my experience, does canvassing the opinions of friends, who often rely on gut reactions that aren't helpful in a discussion like this.

It's important to be reasonable, empathetic and firm. Be free to persist – cover discussions happen months ahead of publication, which allows you time to do so – and perseverance presents a point more effectively than a rant or an argument. Sometimes, though, it is right to bow to the publisher's view. There is no shame in being convinced of a different viewpoint. After all, the cover and its place in the market rightly fall within the publisher's expertise; it is their job! Above all, it's important to remember that preserving goodwill within the author–publisher relationship is ultimately more important.'

From self-publishing to trade

Authors who are unagented sometimes self-publish in the hope of attracting the attention of a trade publisher. This can be a good strategy. If your book does well and has healthy sales figures, then by all means use that in your pitch. You have shown that your book has appeal and that you can, and have, built an audience. A publisher should be able to build on what you have already done. Strike while the iron is hot; approach an agent and publisher in the early days of your book's publication as the process can take up to a year and, while your sales may continue to build in that time, it is just as likely that they could level off.

If your self-published book has sold few copies, it is a good idea to play it down. Effectively you have shown – whatever the reasons – that you were unable to connect with or find an audience for your book and saying you didn't know how to market it won't cut it; this is not something you want to admit to. Whatever your overall strategy for producing a bestseller, if this happens to you, take steps to find out what is wrong or missing in your current approach and put a strategy in place to fix what isn't working.

 Focus point

If you do want to pursue a conventional publishing deal, have a think about your ideal publishing house; the one you would like to see publish your book. Obviously, wanting, and getting, the publisher you would like to publish your book are two different things but, however difficult it might be to attain, when you have a goal, it helps if it is a clear one.

When you have completed your book, you may have some sense of the publishing imprint your book might fit into but if not, find out. If you are widely read, the major imprints should be familiar to you, but to find out more you need to spend more time in bookshops and more time reading. You must know the industry; it's not enough to just write without knowing the business as well.

Knowing which genre your book fits into will help you structure your novel, structure your language and might even tell you how long it should be. Knowing your market will make you, in turn, marketable to an agent and a publisher.

Where to next?

In the next chapter we will look at self-publishing and how the perceptions and practicalities of it have changed radically, creating an exciting new range of choices and options for authors wanting to aim for a bestseller.

10

Self-publishing

We've recently seen a substantial increase in the number of self-published authors making more than $1 million selling books on Amazon, and self-published titles now account for the top 30 per cent of books on Amazon. There's no question that this buzz around self-publishing has encouraged many debut authors to feel sufficiently empowered to take publishing into their own hands. Even its tag, indie publishing, reflects the bold new attitude to what was previously considered second best to conventional publishing.

In this chapter you will learn about the rise of independent publishing and understand what it takes to self-publish successfully, with tips from the experts. You'll also find out about the new hybrid authors who successfully combine trade with self-publishing.

Indie publishing – the new cool

Self-publishing success stories have featured prominently in the mainstream press over the past few years, with a self published book recently named as a favourite book of the year by a *New York Times* book reviewer. And there are even self-published authors who combine self-made success with substantial deals with a trade publisher, enjoying unprecedented advances and advantageous contracts.

According to a survey of Amazon ebook sales and author earnings, self-published authors are not just holding their ground against authors published by the Big Five trade publishers; when it comes to releases after 2011, they are out-earning Big Five authors by a 27-per-cent margin (authorearnings.com). *Fifty Shades of Grey* may have been the firestarter for this indie revolution, but there have been plenty more indie authors providing further fuel since.

The London Book Fair has not always been known for its warm welcome to authors, but it now features a dedicated space for them: curated by Midas PR, Author HQ was launched in 2014 to a full house. Journalist and author of *The Distraction Trap*, Fran Booth, said, 'the atmosphere and welcome for authors and the buzz around self-publishing was palpable'.

This excitement was due in part to the astounding success of authors such as Hugh Howie, whose radical approach to self-publishing and now trade publishing is paving a new route for authors. (At the time of writing, he is published by Random House in the UK and Simon & Schuster in the US, while retaining the e-rights and continuing to self-publish those himself.) The excitement is also due to the barriers to successful self-publishing being swept away; there are no limits or gatekeepers for those who want it badly enough to put in the effort.

 Jon Fine, Amazon

'If the indie author movement was a person, 2011 was the year the movement entered adolescence and 2013 is the year the movement reached adulthood. These newly minted indie ebook authors (old-timers are the ones with three or four years of experience in self-publishing) are experimenting with abandon. Through trial and error, experimentation and rapid information exchange with fellow authors, indie authors are pioneering the secrets of successful modern-day publishing.'

The tide has turned for self-publishers. Previously tagged with the judgemental label 'vanity publishing', indie publishing used to be the sole preserve of those who could not find a trade publisher. Now it is often the first choice, particularly for ambitious authors who know a thing or two about social media and online marketing. And they know that a good product, once read by enough key readers – particularly those who are active on social media and in writing communities – will generate a strong word-of-mouth following.

On the one hand, it is great that self-publishers now have a means by which they can get their book out there without having to rely on a traditional agent or publisher. On the other, the fact that there are no gatekeepers means that the reader finds him- or herself having to wade through huge swathes of books, not all of which are of good quality.

Not everyone sees the volume of self-published books in the marketplace as a problem. Jon Fine believes that digital self-publishing has made it 'easier for writers to tell stories and easier to read wherever you are. And the Alliance of Independent Authors (ALLi) says that 'Booksearch through category and key words offers tailored discovery that is far more nuanced than browsing a bookstore' and that 'good books are easier to find than they have ever been'.

As readers, it is no longer simply a case of buying the books that make the biggest splash because publishing houses are paying handsomely to market them to us. With direct communication from author to reader, readers can search and find what they want to read. Now it is more a matter of keeping alert to the recommendations of trusted readers in reading and writing communities we belong to and making use of the search facility, find new authors and to check reviews. And as we are able to sample books before we buy (via freebies, the look-inside facility and promotional deals), it is a less risky proposition to try out new voices to find the books we'll love to read.

Canny self-publishers are wise to this and know that if their book is good and enough people get to know about, sample and then buy their book, and a conversation will get under way about it, soon a snowball effect comes into play and more and more readers will talk about your book, which gets still more people interested in buying. People like to be part of something bigger than themselves, part of the conversation, and the purchase of a widely discussed book is an easy way to do this.

Successful self-publishers understand the power of free in building their audiences. They know that offering free samples, giving away books, running competitions and dropping their prices for special promotions, will encourage readers to buy their books as well as helping to forge an ongoing connection or relationship. (You'll find tips for how to do this in the marketing chapter in Part 5.)

Is self-publishing right for you?

Putting aside the excitement and enthusiasm about self-publishing, what you really need to know is whether it is right for you and your books. This chapter takes a tour of the pros and cons so that you can reach your own decision.

Should you self-publish?

How many of these statements could be about you? Tick those that are relevant:

- I want full creative control.
- I want all the income from sales and full financial control.
- I want the final decision on title and cover choices.
- I don't want to sign away my rights.
- I am in a hurry.
- I am not writing full-length novels.
- I am writing for a niche market.
- I want to test the market.
- I can't find an agent or publisher.
- I have had a bad experience with a trade publisher.
- I have a backlist of out-of-print trade-published titles.

Consider how important these are to you. If any of them are of paramount importance, then you should try self-publishing.

How much time can you dedicate to the project? The editing of your book, your cover and blurb are among the key steps to increasing discoverability (being found by readers), taking you closer to reaching your bestselling destination, but all these activities take time and effort. You'll have a fuller understanding of the time commitment of self-publishing by the end of this chapter.

It's important to approach your self-publishing project with realistic expectations and an understanding of what your journey will entail:

- Do your research and know what is involved. Ensure that you have a realistic plan and budget to cover the time and money you'll need to publish a book.

- Accept that, while you want to sell many copies of your book, you may sell only a few to friends and family unless you develop a businesslike approach to your book sales.
- In the short-term, view profit as a bonus rather than your sole motivation: publishing is a long game.
- Do it because you love it, you want to and you *have* to.

If you are still keen, the next thing to do is decide how you will self-publish – in what format and with what level of help and support from others.

Laura Palmer, fiction publisher, Head of Zeus

'If a debut author self-publishes an ebook, it will either be a success or it will do nothing. If it does nothing, it is almost as if it never existed in the first place, and you won't have lost much (except your sense of humour, perhaps). If you think that readers will respond positively to your book, and if you are prepared to work very hard to market and promote it, then self-publishing is a good idea. I'd always recommend that authors try to find a publisher in the first instance, though, because publishers can bring books to a global audience via multiple platforms – something that is almost impossible as a self-published author.'

Routes to self-publishing

The options open to you include digital and print, and how you achieve your publishing. While e-publishing itself is free, there are costs involved in preparing the work for self-publishing, including:
- production costs: cover and text design
- editing and proofreading
- audio book production
- distribution costs (digital and print)
- print costs (physical copies)
- ISBNs
- website
- your time
- promotional material
- review copies (physical copies).

It can be expensive and time-consuming to publish a book properly, more so for print. Essentially, once the writing is done, you must morph into a micro-publisher, fulfilling every role in a publishing house, from editing and design through to production, publicity and sales and marketing. Publishing houses have whole teams in place to carry out these roles; you only have yourself or the help you buy in. To get it all done, you'll need to develop a good plan and take it step by step. Decide how much you can actually do yourself, and find out the options for buying in help. Don't forget that, on top of the publishing, you will need to conserve energy for your marketing strategy

If you prefer to focus on developing your writing rather than doing the publishing, a publishing service or one-to-one help may be the best option. Whichever option you choose, be aware of what you are getting and what you have to give in return. Truly independent publishing is when you retain all the rights and meet all the costs. If you give away your rights – as is the case with traditional publishing – you should be getting something pretty substantial in return to make it worth your while.

Both the Society of Authors and the Alliance of Independent Authors (ALLi) warn authors to be cautious about choosing and paying for author services. Don't agree to or sign anything without getting advice from one of these author bodies. Avoid handing over rights to your book or, if the service is free, overpaying for another service – print, for instance. You can quickly compare the costs of their print-on-demand (POD) service and make a decision with your eyes wide open.

What follows is a quick summary of routes to independent publishing. For comprehensive advice and guides, look online to the two organizations mentioned above, as this area is subject to rapid change.

DIY SELF-PUBLISHING

This is where you do everything yourself, or most of it: you should always seek help with the editing. Here you will apply for the Nielsen ISBN application and be responsible for the design, and the uploading of your book to distribution sites. The websites offering free templates, advice and information tend to be print-on-demand businesses that hope you will want to print copies of your book. Find out which sites are most effective and helpful by asking your writing communities.

LOW-COST SELF-PUBLISHING HELP

Many websites offer tools that, for a small fee, will help you organize your self-publishing. For instance, they make it easier to upload your content and have comprehensive lists of everything you need to do to self-publish effectively.

SELF-PUBLISHING SERVICES

You pay, and they edit, publish and print on your behalf; some also offer design and marketing and PR services. The packages tend to be off the peg and somewhat costly for a one-size-fits-all package, and they don't offer good cover and text design. This may not matter as much for an ebook but, for print, a bad cover is a depressing, off-putting sight. Some of these services are for ebook only self-publishing, while others are also faux publishers, offering to publish your book for a fee and, to add insult to injury, do not pass on the profits to the author but only pay a royalty. Approach cautiously with open eyes. If in doubt, seek advice from ALLi.

If you would like to publish a low-cost ebook (distribution is not free) with the option to print physical books on demand, have a look at the packages offered by companies such as completelynovel. com, smashwords.com and the obvious, Amazon.com. An online search will bring up the other companies that offer this service.

ONE-TO-ONE MENTORING

Here you work with an adviser or mentor, who will guide you through the entire publishing process. They can advise on editing, recommend designers, printers and other publishing professionals, help you brief, and then discuss your choices. For advice on finding a good mentor, ask the ALLi or the Society of Authors.

ALLi provides good support to independent authors. They describe their role as to 'help authors take good decisions for their books and their readers; to encourage, enable and empower them to take creative control over their work; and to find good partners that will take them to the widest possible readership. And if using any service, authors need to understand the costs/benefits, what is being offered, and how it compares with the other options for that book.'

ALLi has produced a detailed guide to choosing a self-publishing service. Self-publishing is a big investment, so it might be worth a small investment in their book first.

Key idea

Do not sign any contract lightly. If in doubt, consult the Society of Authors, which offers free contract advice to members.

Assessing a publishing service

Check out your proposed publisher or publishing service online. The indie publishing community is increasingly vocal on all aspects of publishing, so it should be easy to assess the reputation of anyone you're thinking of working with. Thanks to social media, no one can hide.

Look at the following aspects of any service:

- **Cover and text design**

  Don't use their service if you can help it. Hire a professional designer experienced in cover and text design. Ask other authors for recommendations and ask to see samples from anyone you're thinking of hiring.

- **Marketing packages**

  Look for concrete numbers and commitment to detail. This should be agreed contractually. What will they do and how often? What results do they promise?

- **PR**

  Do they offer guarantees or your money back?

- **Distribution**

  Look carefully at what is promised. It can sound more impressive than it is in reality. Are they really claiming that they can get your book into Waterstones? Beware of anyone guaranteeing that they will get your book stocked by bookshops unless it is included in your contract.

- **Having your book listed on Amazon**

  Anyone can do this; it doesn't require a self-publishing service. Your book is listed automatically when your ISBN application is processed. You can use their ISBN but I suggest buying your own ISBNs so that the ISBN is registered to you rather than the publishing service. (ISBNs must be bought in bundles of ten in the UK.)

- **Sales via their site**

  What is that really worth to you? How much traffic do they get? What percentage do they take? Check out their site, find an author in a similar genre and ask to be put in touch with them for their feedback.

- **Royalties**

  Paying to publish your book, then only being paid a royalty is akin to being stung twice. Don't get into an arrangement where you are paid a royalty rather than full profits after costs.

- **Other distribution**

  Will they place stock with wholesalers such as Gardners and Bertrams for distribution to bookshops?

See also londonwritersclub.com for suggestions for vetted publishing people who offer professional, trade-quality publishing services.

PRINT, DIGITAL, AUDIO, OR ALL THREE?

What is the best choice for you? And what do readers want to buy? There's no doubt that digital publishing is easier, cheaper and faster than print and so often a first choice for self-publishers for that reason alone. As to what people want to buy, the sales figures show that digital publishing is here to stay; in 2013, half of total fiction sales were ebooks and they were a fifth of the overall UK book market.

Print is not dead, however, according to publishing pundits – based on a slowing in the growth of ebook sales in 2103. Is this simply because baby boomers won't let go of the physical book, or personal preference, nostalgia akin to that we've seen with vinyl? My guess is that people buy 'keepers', their favourite books in print, and throwaway fiction in digital form. No one can really say for sure; sales in the coming years will show what readers prefer.

What we do know is that ebooks in genre fiction categories such as romance, mystery and science fiction sell incredibly well. If that is your audience, then perhaps ebook with the option to print on demand is the solution for you.

It is worth remembering that the ebook offers more than just a different format. Our entertainment consumption habits have changed radically and we have become used to the enhanced features and storage capacity that e-readers allow, for instance.

Audio book publishing

At the time of writing, only about 5 per cent of books exist as audio books and so the potential for a bestselling audiobook is huge and largely untapped. Hugh Howie recently said that he 'could live on his audio book sales alone'. Amazon launched a new service in 2014 to complete the trinity of Amazon platforms; Kindle Direct

Publishing (KDP) for digital, CreateSpace for print on demand and now acx.com for audio books. Amazon is not the only platform, so have a look around to see what suits you best.

Essentially you can do this two ways:

- Keep full control yourself and narrate and produce independently of Amazon or any other platform offering this service.
- Use Amazon's facility to find a narrator/producer, via a process of audition, who suits your material and make a deal with them (often professional actors or narrators) to narrate and take care of the technical aspects of producing and uploading the audio book. You pay either a flat, one-off fee or go for the no-risk option of splitting the royalty 50/50. (Some forums indicate that narrators/producers will only continue to agree to these deals if they see profit from deals they have already done.) What's clever about this is the ease of it and the quality; all you need provide is your content and the narrating and production is taken care of to a professional standard.

As with any platform you are thinking of using, do look at forums and discussions on how to use a service to your advantage. And make yourself aware of the implications when you sign any rights away. Amazon is a business and while one self-published author said, 'I love Amazon; it bought me a house', be aware that they are not in business for your interests, but theirs. On one forum there were rumblings about Amazon giving away the audio version to ebook buyers, so do check out every aspect of the deals you do with your publishing.

 Key idea

If you want a bestselling book and a bestselling income that goes with it, double-check every decision and deal you make, no matter how small. As these are new and evolving platforms, do your homework before deciding. At the time of writing, Orna Ross of ALLi told a London Book Fair audience that she'd done a 50/50 deal with Amazon for one of her novels, so check her blog for her views on how that turned out.

Challenges for digital and print self-publishing

A big distinguishing factor between trade and self-published books can be the look or design of the book. Many self-published books look awful, falling down in the quality of writing, editing and design. There is no quality control; anyone can publish their book and, on Amazon Kindle for instance, it isn't automatically clear who is trade published and who self-published. Yes, it's all nicely democratic, but readers are now the filter and must look harder when choosing what they buy to ensure that it's of a good standard. Prior to the explosion, of mostly digital publishing, we could rely upon the so-called gatekeepers, the agents and publishers, to find great stories and to publish good-quality, well-edited books.

It's not just inexperienced authors who get the design wrong; people prepared to spend money on their website and elsewhere in their life or businesses fail to get this aspect right. Similarly, authors can spend a lot of money with a self-publishing company, only to end up with a cover that looks depressingly old-school self-published.

This may be unfair, as we usually don't notice when indie books are well published as they blend in, looking exactly like trade books.

If you decide to self-publish and want to avoid such criticism and be taken seriously, you must set and maintain high standards for yourself. We've covered good writing earlier in this book. The following sections highlight some of the areas to be mindful of in self-publishing, with ideas for addressing them.

Professional presentation

Lack of professional presentation will let down your book but good presentation is as essential in self-publishing as in traditional publishing. Presentation includes the quality of the editing as well as the design and overall 'look' of the book.

1 **Have your book professionally edited.**

   Ask authors in your genre for recommendations for an editor, or search the directory of the Society for Editors and Proofreaders. Once you have checked and agreed with the changes suggested, you are ready for the text designer to design the inside text for your book.

2 **Invest in a professional cover and text design – see below.**

   Use a designer who is experienced with books and ask for a fixed price for your cover and text design. If you are printing bulk copies rather than print-on-demand, they may also send the book files directly to the printer for you, eliminating the need for a production role and also reducing the chance of errors creeping in if you handle it yourself.

3　Once the designer has set the edited text and run out proofs, hire a professional proofreader.

You should proofread at the same time. If you can't afford a proofreader, have as many people read it word by word and line by line as possible. Give them proofreading instructions so they know what to looking out for. At this stage, you are not rewriting the book but just correcting any errors. Then add all the changes to one master copy and have the text designer add in the changes from that copy.

4　Your book is now ready for printing or uploading as an ebook.

COVER DESIGN

We do choose a book by its cover. It is widely agreed that book covers help sell books; every publishing house has lengthy, weekly cover meetings with representatives from the sales, marketing and PR departments to discuss the approach for each and every book they publish. If good design helps create a bestseller, your cover is one of your most important marketing tools, so make it work for you.

Unlike trade publishing, where the publisher has the final say, self-publishing means that you, the author, have total control over the choice of cover. Your cover must reflect what is actually in your book and it's your job to brief your cover designer, but only after you've done your research into the sort of cover that is a good fit for your genre. If the cover is inconsistent with the contents, it will quickly lose the reader's trust.

 Researching covers

Get out to a bookshop and do some hands-on research into cover design.

- Look at other great covers – why do they work?
- What are the winning factors of a great cover?
- What have you learned that you would like to apply to your own book cover?

Test your ideas with trusted friends and colleagues, or be completely open and post your book cover roughs on Facebook and ask people to vote for their favourite.

If you don't have the budget for a cover designer, take heart. R.L. Mathewson, author of *Tall, Dark and Lonely* and other paranormal romance, saw her publishing take off in 2012, landing her on the *New York Times* bestseller list. When interviewed on the Smashwords blog, she attributed her increased sales to a number of changes, including re-editing her books, dropping the price from $6.99 to $2.99 and increased word of mouth via reviews. But she says what made the biggest difference was changing the covers.

R.L. Mathewson, author

'The original covers were plain, two shaded covers ... The only problem was the price. Since buying custom-designed covers would have been expensive and force me to raise the prices of the books, I decided to see what I could do on my own. I bought a few photos, played around with photo-editing software and eventually came up with some covers that I liked.'

David Eldridge, designer of classic cookbooks such as *The River Café*, the fiction of Boris Akunin, Caitlin Moran's *How to Be a Woman* and the *James Bond* and *Doctor Who* series, gives his advice on what to consider for your book design. He says that, in laying out a cover, we must think about the hierarchy of information – what is the most important piece of information that you wish to convey? These are the elements to consider:

- **Title:** long titles have poor visual impact, so limit their length where possible.
- **Author name:** don't make your name too small or it may be perceived as apologetic.
- **Typography:** consider distinctive typographic branding that can be carried on to the next title.
- **Endorsements and quotes:** these place the book and can also balance a cover typographically. (Send out review copies to secure these ahead of publication.)
- **Clarity:** for digital versions, always view the layout design at thumbnail size to check that the cover does not appear muddled when small.'

See: twoassociates.co.uk for examples of good design and a tour of an enhanced ebook.

To help with your cover brief, there is a cover design sheet in the Appendices listing everything you'll need to consider and make decisions on, as well as communicate to your designer.

THE BLURB

When we pick up a print book or browse online, one of the first things we look at after the cover is the blurb. Unless you have copywriting skills, your blurb will probably not be easy to write. However, in perfecting your one-line pitch in Chapter 8, you have had some practice at being clear about the top-note of your book.

 Sarah Juckes, CompletelyNovel

'The blurb is the short section found on the back of the book, which describes what the book is about and makes a potential reader want to know more. There is a real art to blurb writing – it is different from writing a synopsis as it needs to capture the thing that is unique and exciting about your book, not tell the reader every last thing that makes the book what it is. As a general rule, blurbs should be:

- *no longer than two paragraphs*
- *written in the same voice as the book*
- *about the main "stakes" of the story – not about the whole thing.'*

How to write a good blurb is a frequent question at London Writers' Club. It is a skill you need to nail if you are an indie publisher. Practise it until you perfect it, or farm it out to someone who is good at it. Study blurbs from successful books that have been published to a high standard and learn how to do it well.'

Draw on your one-line-pitch to convey the most important elements of your story. The nugget of your story will help sell your book. Try it now, but don't be surprised if it takes longer to write than did a whole chapter of your book!

TEXT DESIGN

David Eldridge's word of caution about text design is that, if you get it wrong, a book can read like a long, dull monologue. White space is the speech equivalent of meaningful pauses. If you can possibly afford it, do get professional help. If you want to try DIY here are some useful tips from one self-published writer.

Sarah Juckes, CompletelyNovel

'If you're self-publishing, make sure you pay as much attention to the design of your book on the inside as you do to the cover. Microsoft Word, for instance, has some useful, straightforward tools that authors may not have come across. Adding paragraph styles, justifying text so it meets each margin, adding title pages and page numbers, separating chapters with page breaks and thinking carefully about your use of font, are just a few of the things you need to think about when typesetting. Don't be afraid to emulate styles from other books, and remember, the best typesetting is the kind the reader won't even notice.'

You'll find more detailed advice on this on CompletelyNovel.com.

The best thing about reading print, after a time on an e-reader, is the text design. As a former commissioning editor, I have spent an inordinate amount of time in cover and design meetings, so perhaps I'm more aware of design, but I don't think I'm alone in this view. On an ebook reader, for instance, I find reading more exhausting, feeling that the words are thrust at me in a stream of consciousness. White space and good headings will improve your book immeasurably.

Discoverability

How does a self-published author get *discovered*? The choice of word is deliberate. Many writers self-publish because they are tired of what they perceive to be a 'waiting to get chosen' culture of conventional publishers, yet when they self-publish, often they make the mistake of sitting back, waiting for readers to find their book. You must do everything you can to promote your book, to make it easy for readers to *find* and buy it (see the marketing and publicity chapters for how). Again, this can be costly, time-consuming and a big job. This is not to put you off, but to be frank about what it takes to self-publish successfully.

Now that the majority of books are sold online rather than lovingly displayed on shelves, the key challenge is that readers must discover books by online search rather than browsing them in the flesh. The confluence of digital technology and the rise of Amazon has been a crucial factor in enabling the boom in self-publishing and ebook publishing. What started as a new way of selling and distributing print books, once digital publishing became possible, turned into an opportunity for a new way of publishing and promoting books, too. Now it is also just as much about searching and recommendation, and so the challenge for self-publishers (and the trade) is to make books discoverable.

Things to master include:

- on and offline promotion
- having a good, up-to-date website with SEO optimization
- capturing email addresses via a sign-up box
- using any promotional tools offered by online platforms
- creating good blog content to attract readers to your website.

 Key idea

Criticism of Amazon ranges from the view that they don't pay enough tax to claims that they are killing print and trade publishing. Whatever we may think, the company has changed the landscape and it has enabled and created new ways for authors to be discovered.

There are now thousands of ebook distributors around the world. Amazon, Apple, Ingram, Kobo, Nook and Smashwords are self-publishing's biggest players. You will need to set up an account with each of them or find a distributor who can do it for you. The digital world is constantly changing, so rather than provide information here that will date quickly, see ALLi, a non-profit organization, for up-to-the-minute independent advice on their website.

Print distribution and sales

One of the cornerstones of a bestseller is availability and accessibility across a range of retail channels. Thanks to digital, distributing your book isn't the challenge it once was, but print distribution remains tough for the self-publisher, so how you do this must still be part of your overall bestseller strategy.

In the past, self-publishing was limited by distribution so, unless an author was particularly ingenious, there were always major barriers to the number of copies a self-published book could sell. This is not an issue with ebooks, though it's still challenging for print books, so do factor that into your decision-making. The key is to look at the product and at the market you are aiming for and decide on the route to market that best suits each product.

Some ebook distributors also offer a print-on-demand and distribution service. Many have a website from which customers can buy your book directly. If you sell through these platforms, you must ensure that you don't overpay per copy, so shop around and compare prices. And to ensure that you keep a decent amount of the income, look for a platform that pays a percentage of the income (usually around 70 per cent) rather than royalties. Again, this is in flux, so check with ALLi for up-to-date information on what a fair percentage is.

If you want your book sold through retailers, they won't take print-on-demand books; however some self-publishing companies can help with this. Retailers and distributors will require a cut of the sale price of the book, so you will need to sell the book to them at what is known as a trade discount price. This is between 30 and 50 per cent lower than the retail price, so it may mean that you need to set the price of your book quite a bit higher or take a much lower royalty.

If you distribute the book yourself, you'll need to have the books shipped to you. You will then need to contact bookshops to ask them to stock your book. This is time-consuming because, without the clout of a publishing house, you will need to visit each bookshop individually. Some bookshops will accept a small number of your books on a sale-or-return basis: if they sell, you get paid; if they don't, you take them back at a later stage. It's important to weigh up the value of your book being in a bookshop. Unless they agree to stock a good number of copies, do a promo and make your book very visible – say, cover side up on flatbed or at the front of the shop – it hardly seems worth the effort.

Key idea

When you weigh up the time and effort involved in getting your book into stores, you might find that the time is better invested in increasing your visibility as an author to the point that readers go into bookshops asking for your book.

In the meantime it would seem a wise move to focus your energies on online platforms for digital and print-on-demand.

Many authors concentrate on putting copies into a bookshop in their local area or a specialist bookshop relevant to their book in some way. This can build a solid profile for you as a local author and booksellers can be great champions of your book. Since an estimated 60 to 70 per cent of print and digital book sales are made online, if you combine those potential sales with a focus on local bookshops or bookshops with some other significance to you, you'll probably be doing your best to achieve your bestseller. In other words, don't sweat it that your book isn't stocked in every bookshop; there's a good chance it wouldn't be even if you were published by one of the Big Five publishers.

REACHING YOUR AUDIENCE

While digital distribution means that readers can access your book whenever and wherever they choose, there remains the matter of alerting readers to its existence. This is true for digital and print, though with print there is the added complication of physically getting copies to the reader. One solution is to find your audience and go to them.

Lloyd Bradley, author of *Sounds of London*, describes how the record industry, like publishing, was stymied by distribution in the days of vinyl unless you had a deal with, or were, a large record label. Emil Shallit didn't let that stop him; he established and built Melodisc into the 1950s' largest independent record label by making records available through a network of established retailers, albeit not record retailers. Having identified a black audience, he made Melodisc's records available anywhere black people regularly hung out or shopped, such as Afro-Caribbean barbers and grocers. Taking their product to their audience, rather than expecting their audience to find them, was key to the label's success.

Go and find your audience

Think back to when we profiled your reader. Where do they hang out? Think creatively. Here are a couple of examples to get you started.

- If you are writing chick lit or women's fiction, could you make short stories available on tablet or mp3 at large chains of hairdressing salons?
- If your book is set at a well-known tourist destination, could you find a way to make it part of the tourist experience?

How can you link your work to something already existing? Brainstorm as many ideas as you can. The idea is to capitalize on existing opportunities with ready audiences. Choose the most promising way to reach your audience. Draw up a plan of action to make it happen and break it down into manageable steps.

USING METADATA

Metadata is 'data about data', according to Wikipedia, which could spark a headache just to think of it. And yet the word is that it's essential. It matters because it can make your book easier to discover and every self-publisher can get a start on it. The content and quality of your book's metadata will influence where your book appears within websites or bookshops, and sometimes whether it comes up in recommendation lists alongside other 'similar' books.

Sarah Juckes, CompletelyNovel

'At a basic level, your metadata should include your author name, title and ISBN. The first thing to do before you publish a book is to Google your author name and your book title to make sure the search isn't saturated with similar titles and names, and doesn't bring up a connection to something irrelevant that could hinder your sales. If so, consider changing your title, or creating a pen name that is more unusual.

If you publish on CompletelyNovel.com, for instance, you can choose from a list of subject categories, and add specific keywords that relate to your book. This is a really important and often overlooked step, so make sure you give it the attention it deserves. Your blurb is also part of your metadata and will appear in all sales channels once you publish, so make sure it includes any key terms important to the book, and of course no typos is really important.'

Deciding which platform to use

As we have seen, digital is by far the easiest method of self-publishing and distribution. There are a number of different ebook platforms that you can use to sell your product. They have tools for self-publishers to upload and sell their books through. And many have dashboards where you can check your sales.

Do your research. Find and visit your genre writing communities and ask what others are doing and how it is working for them. You'll find authors very vocal about what works and what doesn't and more than willing to share.

IS THE PRICE RIGHT?

As we saw earlier, with romance author R.L. Mathewson, experimenting with pricing can have a direct impact on helping your book climb to bestselling levels. You don't have control over pricing with a trade publishing but, as an indie author, you can price your book at a level that encourages readers to take a punt on an unknown author.

On Kindle Direct Publishing, for instance, the price you set determines the royalty rate you are paid. If the price is too high you put readers off; too low and your book seems cheap. It's likely that it will be through trial and error that you finally arrive at the right price to encourage your book's sales. One observation is that with daily price deals on Amazon, a book can shoot up the charts but then shoot back down again just as fast, so you need to capitalize on that attention while you have it. If you are fortunate enough to have a choice of deals you're promoted in, a longer-term promotion will have more of an overall impact on your sales and income.

Read indie author forums – especially those in your genre – to find price discussions. And do experiment with price and track the effect on your sales. You can always test to see what works, and change your pricing according to the resulting sales. What works and what doesn't work with pricing is constantly changing, so always research and make your decision at the point of publication. Sylvia Day is an indie author who has experimented with price so it is worth studying her pricing, which she changes strategically. Though R.L. Mathewson enjoyed a boost in sales and eventually a bestseller when she dropped her price, she set her price first and foremost with her reader in mind.

 R.L. Mathewson, author

'When I first published my books, I was more concerned about being taken seriously. I didn't think a low price would accomplish that. So I priced my books as high as the traditional published authors at the time, $6.99. I eventually brought it down to $2.99 because I felt the high price was just too much. This past Christmas I dropped the price to $0.99 as a Christmas gift to my readers. I didn't like the idea of people spending a small fortune to read my books. I also gave one of them away for a while, Playing for Keeps: A Neighbor from Hell novel. When the time came to raise the prices back, I just couldn't do it. I'd received too many emails from readers

> *thanking me for keeping my prices low, sharing stories of*
> *tough times and how thankful they were that my prices*
> *were low enough for them so that they could read my work.*
> *After that, I decided that as long as I could manage the*
> *costs that came along with publishing, I would keep them at*
> *$0.99. I enjoy writing and I would rather someone have the*
> *opportunity to enjoy my stories than to get rich.'*

It's gratifying when an altruistic decision also benefits the author. You can see how the price increases sales but it may also open up new audiences. For 99 cents, people who might ordinarily buy a magazine may be tempted to buy a book instead.

Key idea

In your quest for a bestseller, be prepared to keep testing and trialling your prices to find what works, just as you would if you were in any other business.

From indie to trade

One of the most frequently asked questions at the London Writers' Club is: 'If I self-publish, will it prevent me from finding a trade publisher?' By publishing and promoting your book yourself, you have the opportunity to prove that there is a market for your book and that you are a marketable author. This could lead to you being noticed by a publisher. There is an element of timing involved with this: the publisher must feel that there are enough untapped readers for your book to risk taking a gamble on publishing it. (Whether to accept their offer, and what deal you can strike if a publisher approaches you, is another matter.)

INSPIRING AUTHORS: E.L. JAMES

E.L. James has sold more than 70 million copies of her *Fifty Shades* trilogy worldwide. That much isn't a surprise, but perhaps you didn't know that she began by writing fan fiction stories and publishing them on her website. She then wrote *Fifty Shades of Grey* and self-published it through a small Australian company, which released it as an ebook and print-on-demand. After her enthusiastic fan base drove the book to extreme levels of popularity, Vintage Books in the UK acquired the rights.

James is an extreme example of an author who has self-published and made the leap to trade publishing. But based on her success, you can also learn to generate fans and build a database, a following, a club, an audience – whatever you want to call them, find them, win them over, connect with them while you are writing and looking at publishing options for your book. (This is covered in more detail in Chapter 12, on marketing.) Do this right and not only will you sell more books but you will also be a more compelling prospect if ever you want to seek a trade publisher.

James found an unconventional route to market and worked hard to make her books sell, netting her a conventional publishing deal in the end. It is possible for you too. I've always advised authors, even established authors, to consider each of their books on its individual merits.

For instance, if your book can't find a publisher because it is considered to be a niche title, you needn't necessarily give up. Bookshops are not the right place for a niche book and, given that your audience may be scattered around the world, making shipping expensive, bulk printing doesn't make sense either. Digital and POD books, with their emphasis on discoverability via search engines, are perfect for niche titles. Just be sure to do the work to ensure it can be discovered. The title or subtitle, metadata and social media can all be deployed for that purpose; to learn how to make your book discoverable online, see Chapter 12.

INSPIRING AUTHORS: DANI ATKINS

Dani Atkins' journey from self-published ebook to agent and then publishing house is a great example of how self-publishing can help rather than hinder efforts to get published. Dani published her debut novel, *Fractured*, on the Kindle Direct programme and it was chosen by Amazon to be in a promotion to give away a chapter. (Kindle Direct operates a rolling three-month contract, so there's the opportunity to get out of the deal if you want to publish in another way.)

Fractured was a chick-lit ebook hit that came to the attention of literary agent Kate Burke of Diane Banks Associates, and then was snapped up by Head of Zeus, an independent publishing house launched in 2012 which describes itself as 'dedicated to new authors, great storytelling and fabulous ideas'.

Laura Palmer, fiction publisher, Head of Zeus

'Kate Burke rang me to say that, after reading more than 300 self-published novels, she had finally found an author with the heart, warmth and characters that she felt a publisher could bring to the next level. I trust her taste, so a colleague and I both put everything aside and read the book overnight. The next morning, we signed a two-book deal with Dani.

Self-publishing is a double-edged sword, to be honest. On the one hand, Dani had over 400 five-star reviews, which speaks to the quality of the book and – crucially – proves to us that readers want to engage with her actively, not just passively. On the other hand, if an author self-publishes too successfully, there is the risk that by the time we take over the ebook edition, everyone who wants to buy it has already bought it.'

In terms of PR and marketing, the publisher is able to capitalize on the success of the ebook when publishing the trade paperback version. Head of Zeus did this by doing two things:

1 Selling the book in to the retailers.

   For the sell-in, they created presenters (promotional material) covered with all the great reviews Dani had received on Amazon. This convinced WHSmith that there would be an appetite for the book among their customers, so they stocked a lot of copies.

2 Selling the book out to the readers.

   For the sell-out, they created a digital marketing campaign to lure readers, via teaser adverts, to click through to Dani's Amazon page, where they could see the high ebook ranking and great reviews.'

When moving from self-published ebook to trade book, the practical process, as Laura Palmer explains, is to replace it with the publisher's own version, which has their choice of cover image and might include some extra content (such as book club notes and reader reviewers). 'We had a week-long 'handover' period, where Amazon switch one file for the other, and there were some technical glitches. At one point, we thought we might lose all of Dani's wonderful reader reviews, built up over months, but luckily our digital department whizz-kids found a way round it.'

From trade to indie

As we have seen, in the new and exciting world of digital publishing, it is fair to ask whether you ever need an agent or a publisher. What can a publisher do for authors that they can't do for themselves? Publishers are facing up to the new reality in which authors don't automatically pursue a publishing deal. As with E.L. James and Dani Atkins, self-publishing is not always the end of the road but can lead to trade publishing. But some authors published in the trade discover that it is not the right destination for them, so they break away and return to self-publishing.

Polly Courtney is an example of an author who successfully did this. Polly writes commercial fiction with 'a social conscience' and is best known for her city exposé *Golden Handcuffs*. She had self-published two books before signing a deal with HarperCollins, but she was unhappy with their packaging and, with no marketing budget, she felt she was battling to correct misconceptions created by an overly chick-lit cover and title which didn't reflect the content of her book. She is now back as a proud indie author, most recently publishing *Feral Youth*, the story of the London riots through a teenage girl's eyes. With her combined experience of trade and indie publishing, she now knows what works for her books.

A SELF-PUBLISHING MARKETING STRATEGY

Here are Polly's tips for how self-publishers can build a marketing strategy.

She says that a self-published book marketing strategy should come from answering five questions:

1 **Who are my target readers?**

   You need to find out who your readers are: the people who would pick up your book before any other, the ones who would tell all their friends about it. You might define them in terms of demographics, geography, attitude, cultural likes or dislikes, or it might simply be that your reader is a fan of a particular genre. You can usually tell who your book will appeal to by looking at the themes, style and characters of similar books. Work with a good editor and cover designer who know your market.

2 **How can I reach them?**

   Think about where your target reader hangs out. Is he the type to read newspapers over a long Sunday lunch or does she spend her days in online chatrooms? Once you've worked out which channels your reader uses, try to get more specific. Which programmes on TV? Which magazines exactly? Which websites? Are there events coming up where you think your target might be in attendance? Keep a log of any editors, producers and website owners who you might want to contact.

3 What's my story?

This might be the story behind the book – your own experiences as a writer or the themes you touch on in the book. Maybe you're doing something interesting or wacky to promote the launch.

4 Why is it news?

If you're hoping to use other platforms such as websites, publications, TV or radio shows to promote your book, your story needs to tie in somehow with current news trends. You can't expect your story to make headlines on its own, but if you can piggyback a recent event or issue, you're more likely to get coverage.

5 How should I tell it?

There's an old saying: 'Half the money I spend on advertising is wasted; I just don't know which half.' It's the same with the time you invest in book marketing. You need to put the word out in multiple channels: your website, your social media pages, other websites, traditional outlets ... people will find you and your book via various routes, so you need to be in multiple places at once. The more of a presence you have, the more of a platform you'll build up for the longer term.'

In building your marketing strategy, Polly advises the following:

- **Use channels that work for you as well as your reader.**
  Use a mix of social media such as Twitter, Facebook, YouTube, your own website, alongside more traditional outlets such as newspapers, magazines, radio and TV. If you loathe Twitter, however, don't spend your time there. Experiment with other ways of getting the word out, for example opinion pieces, Q&A interviews, guest blog posts or possibly a blog of your own. If you're a natural in front of the camera, try vlogging (video blogging – check out http://johngreenbooks.com/). If you prefer to stick with audio, try podcasting, like Joanna Penn (http://www.thecreativepenn.com/podcasts/).

- **Collaborate with as many people as you can.**
  If you get people on board at an early stage, they're more likely to do the promotion for you when the book comes out.

Polly Courtney, author

'For my latest novel, Feral Youth, *I decided to make a movie-style trailer to promote the book. Off the back of this, the lead actor went on to record the audiobook version of* Feral Youth, *another actor has performed a series of original songs based on the book, there's a music video in progress and I've even been persuaded to do some prerecorded readings from the book on #SpitItOut TV. The cast and crew continue to be important advocates of the novel.'*

- **Give yourself time.**
  Ideally, plan your book marketing strategy at least six months before publication. Even if you're an efficient person, there will be some elements that are outside your control. If you're planning to use traditional media, bear in mind that glossy magazines work on a three-month lead time. If you're expecting people to review your book, you need to allow editors time to read it. Hold a book launch, no matter how small – but allow enough time to organize it. If you don't plan your launch promotions in advance, there's a risk that you'll get to publication day and think: 'What now?'

Hybrid publishing

With more print and electronic options than ever before, authors can now combine trade publishing and self-publishing to become hybrid authors. Hybrid publishing can apply across your books, where some will be trade and some self-published. It also describes book deals where the rights are split for one book, usually meaning that print rights are licensed to a publisher but digital rights are retained by the author for self-publishing.

 ## Sarah Juckes, CompletelyNovel

'It's an exciting time for authors looking to publish books. Authors no longer need to choose either traditional or self-publishing – they can do both, in any order. Publishers and literary agents are now alive to the opportunities that self-publishing offers, and we are already seeing some of our authors use self-publishing as a way to capture the attention

of traditional publishers. What's more, authors are being more discerning about the areas in which they see traditional publishers adding value. When it comes to some areas such as marketing and publicity, they might instead outsource these to freelancers while self-publishing, if they think this will contribute to better overall success. I think we'll see an increase of "hybrid" authors in the future, making the best out of all routes to publication.'

It is important to note that most successful hybrid authors, such as Hugh Howie, established themselves as successful indies prior to negotiating a print-only deal with a trade publisher. As an unproven debut author, you may find it more difficult, if not impossible, to secure a print-only deal with a publisher, particularly given how hard publishers are working to catch up with indies on their lead in digital.

It is also worth noting that most, if not all, of the big indie authors had a marketing, digital or business background prior to setting themselves up as indie publishers. If you don't have those skills, you'll have to acquire them during the publishing and marketing process or team up with someone who does.

Another important factor is that they write and run their publishing full time with help, so don't be surprised if you find their success difficult to emulate, at least in the short term.

Key idea

As self-publishing has grown, so too has the support available to self-publishers.

Orna Ross, founder and director of the Alliance of Independent Authors

'Our members range from the author who is just starting out and exploring the self-publishing world, to more established authors, some of whom have sold millions of books and are producing work of great literary merit, to professional service providers. We are constantly monitoring a rapidly changing

industry to make sure our members understand what's going on out there and what they need to do to best serve readers. High standards are key to success ... Authors learn best from other authors who have been there, done that and author-publishers are a very savvy community. They learn fast, work hard and aim high. Part of that process is to respect each individual author's publishing choices – we make sure they understand all their options so they can take the best publishing path for each book.

The more successful an author-publisher is, the less likely they are to give up their ebook rights. The trade is stubbornly sticking to a 25-per-cent royalty on ebooks (compared to 70 per cent from self-publishing services) and the boost in print sales and the editorial, design and promotion services that publishers provide does not compensate for the greatly reduced ebook income.'

Orna says that many ALLi members trade publish some books, self-publish others and use trade publishing for subsidiary rights – foreign, print only, etc.She also, rather comfortingly, says, 'We don't call it self-publishing as you don't do it alone.'

Workshop: experiment

If you are not entirely sure of your best route to publication, experiment with this micro e-publishing exercise.

- Polish and publish your opening chapter via your community and ask for feedback. Leave a cliffhanger ending that makes people eager to read more.
- Release a beta version on an electronic platform. If your book is as good as you think it is, you'll soon know whether you're right by putting it to the test.

This is an ideal opportunity to get feedback and to generate word of mouth. The book doesn't have to be absolutely perfect, but don't publish it with flaws that are obvious to you or with spelling mistakes. There is no point in asking for feedback on your work when you already know what its flaws are; it is a waste of everyone's time and a wasted opportunity for you to

You can help your book to be the subject of word-of-mouth recommendation by getting these things right:

1 Tell a compelling story.
2 Edit professionally and proofread before uploading or printing.
3 Have cover and text design done professionally and appropriately for the genre.
4 Engage with readers.
5 Be strategic about PR and marketing so that your book is visible and discoverable.

All of these things will have an impact on reader perception of your book and your chance of achieving a bestseller.

INSPIRING AUTHOR: RACHEL ABBOTT

Rachel Abbott is a hybrid author who has successfully self-published, and she is also represented by top agent Lizzy Kremer of David Higham. Rachel launched her first novel *Only the Innocent* in the UK in 2011 through the Kindle Direct Publishing programme on Amazon, reaching the number one spot in the Kindle store just over three months later. It was the second-highest-selling self-published title in 2012. *Only the Innocent* was subsequently published by Thomas and Mercer in the United States, and reached number eight in the US charts one week after launch. It went on to reach number one, making Rachel's debut a bestseller on both sides of the Atlantic.

In March 2013, she released her second novel, *The Back Road*, which entered the UK Kindle chart at number 100 just 48 hours after launch. It went on to reach number two and has over 450 five-star reviews. Rachel has been described in the press as 'an e-publishing sensation' and 'the trade's hottest property'.

Rachel Abbott, author

'I had the idea for a book for many years before I sat down to write it. I self-published my first novel, Only the Innocent, *without an agent. I sent it to just a few agents and one or two requested the whole manuscript. They liked it but said it was not what publishers were currently looking for.*

At that time it wasn't easy to self-publish in the UK because you needed a US tax code and a US bank account (not a UK dollar account), so the book was put away. When I noticed that systems were set up for self-publishing, I decide to have a go. With my background in multimedia, I was able to do it cheaply by doing the Kindle conversion myself. I was thrilled to get 50 sales in the first day, but these were pretty much all friends and family and then it dwindled to a few per day. Christmas 2011 was the turning point; I realized how ridiculous it was to have run a successful business and yet when it came to my book, I was sitting waiting for people to buy it. I wrote a marketing plan as if it were my business. It was 15 pages long. Now they run to 27 pages.

Only the Innocent *rose to number one in February 2012, where it stayed for a month. Kerry Wilkinson very helpfully tweeted me saying: "Now you need an agent." He had just signed with an agent who was actively seeking a traditional deal for him, and he said that I'd need an agent to sell overseas rights and translation deals.*

He suggested Lizzy Kremer as one of the few agents who had been nice to him when he was pitching. And when US publisher Thomas and Mercer contacted me, Lizzy was able to negotiate that contract. In the UK, there were publishers interested but Lizzy advised me to stick with self-publishing for the time being for my second book. Her advice and support has been invaluable. She steered me into being brave and not to feel obliged to look for a traditional deal. She helped me develop my books and to put together the storylines of new ideas. She acts as a mentor. I don't think I would have kept going without her.

A further benefit of having an agent is membership of KDP White Glove programme for self-published authors with agents. Lizzie negotiates with Amazon on my behalf. I know that some authors look after their self-publishing separately from their agent, who looks after trade published books only.

This wouldn't work for me, as Lizzy has my long-term future in mind; she has to be involved in everything I'm doing. I have to present consistent quality in my work, so I can't and won't publish a book she hasn't looked at.'

Rachel Abbott's advice for debut authors

- If you are going to tackle your own text and cover design, get to grips with Microsoft Word and how to use styles for their typesetting. Look at the styles used in professionally designed books. A badly formatted book stands out immediately as being self-published.

- For your cover, find a professional by posting a brief on one of the sites that gives designers a chance to pitch for your work. They will give you an idea of their design and cost before you choose.

- Analyse what needs to be done from a business perspective to get your book noticed. Dedicate time to marketing. Once I have finished writing, I put writing aside and spend three months on the business side of my publishing.

- When you send off review copies, do so with a formal request for a review. I send a pdf, a bit like an AI, with price, extracts, page length, format, etc. Make it as easy as possible for people to review you.

- If you are not naturally good at or interested in marketing, get help. Look at the Alliance of Independent Authors website for who they suggest.

Rachel, Abbott, author

'I have huge respect for people with day jobs and a family who still manage to write. Even with an agent and doing this as my full-time job, seven days a week, I still struggle to find time to write more than one book per year because I do all the marketing and promotion myself. I'm now wholly self-published apart from foreign language editions. But I am not saying this is the right solution for everybody, and maybe not even for me long term. It's where I am now – but who knows for the future?'

Other indie authors to watch are Brenna Aubrey, Sylvia Day, Barbara Freethy, A.G. Riddle, Alison Morton and Joanna Penn.

Your bestselling self-publishing essentials

In summary, to get self-publishing right, you will need:

- a strong story
- at least a third draft
- a professionally edited and proofread manuscript
- an author biography and author headshot
- a press release and/or Advance Information (AI) sheet – see Appendices for a sample of the latter
- a book blurb for the printed book back cover, also to be used for book description where needed.
- a professionally designed cover
- good formatting
- a platform or platforms such as an Amazon, Kobo or Smashwords account
- a print-on-demand platform
- an author page on sales platforms such as Amazon and Kobo
- an ISBN – do it professionally from the start
- title page, copyright page, and front and end matter
- metadata (see Chapter 12)
- a decision on print, Ebook, audio or app version
- format appropriate to the genre
- the right price.

Indie or trade publishing, or both?

This is not a decision you need make definitively, once and for all, but one you can and should make for each project. Each book should have its own trajectory. Each time you are ready to publish a book, ask yourself, what is the best route to market: should I trade or self-publish?

Don't let the polarization of the two camps force you into deciding one way or the other. You don't have to commit to and stay in one camp; there is nothing stopping you from trying both. They can both be incredibly valuable in your quest for a bestseller.

The pros and cons of self-publishing

Pros	Cons
• Freedom	• It's all down to you unless you pay for help
• Potential for higher income and rewards	• Time-consuming
• Faster to publication	• Needs to be treated as a business
• Easy to test an idea	• Can be lonely
• Ease of updating and producing a new edition	• No advance payment
• Total creative and financial control	• Editing and all production costs must be paid in advance of sales
• Scope to innovate and experiment	• No guarantee of success
• Choice of your support team	
• Paid monthly for sales	

Putting aside the hype and armed with the facts, it remains a very personal decision. When reading the inspirational stories of authors, take note not just of their achievements but also the sort of human being they are, their lifestyles and what their values appear to be. That might give you an additional steer for the route you choose. If it's a large income you seek and you have a good head for business, then the profit margins in self-publishing may lure you in that direction.

The list of all-time bestselling authors who were at one time self-published should be a comfort: Beatrix Potter, J.K. Rowling, Steven King and Charles Dickens, to name a few.

With well-publicized cases of authors choosing self-publishing over trade publishing, we are seeing a shift away from a time when self-publishing was the last resort of those who'd received multiple rejections and could not find an agent or a publisher. For genre fiction especially, there are fantastic opportunities because of the strength of those communities, which means that audiences are readily identified and found.

If you have received multiple rejections but want to persist with finding a trade publisher, self-publish anyway! You may find it works for you and you stick with it or, buoyed by the success of your digital publishing, you resume submitting to agents. Your goal is to write and publish a bestseller so the point is to get your story out there in a way that works for you and your book. Orna Ross defines the independent author as someone 'who sees themselves as the creative director of their book from concept to publication.' Power to the author!

Focus point

If you want to publish your own way, including having the final say on the cover, the title, the way your book is marketed and how it is published, then you should focus on self-publishing. With a trade publisher, you must work hard to become such a huge bestseller that you have enough clout to have the final say in these aspects of publishing. If you'd feel more confident being supported by an agent and publisher, then revisit Chapter 7 and tick all those boxes and keep pursuing that goal.

With self-publishing, you are responsible for everything, from writing, marketing and publicity through to production, design, editing and sales. Ask any successful indie author how they achieved their success and they'll tell you that they dedicate time to both the writing and the publishing side of their business, and they hire the right people to help. You must schedule in separate time for writing and publishing, because they are two entirely different roles needing different hats and attitudes.

Where to next?

In the next chapters we are going to discuss publicity and marketing. Being a published author is like running a micro-business and it requires an entrepreneurial mindset to make your publishing a success. This is even truer for a self-published or hybrid author. So we'll take a closer look at the selling and business side of achieving a bestselling book.

PART FIVE
Sell

11

Publicity

A book won't sell on its own, no matter how beautifully written it is. Around 150,000 books are published in the UK each year; in the US it is more than twice that number. That's a huge amount of competition for your book and a lot of options for the reader to choose from. Your task is to stand out in that crowded market. Publicity and marketing are crucial elements in raising your profile and getting your book to your readers.

In this chapter you will learn how to use publicity to sell more of your books. You'll understand the importance of your own promotional efforts; discover practical tips to help make your book and your brand as visible as possible; and learn about reader engagement and ways of generating word-of-mouth buzz.

Marketing and publicity are all about selling more books. They are therefore big and important subjects for the wannabe bestselling author. We look at publicity first because it's free and therefore more accessible for all. Some of the ideas introduced in relation to publicity also come up in relation to marketing; in practice, it's difficult to separate these two functions. Publicity is an aspect of promotion, which is one of the elements of marketing.

This chapter focuses on the things that you can do yourself, free of charge, to bring your book and your brand to readers' attention. If you know your readers, find the right way to communicate with them, offer them a quality read, and engage their interest beyond the covers of your book, you'll create the right conditions for a word-of-mouth buzz. If this takes off, you'll be well on your way to a bestseller.

What is publicity?

Publicity is about gaining public visibility or awareness for your book via the media. If you think you've done your job as author once you've crossed the last T and dotted the last i, and that now it's over to your publisher, distributor, public relations person (or anyone but you) to get the word out there, then it's time for a big rethink. Whether you have a trade publisher or are self-publishing or combining both, attracting readers to your books and simultaneously building your author brand is a long-haul activity that is pretty much down to you and the efforts you make.

Public relations (PR) are about communicating the right, desirable information about something to the public. It's about influencing opinion and building reputation. PR people do this by carrying out publicity. Often, authors might approach PR people with the request to 'make me as famous as Author X'. These writers think they can hand over all PR responsibility, but that isn't going to happen: even if you have all the money in the world to pay someone to do this job, you can't completely hand it over to another person.

Many authors baulk when they find out how much work is involved in publicity but like it or loathe it, it is a key part of a bestselling strategy so get used to it! Here are just some of the things you can be expected to do on the PR front:

- Speak publicly about your book, at signings (often organized by the author rather than the publisher these days), workshops and other events.
- Be part of the conversation in your genre, including writing and contributing to articles and genre communities, on- and offline.

- Master and be active on social media, including blogging.
- Set up and maintain an up-to-date website.

For more information about all these activities, see below.

The market for your book

The first task is to develop a clear idea of the types of reader who might decide to buy your books and how they make their decision to choose yours and not someone else's. Can you explain which readers will buy *your* books, and why? If not, get to work on this so that when you're asked, you'll be ready. Look to your genre and to bestseller lists for hints, and watch other authors in your genre for how they position themselves.

Choosing a book

Start thinking about readers' decisions to buy books in the following exercise.

How many books did *you* buy in the past year? Answer honestly; this is one of those questions – unlike that of your doctor asking how many drinks you have per week – that people tend to answer with an overestimate.

- Think of the last book you bought.
- Where did you buy it?
- How did you make your choice?
- Were you influenced by the cover?
- Did you buy based on a word-of-mouth recommendation?
- Did you buy in a bookshop or online?
- If you bought on an online site, did you buy because of a review or write a review after buying?
- If not, what might have encouraged you to do so?
- On finishing the book, did you want to find out more about the author?
- What kind of information were you looking for?
- Would you buy another book by this author? If so, why?

Given that you are likely to read in the same genre you are writing in, what insights does this exercise give you about who your readers are and why they might buy your books? What can you do to make your book more enticing for them?

How many of your readers are there in the world? You don't need a precise number, obviously, but develop an informed sense of how large the market is for your book.

As a writer, you're probably at the high end of annual book consumption, whether you purchased or borrowed those books. Many people will buy only a few books per year and a significant proportion of the population will not buy any at all. With so many books on the market and a limited number of readers, your work needs to stand out, so you need to learn creative ways to help readers find your book.

Key idea

What is the most appealing aspect of your book? Why would *you* buy it? Capture that in your pitch, publicity materials and blurb.

Your author platform

As discussed in Chapter 8, when pitching your book, it's a good idea to put in a line or two about your author platform. A strong author platform is key requirement in non-fiction *prior* to pitching to agents. Although fiction publishers are more willing to work together with the author on building the brand and platform, anything you can do yourself enhances your overall offering as an author. (It will help your pitch enormously if you can go further and outline a brief marketing plan; see Chapter 12.)

Your platform is made up of anything that you do to communicate your experience and expertise to others. It includes many publicity activities, such as your web presence, public speaking, classes you teach, media contacts you've established, articles you've published and any other means you currently have for making your name and your future books known to a viable readership.

MOVING OUT OF YOUR COMFORT ZONE

You may be feeling uncomfortable at this point. The demands of publicity and PR may not be what you signed up for when you had the urge to write and create stories. You can happily write alone for days at a time without any problem, but it's different matter when you are being told to create noise around your book, to 'be yourself' and engage with others on social media.

Are any of these statements true of you?

- 'I don't like selling or bigging myself up.'
- 'Speaking in public is not something I'm comfortable doing.'
- '"Being myself" means staying at home and writing, not going out and talking about writing.'
- 'I've no idea how to talk about my book without it sounding forced.'
- 'I chose to do creative work so I didn't have to do this business stuff.'

These concerns are common among writers. Keep an open mind as you read through this chapter, and take the path of least resistance; experiment with all the different aspects of publicity and focus on the one that seems least threatening to you. As you become more experienced, I would urge you to face your fears and find a way to try the more challenging methods of engagement. There are many ways to collaborate with other authors both on- and offline, which takes the heat off you at the same time. For instance, perhaps it would suit you better to be part of a panel discussion rather than standing alone before an audience.

Think creatively and collaboratively, without having to be alone in the spotlight, and multiply your promotional efforts by teaming up with other authors and publishers to create a bigger bang. A clever example of this was the One Big Book Launch, a collaborative launch organized by CompletelyNovel.com with ten authors from across publishers, self-publishers, and genres, joining to celebrate the launch of their books.

Sarah Juckes, CompletelyNovel

'The launch gave each author the chance to increase the number of potential readers at their launch, as well as reach press and literary scouts who love a sense of occasion. We think it marks the beginning of a more collaborative approach to book marketing. Two heads are better than one, and teaming up with other authors and publishers can increase the number of people you are marketing to. Marketing books 'alone' is one of the biggest fears authors have. The answer? Don't do it alone. Get on Twitter, to your local writing group or organization, or even your publisher, and collaborate with other writers.'

Whatever you decide to do to promote your book, think on this. If you have taken the time to write a story that you truly love, doesn't your story deserve its best chance? It's perhaps worth putting aside your fears to nurture your fictional baby.

 ## Laura Dockrill, author

'Author PR and marketing is really crucial. We are operating in a crowded market, with audiences that can be very fickle. If authors engage with their fans, those fans tend to remain more loyal. There are lots of ways to do this – the obvious ones are via social media such as Twitter and Facebook, but that doesn't suit everyone. It could be as simple as building your network on Goodreads or replying to readers' posts on Amazon – or even just writing book club notes to go in the back of your book.

Authors should remember the print retailers too! Making friends with your local bookshop and library is so important. Maeve Binchy used to send handwritten thank-you notes to booksellers who featured her in a shop window.'

PUBLIC SPEAKING ABOUT YOUR BOOK

Being a great writer will help you reach the giddy heights of achieving a bestselling book, but you'll need to get from out from behind your desk and put yourself out there if you want to sell your book in a decent quantity. If you're a good speaker and presenter, or if you can raise yourself up to be one, then you'll do even better. 'Back of the room' book sales can be a real boost to your income, particularly if you are self-published or you have negotiated a generous author discount for your books. Your publisher may even deliver the books directly to a contact at the speaking site.

When you are offered non-paid speaking engagements, here are a few questions to help you decide whether it is worth your while to do it:

- Is it a cause or organization dear to my heart?
- Will it be good practice for my speaking?
- Will my book and I get good exposure?
- How many people can I reach?
- Am I able to sell copies in the promotional period leading up to the talk as well as at the event? (You don't want to miss out on sales to people who don't attend.)
- What promotion will the organizers do in advance of the talk?

You'll need someone to help you sell the books because you'll be busy speaking and networking. The organizers should be able to provide someone to do this for you if you are not being paid.

Don't forget to include local bookshops, libraries, community arts organizations and schools on your list of speaking engagements. You may not be paid, but you can sell books at these events. The more experience you gain as a speaker, the more likely you are to be paid for speaking in the future. And, perversely, the greater your income from your book and the higher you climb up the bestselling charts, the more likely it is that you'll be offered paid speaking opportunities. If you approach it creatively, and find a way to link the themes of your book, you can also sell your books and earn a fee when speaking to trade groups, associations, corporations and large groups.

Audiences seem most interested in what lies behind a book. After all, stories are all about what it means to be human. Audiences like to find out the answers to these questions:

- Why did you write it?
- What does it all mean?
- What were you hoping to express?

Build these topics into your talk.

BEING PART OF THE CONVERSATION

How can you work your book or backstory into a wider conversation? It's all about hooking into the Zeitgeist. Start the conversation about the topic, setting or situation of your book, online or offline. Facebook, LinkedIn and blogs are good places to do this. On Facebook you can set up a page for your book to encourage readers to like, share and comment on your news and conversation about your book. The page should describe your book, the setting, characters and a summary of the plotline.

If you aren't confident about this, your first efforts could be to contribute to Facebook conversations that have already started. Join in and encourage people to carry on existing conversations. When you have their attention, readers following the discussion may be interested in you, and go to your Facebook page or blog, to spend time in the fictional place you have created in your novel.

If the subject or theme of your book is in the news or the subject of debate, then timing is on your side. Get involved. (Bestsellers have been made this way.) Get in touch with the media and offer your contribution. Where relevant, fiction authors are often called to comment on news stories related to the subject matter of their novels. For example, following a high-school mass shooting, Lionel

Shriver, whose novel *We Need to Talk about Kevin* covers this horror, could be called upon to contribute to radio or TV discussions on formats such as *Woman's Hour, Newsnight* or *Question Time*.

Think about your themes, topics and settings. What is contentious about your book, and do you take a particular position? Do you inform, educate, illuminate, cast new light on an old subject? Where and with whom can you imagine discussing your themes? Get involved in that discussion.

YOUR PRESS RELEASE

One of the best tools for helping to add your voice to media conversations is a press release. A press release is an essential bit of an author's PR kit and you'll need to write one yourself if you are self-publishing. If you have a trade publisher, they'll do this for you. Ask them for a copy so that you can use material from it – especially the summary pitch for your book – when you continue your PR efforts after they stop. (Yes, they will stop a month or so after your book is published, though they will still offer support. For example, if a radio or TV producer calls up looking for a talking head on a subject, and if you're right for it, you will be put forward.)

Write a press release

Write a press release for your book, tying it into current concerns in the media. Use the checklist below and aim for one or two pages of text.

Remember these points when writing your press release:

- Get the angle right: make sure your tidbit is newsworthy and that you have sent it to the appropriate outlets.
- The start of the release should be a brief description of the news
- The first ten words or so are the most important. If they don't catch the reader's interest, he or she will not read further.
- Cut adjectives and jargon as much as possible.
- Stick to the facts.
- Follow up! Ninety per cent of the success of any press release is in the follow up.

Mastering social media

Are you already talking to your potential readers? Do you know who they are? How can you connect with your potential and future readers right now?

If you want a bestseller on your hands, you know that you need to get social media (SM) savvy. You can spend hours, days and weeks on SM and not achieve the results you want. The key is, first of all, to be clear about:

- why you are there and what your aim is
- who your audience is and where they hang out.

Social media experts generally advise you not to try to cover all social media, unless you have help to do so. Choose the two types of social media that you are best at and feel most comfortable with and give yourself permission to forget the rest. Many authors favour Facebook and Twitter. But – and it is a big but – do those two properly and thoroughly, with a clear strategy.

Here's how to build your platform on social media:

1 Have a clear understanding of your demographic so that, when you use SM, you know to whom you are talking and you can pitch the communication perfectly.

2 From the moment you pick up your pen to start your bestseller, or perhaps even before, you can start building an audience. Choose the social media that you will focus on – the ones you feel most comfortable with and, more importantly, where your readership hangs out. (YA author Nii Parkes engaged with his audience from the beginning of his writing journey, asking his Facebook group for their view of his characters, cover design, title and so on. By the time his book was published, readers were eager and interested to see it, as they'd been part of the process.)

3 Find and use Twitter writing hashtags to join a popular conversation. There are many thousands for writers including #amwriting. (I like this one as it's not only a well-used hashtag but it also serves as an affirmation ('#I-am-oh-yes-I-really-am-writing' would have been too long, of course).

4 Check out a few of your favourite bestselling authors in your genre and see what SM they use and how they do it. From there, experiment with your own voice and style.

INSPIRING AUTHORS: THE SOCIAL MEDIA EXPERTS

Mastering social media requires a bit of trial and error but it is definitely worth it. Lucy Inglis, historian and author of *Georgian London* and YA novelist, has learned to use social media to her advantage. She advises setting up a Googlemail account and using Google Plus as a first step to be present on SM with little effort. She also says that, if you are short of time, Twitter is your best social media aid for its immediacy and interactivity.

 ## Lucy Inglis, historian and author

'Set up a Twitter account in your own name but, for your book and your writing, choose a name related to your genre; people search for Twitter handles via genre, and you can accumulate a lot of followers by having a genre name.

Twitter is also invaluable for honing your own voice. It makes you think more snappily, to fit the character limit. It really makes you polish up your writing. If you are writing YA, sci-fi or fantasy, romance or erotic fiction, Twitter is a great place for you to find other writers and readers.

Of all SM, Tumblr needs the least interaction for the most results. It's a great place for authors to really speak to writers. And it's particularly good if your audience is a young market, or if you write sci-fi or fantasy.'

The Tumblr website has some friendly, accessible videos to show you how to get started.

Children's and YA author Laura Dockrill uses Tumblr. She told *The Bookseller* that she wanted 'a platform where people are already spending their time looking for book-related content. Instead of asking them to come to me, I'm joining them. I hope that writinglorali.tumblr.com inspires others, igniting creativity and explorations.'

So, instead of overtly drawing attention to yourself, trying to attract readers to your website, you could emulate Laura and reach out to them.

INSPIRING AUTHORS: READER ENGAGEMENT

One author who epitomizes how to get it right is crime writer Peter James. He is an excellent example of an author who does PR well, and keeps on doing it well. Despite being a superstar of the crime-writing world and being in the middle of writing a new book, he agreed to be interviewed for this book. That's reader engagement!

Peter James, author

'Communication channels such as Facebook and Twitter are all great; they allow an immediacy with readers that we didn't have 20 years ago. In the past, my readers would have had to write to me via my publisher, who'd then pass the letter to my agent and eventually it would get to me. This all took time, and the replying process was equally long and arduous. With the instant communication that social media allows, I can learn a lot about my readers and they give great feedback. This means I can build up a picture of what my readers like and dislike, whether that's to do with characters or other choices I make.'

Does the feedback you receive sway you in your writing?

'A while back, I had a few comments like, "I'd like your books better if they didn't have quite so much swearing." It makes you think and, on reflection, I did cut the amount of swearing a little. I can also tell followers what's happening with new books and about events I'm doing. And if I have any research questions, someone out there always knows the answer.'

It's pretty clear from the voice that comes through in your social media that you do that yourself.

'I do, it's important to truly engage. Readers know when its real and when its manufactured.'

Is there any one thing that made a big difference to your career?

'Yes, my early career was not easy and switching to the right genre for me was what changed things. The turning point in my career stemmed from the best piece of advice I've ever been given. At a party, someone from Penguin turned to me and asked, "Why are you writing spy thrillers? You're up against Le Carré and Fleming who both came out of the special services. How can you research the world of spies successfully?"

I decided to act upon this advice, to write about what I had a passion for. What really fascinated me at that time was the supernatural; I spent three years researching and understanding mediums. The book that followed was Possession in 1987. Every publisher in the UK bid for it. It went to number one and was translated into 26 languages. It established me as an author.

But even all of that didn't mean that I could stop evolving and working hard at this business of writing. What happened next was that I was pigeonholed as a horror writer, just as horror writing became a ghetto genre. During this time in the 1990s, although they were bad times for me as an author, I kept working with Midas PR – and I still do – because I knew that year-round publicity was vital rather than just having the publisher do PR around the publication of a book. Often, I spent all of my advance on PR in those days, but it was well worth it.

I then started to work with Carole Blake of Blake Friedmann. I left Orion, and had no publisher for the first time in many years. Then Macmillan approached us to ask if I had considered writing a crime novel. Now I had always wanted to write crime, but thought it was an overcrowded market. They told me they had just lost their number 1 crime novelist and asked if I'd like to have a go. I did, and here I am.

I firmly believe that if an author wants to be a success they need to invest. They can't just sit back and take the advances. The publisher's PR focuses their efforts around book publication time but, if you think about it, they have a lot to do. They have about 600 books per year to promote and there are only two or three per month they can really focus on, so – forgive my rough Maths here – that's probably only about 50–60 titles per year that have any hope of getting on to the bestseller list. With publishers, you have a maximum window of about one month. So what about the rest of the year? You should still be out there, either under your own steam or with PR help.

Macmillan's current marketing strategy for me is a Facebook campaign comprising competitions and book giveaways. And it works. Last week I offered six advance proof copies and had 800 entries in 12 hours.'

A stage production of your book *The Perfect Murder* is touring theatres. How has this affected your book sales?

'It's been a really good thing; there is a knock-on effect from all the publicity surrounding the play, so the book has stayed selling strongly in paperback for far longer than the others did.'

Peter James's advice for debut novelists

1 **Write a story that really matters.**

'What is it that makes people interested in a book? What do people worry about? Make sure your story has that element to it.'

2 Promote your book tirelessly and don't ever stop.

'Get out into the world. Do library events and bookshops, which encourages bookshops to stock your book. The day of my first book's publication was "the worst in my life" as I couldn't find a single copy anywhere; I soon learned that I had to be part of the marketing push myself.'

3 Remember that writing is work.

'I like this anecdote about Margaret Atwood being at a party where she is introduced to a brain surgeon. It went something like this:

BS: What do you do?

MA: I'm an author

BS: Ah, very nice. I'm going to write a novel when I retire.

MA: What do you do?

BS: I'm a brain surgeon.

MA: That's funny; I'm going to be a brain surgeon when I retire.'

4 Engage with your reader and have fun doing it.

'Do book launches, talks and speak anywhere you will encounter your reader. Think about the reader; make a proper connection, be entertaining, and don't bore them by reading from your book. Make them fun events, perhaps with cocktails themed around the book you're launching.'

Peter James, author

'To launch Dead Man's Grip, I wanted to rival a Bond book that was coming out at the time. A character in the book had his hand superglued to a steering wheel (and was pushed into the sea) so we re-enacted that. I was submerged in Shoreham Harbour in a van and hauled up by a crane. Out I came in a dry suit over the top of a tux.'

This shows engagement, and it tallies with something else about Peter, which is that he invites the people who read his books, such as policemen, to his launch parties; he's a crime writer, after all. He engages with real people who buy books, instead of just the press and booksellers.

Key idea

If you can afford to pay for PR – as Peter James did even in
the early days when the PR cost all of his advance – then don't
hesitate. Do it. If not, you'll need to do it yourself. Be adaptable –
note how, instead of defending his genre choice, Peter acted
upon a challenging insight that required radical changes to his
writing career.

PR and publicity tips

Peter James has worked with Midas PR, one of Britain's leading
book PR companies, since the early days of his career. Midas
successfully curated the London Book Fair's author lounge in 2014.
I asked Tory Lyne-Pirkis, Account Director at Midas, for her top tips
for authors wanting to be noticed:

1 **Get your book jacket right.**

   The old adage, 'Don't judge a book by its cover' is untrue:
   everyone, including book reviewers, judges whether a book is
   right for their audience by looking at the cover. Do your research
   and find out what the covers of bestselling books look like,
   because you will want to make sure that the jacket of your book
   is able to compete with other books in the same genre. This is one
   of the times when it pays to not stand out from the crowd but to
   follow the designs and styles of other similar books, as readers
   are more likely to be drawn to buy new books that look similar
   to the ones they have read.

2 **Make friends with your local bookshop.**

   Bookshop owners and managers are the champions of local
   authors. Bookshops want to sell books, and they will be very
   happy to help you organize a launch or an event if you can
   guarantee that all your friends will come to the shop to buy
   copies. If the bookshop doesn't stock your book, offer to come
   in and do a stock signing, as signed copies are easier to sell. By
   offering to do a stock signing, you are also ensuring that the
   bookshop is ordering in copies of your book from your publisher,
   creating supply and demand.

3 **Get to grips with book bloggers.**

   Research has proved that the more positive reviews you can
   post on your Amazon page, the more copies of your book will
   sell. If you can't secure a review of your book in a newspaper or

magazine, get in touch with book bloggers who review books in your genre. In return for a free book, they will run an often very positive review of your book, which you can then use for a review quote on Amazon.

4 **Network.**

Runaway bestsellers always start out as word-of-mouth sellers, with friends recommending the book to one another until everyone is reading it. You need to spread the word about your book as far and wide as possible. You can do this in the real world by attending book events and getting to know your local bookshop, local librarians, English teachers at your local school and organizers of your local festival. In the virtual world, you can network using Twitter and Facebook. On Twitter, you can follow and tweet at influencers in the publishing industry, and you can build a following of people who are interested in your work and who may well recommend your book to others.

5 **Start local.**

If you want publicity for your book, talk to your local newspaper, radio station or county magazine about an interview or a book review, as they are always on the lookout for regional interest stories. For coverage in national newspapers and magazines and TV and radio, you will need to hire a professional book publicist.

6 **Never give up!**

It takes years for professional publicists to build relationships with journalists, bookshops, festival organizers, librarians and so on. PR takes time, and you're not going to be able to persuade everyone you talk to that they want to review your book, or that they want to help you. If you get a 'no' from someone, don't let it get you down. Just pick yourself up and keep going. If you keep trying, you'll be surprised by the number of people willing to support you in your quest to get noticed. Tenacity is key!

This is all good and proven advice from a leading book PR. What will you use in your own campaign?

The importance of reviews

When your book is on the market and being read, it will be reviewed. All book PRs stress the importance of good reviews and good reviews are especially important on Amazon. It is believed that readers are more likely to buy your book if it has been rated on Amazon than if it hasn't been rated. A well-written, positive review that explains why your book is good (not just that it is good) is highly desirable.

Nathalie Nahai, psychologist and author

'When we're appraising a product for the first time without much contextual information, we look to social cues to help us decide whether or not it's a good choice. Any kind of earned media (such as likes, shares, reviews and recommendations) will increase your chances of selling to new customers. In fact, research shows that if you do decide to buy an item, you'll actually be more satisfied with your purchase if it's been (positively) reviewed by others.'

What do you think when you read five-star reviews on Amazon? Do you find them convincing? Beware: many of the reviews on Amazon seem too positive, too comprehensive, well written and sales-focused to be true. To counter this, when you ask friends to read and review your book, ask them to comment on whether it was useful to them if it is narrative non-fiction or, if it's straight fiction, ask whether it was entertaining or fun. Whatever you had set out to do, ask them if it lit that spark or fulfilled that function. That way, they will be honest in their critique of the book, and you'll get a review that is constructive as well as helpful to any potential readers who encounter your book.

Scott Pack, publisher, The Friday Project

'Given the priority and prestige accorded to newspaper reviews, you'd think they were crucial to book sales but, when it comes to the broadsheets, they aren't really. A big rave review in the Mail *can definitely shift numbers but the same exposure in* The Times *or* The Guardian *rarely has the same clout. Even when a book or author receives blanket coverage across the literary press, it doesn't mean big sales. Take Karl Ove Knausgaard, probably the most written-about author of the past couple of years in the literary pages; and yet his first book has yet to sell 10,000 copies.*

I would argue that Amazon reviews also have little direct impact on sales but, like press reviews, they can contribute

> *to the overall noise around a book. Clearly, no one is going to see an Amazon review unless they have already searched for the book itself, but they can help support a decision to read something or try it out. Most consumers are aware that Amazon reviews need to be taken with a pinch of salt as well. Lots of positive reviews are hardly a bad thing, though.'*

Perversely, then, bad reviews on Amazon can help, as long as they don't outnumber the positive ones. The ratings will seem more trustworthy if they're not all good, and the number of reviews your book gains is considered a reflection of its visibility and so will affect your ranking. There'll always be someone who'll slate your book, or any book for that matter. Some reviewers get personal and really seem to have it in for the author. It can be upsetting but don't worry too much about these; the madder and more unreasonable they sound when they do criticize your book, the more easily the reader will discount those reviews. What Amazon ranking seems to like is attention; they don't mind if a book is reviewed badly as long as it is not being ignored. Remember *Fifty Shades* and the slagging off it received on Amazon and elsewhere – sales of the book were boosted by a fascination that went beyond whether the writing was any good or not.

Key idea

A group of YA writers canvassed via Facebook said that they have bought books that had bad reviews, and that they don't choose to buy a book just because it has a good review. You need the right mix of good and bad reviews – mostly good, a few bad. If a trusted friend recommends a book, that's a different story.

How do you get reviews? Ask people. Send out review copies and ask people to give their honest view. To save money, send a pdf or e-version. Email people you know as well as people in your genre communities. Author and entrepreneur, Mike Michalowicz has really helpful step-by-step tips for getting your book reviewed (http://www.mikemichalowicz.com/how-to-get-tons-of-amazon-reviews-for-your-book-or-product/).

OFFERING THE READER MORE

Through your publicity efforts, a reader needs to hear about your book, seek it out, buy it, and read it. But your relationship doesn't have to stop there.

Think about one of your favourite books. Now recall how you felt when you read the last line, closed the book and sat back with a mixture of satisfaction at having enjoyed a good story and woe at having finished. You may have felt bereft, with a sense of loss in your life where the book had been. At this point, imagine that, having reached the end but while still in the story world, you could have more, staying in that place a little longer before returning to reality. Some trade publishers do this well, including author interviews at the back of their books. Offering more allows readers to linger and further cement their relationship with the author. If you are self-publishing, then think about how you'll offer this reader add-on for your book.

For maximum reader engagement, invite them to join you in conversation. Point readers to your website (via social media, and the offer of useful or interesting content on your site). Make it a compelling invitation and a satisfying experience by offering them something extra when they get there.

When they link to your website, for example, they might find additional content such as:

- a look behind the scenes
- the backstory to the book
- an alternative ending. If you wrote a happy ending, give them sad instead; if sad, give them happy. If the heroine got her man, give an ending where she skips off into the sunset alone.

Give readers a reason to engage using social media:

- Ask them to vote for their favourite ending.
- Ask them to rewrite the final line or paragraph of your book, or their favourite book.
- Ask them for contributions or input while you are writing. For example, they might suggest a setting, a character's name, or vote for whether or not the heroine should end up with her man.
- Ask their pet's names and incorporate some of them into your next book.
- Before they leave, ask for their email address with a promise to send news and updates.

Be yourself, and be enthusiastic about your own work and other writing you admire, and you'll attract the sort of people who will like and understand your work.

Word-of-mouth recommendation

In a quick Facebook survey, I posed a question for 100 writers:
'Thinking of the last book you bought, why did you choose that
over any other?' Of 100 responses, five identified the cover as most
important, 27 mentioned choosing from a specific genre, but the
highest score of 59 went to personal or Facebook recommendations.

These recommendations from people we know, or know of, and
trust is known as 'word of mouth' (WOM). WOM is the holy grail
of bestselling books. According to a World Book Day survey, 'Word
of mouth is, arguably, the most important factor in making a book
successful.' It's heartening to know that appeal can't wholly be
bought via advertising.

How do you create a WOM buzz around your book? Let's first cover
the fantasy angle, where you can have anything you want to help you
to sell copies. You suddenly find yourself with a bottomless purse, able
to hire a team of marketing and publicity professionals. They create
a dazzling launch party that attracts huge media attention. From
their incredible connections, your book finds its way into the hands of
Richard and Judy. Soon, Oprah discovers your book and waxes lyrical
about it on Twitter. All of this kickstarts a word-of-mouth reaction.
You're invited on breakfast TV and radio and everyone is talking about
your book and debating your subject matter. The bookshops all display
your book cover up in huge stacks. It's selected by WHSmith Travel as
book of the week, so it is prominent at every train station and airport.
And your book ranks in the top ten bestsellers on the Amazon chart in
its first week. Waterstones increase their order as they see how well it is
doing on Amazon, and it becomes a 'staff pick' in every store.

Let's break apart the fantasy to see what realistically can be done:

1 You can do your own publicity.

2 You don't know Oprah? Don't despair: for endorsements, be
  strategic. Start with low-hanging fruit, with people you already
  know, and work your way up to your ideal endorsement,

says author and entrepreneur Shaa Wasmund who received endorsements from leading thinkers, though not by approaching them directly at first. She identified the experts she wanted to target, then, starting with people she already knew, she built a chain of endorsements, using each as an introduction to get her a step closer to her targets. She ended up with quotes from Sir Ranulph Fiennes, OBE and Seth Godin.

3 To get people talking about your book, start with your local book clubs. Send them free copies. (There's more about book club books in the next chapter.)

4 If the content of your book matters to people, then you can generate debate by being part of the conversation. Identify places online and start contributing.

5 Local radio is a good place to start. Identify a programme that your book would sit well on and be bold: send in your book with a press release and a covering letter offering to talk about it on air.

6 Build your name as a local author in schools, libraries and bookshops, and branch out from there.

Even if you have budget, paying a whole team of publicity and marketing people works only up to a point. You will still have to work hard along with them. And you need to have written a book that has conceptually strong material; a theme that generates debate, that nails a subject that's hanging in the air but that nobody else has quite covered yet, and certainly not in the way that you do. You also need to write good marketing content for them to use, make yourself available for interview, talk to the media, and go out and speak to your readers.

 Key idea

The key ingredients of a WOM bestseller are:
- great storytelling
- writing that is good enough
- a 'you must read this now' factor that gets people talking
- good timing, based on the Zeitgeist – what the reading classes are concerned about
- luck — a news story breaking on a subject close to that of your book
- fashion – your theme or genre is 'in'.

BUILDING WOM FOR YOUR AUTHOR BRAND

Here are some top tips for building WOM:

1 **Be consistent in your output.** This doesn't mean your writing has to be the same, but it does have to be consistently good in all aspects.

2 **Don't reinvent yourself for each and every book.** If you want to explore and innovate with every book you write, that is of course entirely your decision. But you can't expect readers to follow you from book to book. Don't be surprised if you lose some of them.

3 **Provide a common thread.** What are you best known for? If you do leap from genre to genre, what skill, strength or signature can you use in the promotion to display what you are known for?

4 **Build relationships.** Engage with your readership. Spend time online and offline in real communities. Be interested in other author's books and in helping them with their promotion.

5 **Build trust.** Be helpful and engaging on social media rather than acting like a door-to-door salesperson. It's off-putting when authors that follow, friend or connect on social media don't skip a beat before trying to sell their book – usually in upper-case sentences.

6 **Be patient.** It might not happen for book 1 or even book 2 but, if you want to write a bestseller, be in it for the long game.

7 **Keep writing more books.** If you do create a hit book, there will be a flow-on effect to your earlier books. Readers will want them all and they won't want to wait, so don't stop writing.

Tweet @blakefriedmann agency

'*Go to writerly events, mix with other writers, form friendships – your best contacts often turn out to be your peers. Solidarity!*'

If you are self-publishing, you need to take responsibility for all aspects of publicity, including handling your own launch. Below is a list of ten key steps to generating and maintaining a successful online launch; use this list to draw up your own launch schedule.

Because many of the steps are about building your platform, they'll help if you're being traditionally published, too.

1 Build up your database. Don't worry if this is tiny at first; it will grow once you provide people with an easy opportunity to opt in on your website and blog. London Writers' Club started with just 35 people on its mailing list and it now has over 10,000.

2 Start mentioning your book early on. Don't give everything away – just drop hints in your blog or e-zine and give them the date of publication and perhaps an online book launch party so they can put it in their diary!

3 Tag your email signature with a jpeg of your book cover. Add a line about the book and a link to your website, Amazon, other book-selling sites, or wherever else you want to direct people.

4 Create your sales page. Do this ahead of launching. Your site needs a full page about your book and a link to where people can buy it.

5 Upload the book cover to your site. State the title and price, remembering to add on the shipping costs if you are selling print copies yourself.

6 Draw up a priority list of supporters. These are people who have already engaged with you in some way. Give this priority list a chance to buy your book at a discounted price. Send them a short email, directing them to your sales page. Remember to always give your customers a deadline to respond by and send your priority list a reminder: 'Only 24 hours at this special discount price'.

7 Send out a more general selling email to your database (e.g. your e-zine list). They may not have bought from you yet, so direct them to your sales page. Again, give them a discount and remember to include a deadline date.

8 Build an affiliate programme. Talk to authors in your genre about your new book. Are they interested in doing cross-promotion with you? Tell them how they can promote it and whether you are offering a promotion. Give them an individual affiliate link that gives them credit on any referred sales. Make sure you give them the full information and are clear on how much commission they will receive per sale. (You'll find more detailed information on how to do this on londonwritersclub.com.)

9 Keep promoting your book. Think about a bonus you could offer a few months after the launch to keep a conversation going around your book. This might be an additional chapter, a free

teleclass on how to write and publish in your genre or a more exclusive personal event.

10 Ask every buyer to give you feedback. Use this feedback on your site and as quotes for the media and offline publicity and marketing.

Where to next?

In the next chapter, you'll find out more about marketing within the publishing industry and how you can work with professionals to raise your book's profile even further.

12

Marketing

In book publishing, marketing is traditionally defined as anything paid for, including catalogues, advertisements, posters and bookshop promotions. The focus in book marketing is on building brands, manoeuvring around the digital explosion, making the most of the opportunities provided by social media, and keeping abreast of shifting marketplaces.

In this chapter, you'll learn about the role of marketing in modern publishing and find out where you need to spend your time, money and effort in marketing to maximize your sales. You will create your own marketing and publicity plan that will let you reap the benefits of being a published author, and find out who are the best people to help you.

Marketing in the book trade

Once you've completely nailed your story, you will need to be businesslike. The thought of packaging up and selling your book as a product might grate, but it is necessary. If you've got the hook of your story absolutely clear, then the marketing should not only be true to and representative of your book, but also stronger for having the hook. We hear everywhere that content is king and yet it is marketing that appears to rule as we see pretty average books succeed because of the marketing splash. There's a sense that our books, known in this context as a 'product' or 'content', are in danger of becoming secondary to the marketing machine.

By using the word 'content' or 'product' to describe your novel, publishing professionals do not mean to devalue or reduce it to a widget but, once you reach the marketing phase, your book has been 'put to bed'. (If you are not sure that it is as good as it can be, now is the time to go back and make it exactly how you want it to be.) The focus now is on making what you've produced easy to explain in the short time available in any selling and publicity opportunity that presents itself. So, that explained, I'll be talking about your book and your product interchangeably.

INSPIRING AUTHOR: A BUSINESSLIKE SUCCESS

Sylvia Day, bestselling *New York Times* author whose *Crossfire* series has sold more than 13 million copies since its first release in 2012, is a news-making hybrid author whose success is due to her incredibly focused and businesslike approach to her publishing. She has made the publishing business her business. Originally self-published, she has since done an eight-figure deal with St Martins' Press.

Some of the efforts she has put into her publishing are:

- changing agent five times to find the one that suited her publishing aims
- displaying market and business flair in all aspects of her publishing
- negotiating hard for her publisher to keep prices keen rather than hiking them up when they acquired her book (selling at $4.99 rather than $9.99).

Despite her success under her own steam and on her own terms, she says that 'the world cannot survive without the publishing industry' because it provides a viable channel which enables a wide distribution of books, whereas self-publishing doesn't have that network.

Sylvia Day, author

'Some of the gatekeeper functions that we have in New York (shorthand for the publishing industry) are also important. Foreign sales are still dependent on how books perform in the US. As the foreign market opens – and it is opening – many publishers need to have a US-based partner in order for them to adequately market titles in their territory. I've worked with 12 different publishers and some of the best people in the industry. These people are repositories of information about books and the industry ... and you need that vibrant community. Booksellers tie into this, of course. There's a network in place that serves a purpose and I think that reading and the types of books available and the quality of the books available would be dramatically changed by the loss of the publishing industry.' http://www.digitalbookworld. com/2013/hybrid-author-sylvia-day-the-world-cannot-survive-without-the-publishing-industry/

Day's journey to where she is now – a blockbuster author selling millions – has been achieved with a good story to start with, in a genre where readers read voraciously, with a willingness to trial different modes of publishing, and by making an-depth study of how the publishing industry works.

MARKETING MYTHS

When you see a bestselling author enjoying the limelight, it might look like one big splash, an overnight success. This is one of the many myths and misconceptions about being a writer and publishing. What you see is actually the result of much hard work and joined-up effort on the part of the author, agent, publisher, PR and marketing people over a number of years.

Another myth relates to the role of agent and publisher in marketing. I overheard one author at the London Book Fair saying to another: 'I can't wait to get an agent so I can forget about all that marketing and publicity stuff and concentrate on my writing.' The role of the agent (covered in detail in Chapter 7) is not to do your marketing; however, your agent will keep an eye on your marketing and PR, will offer advice and feedback, and will champion your cause should it go wrong. If they are active on social media, they may also share your posts or tweets and announce good news and events. They aren't actually responsible for the marketing itself, and they won't do it for you.

If an agent is pitching on your behalf and your book goes to auction (when multiple publishers are interested in your book), your agent may push for a marketing plan to be included as part of the offer. They do so because a good marketing plan, and the publisher's commitment to it in writing, should result in healthy book sales. The addition of a stand-out marketing plan can sweeten a book deal to the extent that the publisher paying the highest advance may not be the publisher of choice.

Your brand and platform

Branding is the process involved in creating a unique name and image in your readers' minds for you and your books. Branding aims to establish a significant and differentiated presence in the market that attracts and retains loyal customers. The starting point for branding is the author's platform. A publisher will have a strategy for building author platforms.

 ## Laura Palmer, fiction publisher, Head of Zeus

'The first aspect of building a debut novelist's platform is undoubtedly to have the right novel. A story with a great premise, a gripping plot and a theme or issue that lends itself to discussion is the ideal combination to launch an author. The second is to have the right title and cover – something that places the author firmly in a genre but also looks fresh and inviting. The third is not to worry too much about revenue, and concentrate instead on building readership – even if that means discounting the price of the book, or paying marketing costs that you may not recoup against this title. The last is to encourage the author to take part in anything that could aid reader recommendation. Whether that is local signings, blog posts or book group visits, nothing is too small when it comes to securing the elusive word of mouth that helps create bestsellers.'

YOUR ONE-LINE PITCH

What is the one-line pitch that encapsulates your book? In this phase of the making of a bestseller, this is your marketing gold dust.

Think of all of the people who may be involved in the publishing of your book – agent, marketing, PR, sales, booksellers. They need to sum up your book for one another in turn. If there's only time or space for one line, how might you refine your pitch, using your three-sentence pitch (see Chapter 8) as the starting point?

Pitch your one-line pitch

If you're not sure how to improve your one-liner, pitch it to some writing buddies and ask for their feedback.

- Do they ask for clarification? Don't explain, but try to find out what wasn't clear. This lets you build clarity into your pitch and into your book.
- Do people ask what happened next in an excited way? This is good. While they are engaged, ask them what most intrigued or excited them about the book. Carefully note which aspect of the overall concept they most connect with. Use what you learned for your future pitches and for your blurb.
- Do they glaze over? This may be because your pitch doesn't adequately describe your book, or it is a true representation of a book that isn't working yet, or it may just be that they are unfamiliar with the genre. Ask open questions to find out why they think it isn't working and how to fix it.

INSPIRING AUTHORS: LONG-TERM MARKETING

Prolific children's author Michael Rosen was recently interviewed on Radio 4. His bestselling book, *We're Going on a Bear Hunt*, was first published in 1989 and has sold more than 8 million copies in 18 languages. I don't know a child under the age of 7 who doesn't have this book and, remarkably, now that booksellers tend to stock as little of each book as possible, you can find multiple copies of it in any bookshop you walk into.

You'd hardly think that Michael would still need to keep plugging it, yet there he was, still doing interviews to talk about his writing and to connect and share with his readership. Despite his huge success, he continues to work hard at marketing his brand and his books, not that he necessarily thinks of it in that way.

On Michael's website, there's further evidence of his commitment. He works his market. He regularly talks to schools and festivals, keeping his name and his books in front of his readership. If he hasn't relaxed on the promotion front, even with such a bestselling book under his belt, why do unestablished authors think they don't need to do this? It's an ongoing process of keeping your brand and your books visible.

Marketing with a publisher

If you have a publisher, they will have some marketing budget to spend on you, even if it is just the allocation of their own time and staff resources. Publishers (and agents) like fiction authors to write series because promotion turns into brand marketing: every time they promote a book, they are promoting the whole list. If you write stand-alone books, publishers prefer multi-book deals for the same reason. Marketing investment in your current book promotes your entire authorial brand: readers who like your second book will seek out your first.

Authors often complain about how trade publishers promote and market their books or, rather, how publishers fail to promote and market their books. Like the choice of cover and title, this is another trouble spot where authors, their agents and publishers can fall out.

Many debut authors say they prefer to have an agent and a publisher rather than self-publish, so that they don't have to bear full responsibility for their marketing and PR. But, as we have seen, publishers do not have limitless budgets and nor do they want to risk too much of their budget on a title that they're not sure will pay dividends. They need to see evidence of your commitment to promoting your book. Your own marketing plan (see below) will provide that evidence.

Stretching a small marketing budget

Regardless of your route to publication, if you are lucky enough to have some money of your own to spend on marketing, you'll want to spend it wisely. So what should you spend it on? A combination of sleek, professional promotion and more personal touches will take your marketing budget further.

Things you could pay for include:
- help with devising an effective social media strategy
- incentives to get people to engage with you, connect with your work and ultimately buy your book –for example, competitions and giveaways via Facebook or Twitter

- a book trailer for video promotion if you want to reach a wider audience (these can be done well for around £350)
- mp3 podcasts, which are easy and cheap to do yourself.

Things you don't need to pay for include:

- a video for YouTube that is just you talking to camera. Keep this short and sweet, explaining your book's concept.
- a call to action: most traffic on YouTube stays on that site, with little of it channelled back to your web pages, so mention a giveaway, such as a chapter of your book, to encourage visitors to go your site, where they can sign up to your database (there's more about databases below).

Key idea

It's important to spend money and make effort at the right time with a specific goal in mind, rather than adopting a scattergun approach. There's information on how to schedule your marketing activities, and more ideas for low-cost actions that you can take yourself, in the next section.

What kind of marketing campaign can a debut novelist expect to get from a trade publisher?

Lisa Highton, publisher, Two Roads at John Murray Press

'When we acquire a debut novelist, we engage in a partnership, deciding upfront how we're going to establish both the author and the book through sales, publicity, marketing and what our strategy is. Essentially, there is a roll-out campaign of action and as much as possible the author is alongside and is engaging both with us and readers, through social media, publicity, appearances and general profile raising. There isn't a one-size-fits-all approach; each campaign is bespoke. We don't browbeat authors into social media or appearances but I'm always surprised at how good authors are – they find their best voice and use it to advantage.

Our activity on a book starts on acquisition and doesn't stop. Obviously there are key points in the life cycle when more

*people are involved, but it is genuinely ongoing. If there is
a common denominator for success, it is engagement. The
alchemy seems to be: great book + active publisher + active
author = success. If the events and conversation with readers
don't stop then, in my experience, neither does the book.'*

When thinking about publishers to approach, it is worth looking
at the size of the imprint. The Two Roads imprint, for instance,
publishes only around ten authors per year, which allows more
marketing attention to be given to each title.

- Debut authors are often disappointed by their marketing
  campaign as budgets are seldom large. Tube advertising would
  be a dream but, given the cost, it is only the biggest debuts that
  will attract that level of marketing spend. If your book does
  attract this sort of investment, it means that your publisher has
  high sales expectations of your book.
- Video trailers might be something a trade publisher will do for
  you but, if not, you can always do this yourself.
- Book launches are rarely organized by publishers these days,
  unless they are for celebrity titles. Most launch parties are paid
  for and organized by the authors themselves. That said, don't be
  afraid to ask for a contribution towards drinks or their support
  in some way, such as fliers or other promotional material.
- Do for yourself whatever marketing activity you are capable
  of doing and are good at. If you have a trade publisher
  communicate with your marketing contact in advance of
  publication and keep them informed of your plans so that each
  of your efforts complement the other. They may not be able to
  do everything for you but often they can contribute or advise.

Publishers and reader engagement

Until the rise of social media, publishers often had no idea who their
customers were. They didn't have a way of capturing the names of
readers, let alone engaging with them. Even with a hugely successful
TV tie-in, or a bestseller in a book series, marketing was much more
about general advertising and promotion than direct engagement
with readers. And with bookshops still the key outlet for books,
publishers didn't perceive the need for it.

Now, with the instant communication that social media affords, there is no excuse for not finding and engaging with your audience to build author brand loyalty. Indie authors were ahead of traditional publishers in cottoning on to this, with trade publishers attracting a lot of flack for doing it badly. However, recent years have seen huge leaps in publishers' efforts to engage directly with readers on behalf of authors and on their own behalf as publishing houses.

Indies and publishers alike are becoming much better at reader engagement, and there are all sorts of initiatives, including the Authonomy writing community and a romance festival from HarperCollins, that tap into this.

WHAT MAKES A BESTSELLER?

From a PR point of view, many factors go into the creation of a bestseller. Joe Pickering, Publicity Director, Cape and Bodley Head at Random House, won the Publishers Publicity Circle award for Paperback Original Fiction Campaign for his work on *Legend of a Suicide* by David Vann. He was kind enough to let me interview him about how a novelist can build a platform.

Joe Pickering, publicity director

'There are lots of factors that go into the creation of a bestseller. Quality, market, timing, Zeitgeist, trends, competitor titles, economy, cultural climate … As I list those, I wonder how bestsellers ever happen. Which makes me think that luck, or fortune, plays a large part. Realistically, though, it's about the right things coming together at the right time: a good book (in any sense, from "masterpiece" to "commercial"); a publishing house aware of what they've got and the dedication and ability to make it work; and readers responding. In my experience, from the publisher's perspective, it usually seems to involve a number of people across various departments regularly meeting to discuss ideas, progress, what's next and how things can be kept going. I'm not sure I've ever seen a bestseller happen without at least that.'

Joe Pickering's top tips for platform and profile building

1 Work with your publicist, not against them.
2 Write a good author biography for yourself – your publicist will find it useful.

3 Think about what you can offer in terms of your profile, things you've done, interests, etc. No one wants to talk just about how you wrote your novel; they want to know what it was based on, what research you did and whether it links to current events. Share your interest in anything that might be a different hook for media.

4 Think about social media and whether it's for you. Look at Twitter, Facebook, Instagram; if they don't immediately grab you, they may not be right for you, and that's fine. It's not a silver bullet. But if you have any questions about them, ask your publicist.

5 Don't retweet praise on Twitter. It's OK – just about – to humbly tweet a good review. If someone tweets something nice about you, or someone else tweets a link to a review, reply with a 'thanks' or similar but don't RT it. Think about it; if you were speaking to someone at a party and they said 'You're really funny', would you then stand up on a table and say 'Hey, everybody! This person just said I'm really funny!'?

6 If there's anything you really don't want to do or you feel uncomfortable with, tell your publicist. If you freeze on live radio or on stage at an event when faced with a certain question, you'll wish you'd said something, and so will they.

Joe Pickering, publicity director

Do we need to be original and quirky to stand out?

'Off the top of my head I can't think of a single individual bit of quirk I've seen that I've thought was brilliant. Anything like that needs to be backed up with some solid, traditional PR/ marketing, a good book and other creative ideas. One single bit of bestseller-creating quirk would be a stroke of genius, and I've certainly never come up with it.'

When you are promoting, are you thinking book PR or author PR? How far are your sights set?

'Both, which is why it's important to know about the author. You start thinking about the book around six months ahead of time and work from there. It can take a while to work out exactly what you're saying about the book, where it sits with your list and the market, and then it's important to get the author's viewpoint and input.'

Apart from the writing, what author attributes most light you up?

'Good contacts, good personality, intelligence, sense of humour, ability to talk about their book, original thoughts, interesting background. But of course not everyone has all of those things, so you look to tease them out or work with whatever you have. You buy the book, not the author, but if the author's an asset, so much the better.'

What happens in the PR department when an author is commissioned?

'Someone from the PR department reads the submission and gives feedback. The author and agent might come in for a meeting (if they're meeting other publishers) and someone from the PR team will usually go to that. After it's acquired, they might come in to meet other publishing people, and a PR person will be at that. Roughly a year before, we'll be involved in pitch meetings and such things, discussing the general approach. In any journalist or festival meetings, we'll be talking about and pitching the book.

'Around four to six months ahead, we'll have advance proofs (reading copies in the United States) sent out to journalists and various people. Around that time, we'll make direct contact with the author and start working with them more closely. That's a very rough timeline!'

Book clubs and the 'sweet spot'

For traditionally published books, book club appeal is widely acknowledged as a vehicle for building audiences. Charlie Brotherstone, agent at A.M. Heath, says that his top tip for producing a commercial hit is 'Always aim for the sweet spot if you want a word-of-mouth bestseller.'

What is this sweet spot and how does it help you in your quest for a bestseller? It refers to accessible novels – books we want to discuss and communicate about with each other. They can be issue-led with big concepts (see Chapter 2). They often emphasize an uncomfortable situation or work at fathoming something we don't understand. They are ideal book club books.

A good book club book has three key features:

1 **It has an engaging, compelling story.**

   Some book club members will only have time to read one book between meetings, so they need a story that will keep them turning the pages right until the end, that they'll be keen to pick up at the end of a busy day, and that they'll be motivated to finish in time for the next meeting. Other members may read many books over the same period, so they need a story that can compete with the rest of their reading material and that they will remember long enough for the book club discussion.

2 **It is a source of new information.**

   Members learn from their reading. This learning is often about a different culture, whether that culture belongs to a different racial group, a different country or segment of society, or a period in history. Readers also learn technical information about characters' jobs, hobbies, or the challenges that they face in their lives.

3 **It is often literary fiction.**

   Pure genre fiction can be an interesting sideline for general book clubs, but pure genre may not generate satisfying discussions about the subject matter, the writing techniques used or the readers' responses to the story.

The generation of a good discussion is the hallmark of a successful book club. Clubs remember the books that polarized their members' opinions because the stories raised questions about moral issues, social issues, or even literary issues that couldn't be definitively answered.

Here are some examples of acclaimed book club reads. Many of them have been made into films:

- *The Help* by Kathryn Stockett (Penguin, 2010)
- *The Time Traveler's Wife* by Audrey Niffenegger (Scribner Book Company, 2014)
- *We Need to Talk about Kevin* by Lionel Shriver (Serpents Tail, 2010)
- *Cutting for Stone* by Abraham Verghese (Vintage, 2009)
- *The Poisonwood Bible* by Barbara Kingsolver (Faber & Faber, 2013)
- *And the Mountains Echoed* by Khaled Hosseini (Bloomsbury Publishing 2013)
- *Suite Française* by Irene Nemirovsky (Vintage, 2007)
- *The Road* by Cormac McCarthy (Picador, 2009)
- *The Gargoyle* by Andrew Davidson (Canongate Books Ltd, 2009)
- *Never Let Me Go* by Kazuo Ishiguro (Faber & Faber, 2005)

Is it possible or desirable to write for a book club audience? An awareness of what makes a good book club read is an awareness of what makes books popular in general; this will do your book no harm. Again, don't twist yourself in knots writing for the market but be aware of the market so that, if choices present themselves, you may opt for the one that makes your book more marketable.

Joining a book club

Introducing yourself to book clubs may be a way to generate local buzz and is a good strategic step in developing your author brand. If you're not in a club, use your contacts to find someone who can talk to you about their book club experience.

Think about joining a club – many local libraries run them, as do bookshops. If all else fails, search the Internet for information about book clubs; for example, see www.litlovers.com.

CURRENT BOOK CLUB BOOKS

Spend some time on the Richard and Judy website to get a feel for current book club books. If you are feeling at all snobbish about this, perhaps you don't want to accept the reality of writing commercial fiction. There have been many fine books in Richard and Judy's recommendations. For example, look at this review from the Richard and Judy website.

On *Apple Tree Yard* by Louise Doughty

'Yvonne Carmichael has worked hard to achieve the life she always wanted: a high-flying career in genetics, a beautiful home, a good relationship with her husband and their two grown-up children. Then one day she meets a stranger at the Houses of Parliament and, on impulse, begins a passionate affair with him – a decision that will put everything she values at risk. At first she believes she can keep the relationship separate from the rest of her life, but she can't control what happens next. All of her careful plans spiral into greater deceit and, eventually, a life-changing act of violence. Apple Tree Yard is a psychological thriller about one woman's adultery and an insightful examination of the values we live by and the choices we make.'

Let's identify what makes *Apple Tree Yard* commercial and appealing:

- The *story* is very **Zeitgeisty**. The market has been softened for an erotic/romantic novel by other books dealing with women's sex lives, although oddly there's no real sex in this book. It really is a story about a story. But what makes it really buzz from a word-of-mouth perspective is the shock ending.
- Readers always seem to want a bit more from books and this book provides that **extra hook**. They're not content with just a domestic account (although there is still a market for those, despite claims that chick lit is dead). Domestic psychological thrillers are hot right now.
- The **writing and the plausibility** have been criticized, but that hasn't dented its success; they are good enough. It is rated as liked by 96 per cent of its readers on Goodreads.

Here is the review of another book featured on the Richard and Judy website.

On *The Rosie Project* by Graeme Simsion

'Love isn't an exact science – but no one told Don Tillman. A thirty-nine-year-old geneticist, Don has never had a second date. So he devises the Wife Project, a scientific test to find the perfect partner. Enter Rosie – "the world's most incompatible woman" – throwing Don's safe, ordered life into chaos. But what is this unsettling, alien emotion he's feeling?'

Unpacking its commercial appeal, we know that science is hot right now and online dating is bigger than ever before. This book begs a frequently asked question: must a bestselling idea be wholly original? The answer is no, it doesn't have to be original but, as in *The Rosie Project*, it does need a fresh spin.

Analysing book club appeal

Talk to some book club members and find out the following:
- The club's top three books. What did they love about those books?
- The book they all hated. What did they hate about it?

- The red flags – the kinds of books they never go for, and the elements of stories that they avoid if possible.
- The trends in theme, character type or setting that are over, as far as that club is concerned.

What advice would they give to an author?

Is there any evidence that book clubs read the kind of thing you write? If not, what are the minimum actions you'd need to take for your future releases to make them more appealing? Can you change the marketing emphasis, making it easier for clubs to understand the appeal of your book? If your book is a good match, how can you encourage your local clubs to read your work?

Make a list of three actions and schedule them as part of your marketing strategy. For example:

- Present a free copy or additional marketing material to your contact and ask for an introduction to someone they know in another book club. Build your local network, club by club.
- Offer to go along to a club meeting and talk about your book, or arrange a Skype session, or initiate an online discussion.
- If you're at an appropriate stage of development, try pitching your next story to them and make note of the feedback from these informed readers.

Your marketing strategy

Pulling it all together, this step-by-step checklist will take you through the key points in marketing your book. If you are self-publishing, you have full control and responsibility for marketing, so get started as soon as you possibly can.

1 **Create the best book possible.**

This is a no-brainer. Check and recheck that you've written the best book you can write, from idea to execution. Ensure that you have a good hook, an interesting backstory, professional editing and appropriate text and cover design.

2 **Set goals and a timeline.**

Count down to your publication date with a step-by-step action plan to make the marketing manageable. You might be sturdy enough to start this while still writing. Most of us do a little marketing but leave most of the work until we have finished writing. If you have a plan in place, you can start with some PR and build up as you get closer to publication.

When your book is finished (six months before publication), create a publicity and marketing plan. This is essential. If you are self publishing, you must create this ASAP or hire a publicist to do it on your behalf. If you have a publisher, you need to be aware of and involved with the publicity and marketing that is planned for your book, and dovetail your efforts with theirs. They are looking for you to identify and execute those marketing activities that they don't carry out. What contacts do you have? What specialist publications can you contact?

Two months before and after publication, be available and prepared to eat, drink and sleep your book for at least four months, if not the rest of your life. Making a big impression now will really help your book sales. Remember that getting on to the bestseller chart is about reaching the highest number of sales within the shortest period of time, so do concentrate your efforts at this stage rather than doing a little here and there.

For publication, plan a launch party that is strategic as well as fun; invite people who will buy your book, not just friends or people looking for a freebie.

3 **Work on your backstory.**

Be it your expertise, your hidden talents or your life story, use your own backstory to promote your books. Do you have any crossover or similarities with your protagonist? Did you live in the area where your book is set? Why are you the right person to write this book? How did you get the idea? This often makes a good hook for PR.

4 **Prepare a marketing and publicity pack.**

This includes a press release, an AI, and an author biography that includes a paragraph of your backstory. A press release should be one or two pages long. Include a photograph of yourself, a short summary of your book, a paragraph about yourself, the front cover image and your contact details. If you send out copies of your book with the release, label them with your contact details in case the letter becomes separated from your book.

For your author photograph, have two good head shots, one in colour and one in black and white. It pays to use a professional photographer, so don't use a holiday snap. Make sure the back is stickered with your contact details and with the photographer's credit, if needed. Think about having a style of shot that fits with your book.

It would be great to include a quote or testimonial from a well-known person, especially if they are someone who also has some affiliation or association with your subject matter, no matter how slender.

5 **Be creative and innovative.**

Take chances, particularly with low-cost or free PR and marketing ideas. What have you got to lose? Remember that book launches can happen anywhere; come up with a venue that's relevant to your book and that will particularly attract your target audience. The more original your book launch, the more media attention it will receive.

Where are your readers? Perhaps there are half a million of them but they are spread around the globe. Or perhaps you have a similar number but only in the Welsh countryside. Compile a list of the places where they might be found, no matter how weird, and come up with creative ways reaching them.

6 **Know your book's unique PR angle.**

Is your book Zeitgeisty, or about something that's often debated? Is your setting or theme unusual? Does it tie in to something that happened in real life? Look for PR hooks.

Monitor the media for chances to contribute to discussions. Include radio, press and TV. If you know your angle and the thesis of your book thoroughly, you will have your ears pricked and ready to react to any relevant news or human-interest story. You are now an expert of sorts on the subject. You'll have thought long and hard about it and have researched it, too; you'll be able to contribute to wider discussions in your own way, as an author. Offer yourself for talks and events. If you hear a radio discussion on your topic or theme, then engage by calling in, emailing or tweeting. Brief friends and family, asking them to keep an ear out for opportunities.

Did you discover something interesting in your research? Write an article about it for a specialist magazine. Or hold a free workshop for journalists in exchange for an article or review; be imaginative and get their attention. It may only generate one article, but that's good publicity.

Try to ensure that you have some events planned during publication month. Think about offering free speaking events to different groups of people. They can organize and promote the event and generate a good-sized audience; if even half the audience buys the book, the event has been success.

7 **Build your online presence.**

Even if it is just the basics of having a website and setting up an email and Google Plus, start to build your online presence as early in the process as you can. Your website can be simple, and dedicated to your writing and your books. It should also be a visual and with content fit for your genre. If you're stuck about what to put on it, gather ideas for blog posts around the theme of your book. Have a sign-up box on every page that feeds through to your database (see point 10.) Focus on web optimization – all authors should aim to improve their website ranking on search engines. Check that the title of your website is search friendly.

Include a sales page on your website that includes a call to action so that, every time a potential reader visits your site, they are able to buy your book, or to buy into you as an author in some way. Develop some author Q&As for your site – these can be used as quick PR material if needed at short notice. Ask readers of your book to write a testimonial – you can put these on the back of the book for later editions, or put them on your website.

8 **Build a database.**

Make this a priority. Start collecting names and addresses – the database – by offering free stuff in return for signing up. You could offer book club notes or your first chapter as a free download for anyone subscribing to your mailing list. You could also link to a Facebook page for your book so that readers can 'like' your book, add testimonials, comments and give feedback.

There's some great software that will build a database for you, software that allows you to keep all your contacts in separate lists, letting people subscribe and unsubscribe themselves. The most popular are Constant Contact and Monkey Chimp.

You'll soon build up a picture of what most interests your audience and you can put this knowledge to use by composing an e-zine and sending it out to your subscribed readers. Experiment by sending it on different days and at different times of day to see when your audience is most receptive. The clever software tells you how many people open each edition. You also receive statistics about the number of click-throughs for each item in your e-zine so that you know what people are most interested in reading. To see an example, pop your email

address into the green sign up box on www.londonwritersclub.
com and you will receive an edition of the London Writers'
Club e-zine.

9 **Don't get hung up on press review coverage.**

Yes, it would be nice to see yourself in the *Sunday Times
Review* pages, but there is evidence that such coverage doesn't
necessarily sell books, so it isn't of great value unless you are
writing literary fiction.

10 **Focus on editorial coverage.**

This can sell books, more so if the paper is the *Daily Mail*.
Check out your competition; identify similar books and check
out their websites to see what media coverage they've had and
try to figure out how they might have angled their pitch. If your
theme, your backstory, your book sales or how you've published
your book are newsworthy, then approach those outlets offering
ideas for features or to contribute top tips or quotes on the
subject you are writing about.

Promoting your book to conventional media should begin long
before a book is released; find out the lead times for the press
and magazines you want to pitch to. Your subject matter or
backstory is the hook. You must line up reviews and interviews
well before your book's publication day and, if you keep up
the promotion, you will continue to receive requests after your
book is published. This will keep sales ticking over.

Your media hotlist may include bloggers, on- and offline
reviewers, literary journals, newspapers, magazines and other
relevant forms of media. If available, check the guidelines of
the publications you're submitting to. Send your press release
with an offer of a review copy. Target editors and reviewers
using their correct name. When you contact journalists, the
letter should come from your publishing company (or use a
pseudonym), since many journalists prefer not to deal directly
with authors.

Local media can really help sell and may be easier to access.
Send a suitably revised press release to local newspapers, radio
and TV stations; create a story with local and timely interest
and they may just bite.

Is there a bookshop that specializes in your field of expertise?
Ask if they will stock copies of your book and then offer a free
book signing event or reading. Offer a free copy of your book
to the manager and politely (rather than egotistically) suggest

why their customers might like your book. Local bookstores like signings because they bring customers through their doors. Promise the bookstore something in return. For example, put their shop details on your website and on all publicity.

11 Follow up.

Not hearing from a journalist doesn't mean a 'no'. Be polite and professional (and definitely not pushy); if you haven't heard anything, follow up after ten working days from sending out. Don't forget the telephone. Yes, people are busy and it can be nerve-racking to pick up the phone but, with email and text, the telephone hardly ever rings these days. It can make a refreshing change to hear someone's voice. If you are able to, find out when is a good time to call. Don't call on press day.

12 Affiliate, co-operate and piggyback with others.

Send your book to other authors to ask for quotes, ensuring that the authors are relevant to your genre, theme or area of expertise. Offer to interview other authors, have them write a guest blog and do the same in return for them. Support each other by cross-promoting each other's books.

13 Repeat what works and drop what doesn't.

Keep a record of your marketing and publicity activities and record the sales results. Was your effort worthwhile? Whatever you do, don't keep doing the same thing expecting different results.

Do an audit every six months. Stop and look at what doesn't work and consider changing what you've been doing. Sometimes you may have to try a new approach to marketing your book, whether it is changing the look and presentation of your website, trying a different marketing strategy, getting additional help with your online promoting or improving your copy writing skills. Ask for feedback. Look at what other authors are doing and try out their tactics.

14 Be prepared for the long haul.

Don't stop. Marketing and promoting are an ongoing job for any author who wants to have a bestseller. Your marketing plan should reflect this continual process. You can't do something once and hope that it will work.

Draw up your marketing plan

Brainstorm a longlist of all the things you can do to promote your book. Don't hold back – just go for it and put down all your thoughts on a piece of paper. Sit with the list for a week or two. Refine and prioritize it later.

You might include the following.

- Offline activities: signings, appearances, readings, launches, press, radio, trade magazines, specialist magazines and outlets.
- Online activities: giveaways and competitions, reader engagement via your website, blogs and other online spaces and last, but definitely not least, social media.

Using the marketing strategy steps listed above, transform your longlist into your own marketing plan:

- Identify your goals.
- Break down each goal into manageable action steps.
- Put dates against each step, up to and beyond your publication date.
- Create a spreadsheet, a flow chart, a poster for your wall or a mind map – whatever works for you.

Focus point

As we've seen in this chapter, the chances of being an overnight sensation are very slim. To increase your chances of a bestseller, start marketing as soon as that first inspiration light bulb goes off in your head. Keep going at it until you start to see the sales you're looking for, and don't stop even then.

If you start with the right product, nail the marketing and put your book in front of the right readers who love your genre, you should be able to achieve impressive book sales. Monitor your marketing and PR efforts and track the results so that you know what is most effective.

Where to next?

In the next chapter, you will find out how being an authorpreneur is an essential part of creating a bestseller. It is your final and crucial step in boosting your bestselling potential.

13

Be an 'authorpreneur'

What is an authorpreneur? It's is a mash-up of two words, author and entrepreneur, reflecting the dual roles required of the modern writer. They're very different roles and sometimes they'll clash and get in each other's way; at other times, moving from one to the other will provide a welcome break.

Hazel Edwards, author of more than 200 books, is credited with coining the word. She says, 'Apart from crafting words … this means learning the marketing, publishing, technological, legal and entrepreneurial skills to establish and maintain creative self-employment.'

If you want to make a decent income from books, you must become an authorpreneur, applying a businesslike approach to your writing and publishing. In this chapter we will look at how you can become one in the final step to achieving a bestseller.

The key difference between an author and an authorpreneur is that the authorpreneur regards their book as they would a business. They take risks, invest money, time and energy, and discover what works through trial and error and evaluation. And they wholeheartedly commit to being in the business of creating a bestseller by monetizing their publishing at every possible opportunity.

Hazel Edwards' book *Authorpreneurship: The Business of Creativity* is a practical resource for any writer looking to adapt to changing times.

Hazel Edwards, author
Authorpreneurship

'Many find it difficult to reconcile the notion of being creative with being a solo operator in the business of ideas. When you're the one who has to plot the book, and pitch the concept, it's hard to switch roles or keep all running simultaneously. But unless you're reasonably well organized and have some control over how much time and energy you can afford to spend on a project, you'll go broke and become exhausted.

My use of the term "Authorpreneurship" credits the originators of ideas as the "brand". And suggests that in fast-changing times, they need to better manage the rights to their intellectual property, so they continue to gain financially and morally, as the story may move into new formats.

The "Business of Creativity" is not a contradiction in terms. Being a writer isn't just about writing. You also have to allow a percentage of time for all of the other stuff as well as learning aspects of new technology that are relevant for your subjects.'

Key idea

If the writing gets tough and you've done all you can, moving into your to-do list on the business side of your writing can be a good thing. Similarly, when the marketing becomes relentless, you always have your notebook and the book you are writing to escape into.

The authorpreneurial way

Write your own authorpreneurial action plan. Think about what you are good at and how you can use that in your publishing – perhaps skills from a previous existence in business or administration or working with people. Here are some ideas to include:

- When invited to speak, always use your latest book title as your talk title.
- Choose and learn to use social media selectively, so you have the skills to use them effectively.
- Be strategic. Have a plan for where you are heading in the long term; don't expect a bestseller to happen overnight.
- Be prepared to invest in your career.
- Be persistent, but don't be pushy. Do not urge or even ask people to buy your book. Give them a free sample of it. Ask them what they are reading. Find out what your readers are interested in. Engage in conversations, not a one-way monologue.

Develop resilience and a thick skin. Be flexible in your plans and approach. Above all, be professional: entrepreneurs have good websites, promotional material and business cards. None of these things need be corporate or boring: small companies like Moo.com do a pack of cards where you can get a lovely mix of cards featuring a different image on each card. (Find images that reflect your book titles or main characters or themes.) They're a great conversation starter.

The new reality for authors

Back in the good old days, an author could scribble an idea on the back of an envelope, shove it across the table to (usually *his*) agent after enough claret had been consumed and the industry gossip gotten out of the way. The agent would then telephone or mention the book to a publisher when *they* were next lunching and a deal would be struck. The author would then receive a contract for the book with a generous advance and a delivery date, which they might or might not adhere to, but in reality they had plenty of time to write and deliver the book.

After a careful and consultative editorial phase, the hardback book would then be lovingly wrapped in a stunning book jacket, the publicity campaign would kick off with a book launch which journalists would attend. Signings would have long queues of adoring readers. Everyone in the process would be happy.

Then they would Write, Publish, Launch, Repeat.

Whatever the accuracy of that fantasy – or how long ago it existed – there is a new reality. Most people in professional or creative roles now need to be entrepreneurial, whatever it is they do. The rise of the concept of personal branding not only applies to pop stars and CEOs but also to authors who would like to rise from the slush pile – or from selling few copies of their book – and be noticed by agents, publishers and readers.

Key idea

An authorpreneur is an author who thinks with the mindset of an entrepreneur.

Authorpreneurs regard their author brand as a micro-business and they apply business techniques to building their brand, quite separately from their writing. They also take a businesslike approach to marketing and publicity and every other aspect of finding readers for their books. Authorpreneurs drive, and are involved with, their own marketing, whether they're traditionally or self-published.

Becoming an authorpreneur

A really good start to setting up your authorpreneurship as a micro-business is to look at what someone like author John Williams is doing. His non-fiction book *Screw Work, Let's Play* describes how to do what you love and get paid for it. Passion is the beginning and telling people about it is the second but equally vital part.

John Williams, author

'The key to getting paid for playing is choosing the right things to play, things that you are naturally good at. Your aim must be to get in flow … Real pioneers in any field get there by experimenting and playing. Test out new ways of doing things and notice what happens. Report what you find and invite others to join the conversation.'

If you study the careers of just two of the authors already mentioned, Peter James and Sylvia Day, you'll see that's exactly what they did from the beginning and still do today despite their publishing success. They could sit back and just enjoy their success but instead they keep on experimenting and growing.

The good news is that you don't need a Dragon's-Den-like investment or to have a five-year plan to get off the ground as an authorpreneur. You just need to be willing to invest your time, energy and every particle of your story-telling talent. In terms of financial investment, you could probably make a professional start for the price of a last-minute package holiday to Malaga.

LEVERAGING YOUR BOOK

Here are some examples of how to build your own brand and platform:

- Build a series (see below).
- If you've done the research, work it; speak and become known as an expert on the subject or setting of your book. (*Georgian London* author Lucy Inglis is a good example of how to do this.)
- Make appearances wherever appropriate. Libraries and schools can be incredibly supportive. Childrens' and YA authors should know that schools will work hard to promote your book to the children and parents of the school you visit.
- Film/TV series. Don't wish and pray to be optioned or commissioned, though; make your own video or short film which not only brings your work to life in another medium but is also useful as a promotional tool for YouTube – or your website, if it's very short.
- Establish yourself as an expert in the subject or setting of your book. If you aren't an expert, then talk about what you are an expert in and invite other experts to take part. Your aim here is to get a debate or discussion going that's based upon, and perhaps even broader than, what you covered in your book. Again, the book is just a seed.
- Use the full range of opportunities open to you. Every online platform offers ways to help indie publishers sell books. Amazon, for instance, has a range of marketing opportunities for you to use including: 'also-boughts', tailored recommendations, popularity charts, mailing lists and 'also by' pages.

Key idea

Don't expect too much in the short term; it is tough selling a first book. You just have to keep putting new work out there and do as much promotion as you can while focusing on new writing.

BUILDING A SERIES

A more direct route to a bestseller is to build a series. In this way you build your brand so that your authorial brand and your book benefit from the compound effect.

This is an obvious decision to make, because all the hard work that you and the publishers put into promoting you and your authorial brand is built upon every time you write and release another book. In the American idiom, 'what's not to like' about this idea?

If you write outside a series with each book, you and the publicity department must promote afresh. They can still use your authorial branding, of course, but it is far simpler if they can go out promoting the next instalment in a series that readers are desperate to catch up on to find out what happens next.

Traditional publishers generally publish one book per year; indie authors are finding that it really pays to strike while a series is hot, often pushing themselves to publish two books per year. This level of supply and demand does have an impact on the quality of the work, which is why many indie authors make good use of editors.

Promoting your brand

In Chapter 12, on marketing, we talked about building your audience by consistently remaining engaged and visible. As we have seen, this is vital to your success. An authorpreneur thinks bigger than a single book. Instead they think long term, by not just promoting their book or books, but by also promoting themselves as an author brand.

JOINING THE WRITING COMMUNITY

You can promote your brand by engaging with other writers in your genre. These are generally also readers in the same genre and, whether they are buying books to keep themselves entertained, to see what others are writing or because they like a book cover, they are buying books, possibly including yours.

To maintain your visibility, don't just engage but offer to help other authors, not just in a calculated attempt to curry favour but because it is an enjoyable way to be connected and involved in writing communities, particularly those in your genre. Do what you can to help other authors you respect and admire. Comment on their ideas, congratulate them on their new book and on their successes. Give feedback and offer helpful suggestions when they call for input for book research. When they post their book covers, tell them what you think. If they ask questions when they are doing their research, make the effort if you can to respond and help.

On Facebook and Twitter, don't wait until your book is published to engage with other authors in your genre as well as readers.

Promoting yourself and your books

What is the one thing you will do today to tick the authorpreneur box for your book? You can start small and work up from there. Perhaps try a workshop or event at your local library or bookshop.

Decide on what it is that you will do, and what tasks need to be done, break down the task into actionable steps, with mini-deadlines, and commit to a date for completing it.

Remember, it is your time and money you are investing. What are the most effective ways you can achieve a balance between writing and promoting your books? Focus on methods that are effective but cost little in terms of time and money.

John Williams, author

'Ultimately, the best advice for any authorpreneur is to be crazy about what you're doing.'

The most successful authors are those who write good books, are passionate about writing but who also acknowledge that it is a business. Tim Winton is one such author. He's a wonderful writer, passionate about his stories but also very clear that writing is how he makes his living.

Figure out what you don't know and be honest about it; ask other authors. When you find out, tell them what you found out. Use your contacts book and anything else at your disposal. Don't be shy of asking people for help and who they know who could help.

Ask for and use any testimonials and reviews from happy readers on your website and if you can get any well-known names, use them for cover endorsements.

If you have great endorsements, use them. One author who didn't have any famous names to endorse his book made his quotes up, and they were so obviously made up that they became a hook, a talking point in themselves. It did him good rather than harm as he showed that he was not only prepared to laugh and take a risk but that he had a clever way of going about it.

RESPONDING TO REVIEWS

Relish the bad reviews as much as the good ones, remembering that any review – not just the positive ones – will increase your rankings. Respond politely to reviews if they point out a problem with your book, not to defend it but to find out why they think what they do. The information could be useful to you or, when you've explain your point of view, you might convert a disgruntled reader into a fan. I've heard many an anecdote where this has ended happily.

Key idea

Be agile and don't worry about starting small as it means you can react and respond to whatever works best for your publishing. Find a way to build flexibility into your publishing, remembering the cruise liner and the speedboat analogy: a speedboat can turn with ease but it takes a whole day for a cruise liner to change direction.

REACHING OUT TO YOUR READERS

As we have seen, once your book is written and you are in the selling phase, it is helpful to think of your book as a product and yourself as a brand. It helps you to distance yourself from the writing and think of the business side of being an author. It also helps to borrow from what works about branding. However, like Orna Ross, speaking at the London Book Fair in 2014, you may prefer to talk about authors reaching out to their readers than about the marketing of books or of authors as brands. If you reach out to readers wholeheartedly, book sales can come about, not from pushing a sale, but from interesting the reader in you and then your book.

John Purkiss, co-author of *Brand You*, says that we buy into brands 'because we think we know what to expect. We know exactly what we will be getting.' So it is with an author name and with a series. As a starting author it's much easier to promote a series of genre books than it is to try to get your name known. First you entice them with a genre you love, and then they get to know you, the author.

IS IT WORTH THE INVESTMENT?

Can you really make money from publishing a book? Authors frequently mull over this question. The answer is yes, you can, or publishing wouldn't have been such a viable business for so long. Whether you can make a living as an author – or your fortune – is an entirely different question. As with any other enterprise, you first need to have a great idea that readers want to read about and then be either extremely lucky or enterprising and hard working to get your book in front of those readers.

Being an authorpreneur, according to Hugh Howey, involves 'more risk but the potential for more rewards'.

Seven things to remember about the business of writing

1   It is a business. You can't treat it wholly as an art form or a hobby. If you can, put on a (mental if not physical) suit jacket for several hours at least once a week. That's your authorpreneur jacket. Wear it, and act like one.

2   You need a writing and publishing strategy that pushes you towards your bestseller. Stick it up where you can see it. Consider which parts of it you can do yourself and which you need help with.

3   The income of an author is uncertain, but there are tax breaks in which – like farmers and musicians – you can average out your income over two years. The effect of this is that if you have a year where you are writing and researching and earn little in that tax year, you can average it out over the following tax year to help you with the unevenness of your income. Similarly, if you are lucky enough to be paid a large advance and so earn a lot in one tax year, you can spread that income over two years.

4   Grants and funding are available to support writers when they are writing. Look at the Arts Council guidelines and search online for other grants.

5   Book PR and marketing lasts for the entire life of your book. You can't simply hand your manuscript over and relax about marketing or sales for your book, leaving someone else to get on with it. You must live and breathe your book or it will wither and die. Help it to make an impression on the world.

6   Don't wait to be chosen. You're free to do what you want. Set writing and publishing goals that you can work towards and go out and make those goals a reality.

7 Be flexible: do pitch to an agent if that's the route you prefer, but consider self-publishing if trade publishing doesn't work out for you. Be agile and change your publishing plans as you need to, whether that's to respond to the market or to your own changing circumstances.

 Key idea

Be realistic about the financial side of being an author. In most cases it is a slow build rather than an overnight moneyspinner.

Workshop: your authorpreneur kit

As an authorpreneur, you need to have the following items in your kit:
- A website with an up-to-date blog
- A free giveaway tied to an email autoresponder system
- An email list and a regular email newsletter
- Top tips ready for journalists and other requests
- An author biography and headshot
- A press release
- A Twitter account
- A Facebook page
- A Facebook or LinkedIn group
- Video tips on YouTube
- A marketing strategy
- Good promotional materials
- A business card
- Flyers

Pick one of these right now and get started.

We've seen that, while there are no guarantees of a bestseller, certain measures and strategies will increase your chances of achieving one. Write well, edit and design professionally, make your brand and your books visible, build your audience, run your writing and publishing as a micro-business and then write another book. All of these things together dramatically increase your chances of a big-selling book.

While it might seem that publishing is narrowing, with bookshops closing and with just one online retailer dominating, there is breadth and opportunity in the new choices that technology allows. Authors no longer need wait to be chosen by agents or publishers but can publish and reach readers directly if they choose to.

Print books seem here to stay, though in smaller numbers, and digital, while it has become a normal part of the publishing landscape, seems set to continue to innovate and surprise, so the future of publishing is wide open and loaded with opportunity. I spoke with many people in the publishing world for this book and there seems to be more optimism than gloom. There's a sense that there is room for everyone and that in future there won't be any distinction between trade and self-publishing for the reader; there'll just be books, authors and readers who want to read them.

Many authors have good relationships with their publishers and are content to be with a publishing house. If that option is not open to you, or if you prefer to self publish, know that there are many other successful ways of publishing and routes to market for you to try. All that is stopping you is your own willingness to make it a success, whether this a temporary or life-long obsession for you. Do it properly and you might achieve the bestseller that you desire.

For indie authors, it's up to you to learn from successful role models how to use the technology and platforms available – which allow global reach from your desk – to maximize your book sales.

There are no mistakes in how you choose to publish, as experimentation has never been easier, faster or cheaper. Study the bestselling authors, the ones who have made mistakes as well as the successes in self-publishing, because they've learned the hard way what works and what doesn't. And then go out and do your own experiments. Make them enjoyable and bestselling ones.

There are many options when publishing digitally, including testing in beta, trying out an ebook, giving away an excerpt, print-on-demand or audiobook, and if you do that well enough and prove there is a market, carry on as a fully fledged authorpreneur or find a publisher to take your books forward.

The most successful authors are those who have a good book that tells a compelling story, are clear about what they offer and genuinely care about their readers, and who reach out to and engage with their readers. That's how to grow readership.

However you reach readers to tell them about your book, always respect your audience and don't oversell or be too pushy. If you have a good book and you find and build the right communities for your book, then interest in your book should follow. Know what your readers want, find them where they spend time and interact with them, respect them and let them know what kind of writing they can expect from you. Move them, inspire or make them laugh. Give them the very best book that you can write. And then when you've written a great story and given the marketing your full and best attention, keep all those balls in the air and then schedule in time to get back behind your desk and start writing another book. It will all be worth it in the end.

Happy publishing!

Appendices

Cover briefing sheet – for your designer	
Title	
Subtitle	
Author	
Publication date	
Price	
ISBN for barcode	
Format	
Page extent	
Binding	
Cover finish: • Spot varnish • Embossing • Foil • Matte or gloss?	
Inside cover printing, if any	
Author photo on jacket? Where?	
Quotes or endorsements	*Attach separate sheet and indicate where they are to be used.*
Book genre or category	
Cover copy with author biography	*Attach on separate sheet as above.*
Comparable books/competition	
Number of copies	

Acquisition overview sheet

Editor

Title

Author

Agent

Rights available

One-line pitch

Why do we want to buy this book?

The difference:

The approach:

The market:

On trend:

The author:

More about the author

How will we reach our readers?

Comparable books & sales

How will we publish?

Sample advance information sheet

Masterclass: Write a Bestseller: Teach Yourself Book

Jacq Burns

Keynote

An inspired insider's guide to pinning down your bestseller concept, executing, pitching, selling or publishing it yourself.

Description

There is no precise formula for writing a bestseller, but there are secrets, skills and techniques that will dramatically improve your odds of publishing a bestselling novel.

Whatever your motivation - whether sick of rejections, getting ready to approach a publisher, or with an idea you think is unbeatable - you need to read this book before you do anything else. It gives you the key insights into what makes a bestseller and explains the trends and conventions of different genres, before helping you get a real handle on the writing (and revising) process. A third of the book is devoted to pitching and selling your novel both to traditional agents and as a self-published author, with incisive and cutting-edge insights into writing for Amazon and becoming an 'authorpreneur'.

Sales Points

- Brilliant insights on creating bestseller ingredients from a former publisher now agent and literary consultant.
- Covers both the creative principles behind the bestseller format and the rules behind pitching a potential bestseller
- Innovative and cutting-edge coverage of the rapidly changing publishing world - and how to take advantage of it

Author Biography

Jacq Burns commissioned books at Random House and Harpercollins prior to setting up as a literary agent and co-director of London Writers' Club. In non-fiction her focus is broadly on personal development and business topics and in fiction she helps develop writing across most genres. She has ghosted a wide range of subjects and also written a series of humorous books under a pseudonym.

Publication date	**Friday, October 31, 2014**
Price	**£12.99**
EAN/ISBN-13	**9781473600034**
BIC 1.1	**Literary Reference Works (CGL) Creative Writing & Creative Writing Guides (CGV)**
BIC 2.0	**Creative Writing & Creative Writing Guides (CBV)**
Binding	**Paperback**
Format	**Demy**
Extent	**256 pages**
Word Count	
Exclusively for Sale	**World (ex USA, Can)**
Not for Sale	**Can;USA**
Book locale	**UK**
Author living in	**UK**

Hodder & Stoughton.

www.hodder.co.uk

9 781473 600034

Sales Office: 338 Euston Road, London, NW1 3BH, UNITED KINGDOM
Tel: 0207 873 6000
International Tel: +44 (0) 207 873 6000

Orders to: Bookpoint Ltd, 130 Park Drive, Milton Park, Abingdon, Oxfordshire, OX14 4SE
Tel: 01235 400400
International +44 (0)1235 400 400
Tel:

Resources

http://www3.cs.stonybrook.edu/~songfeng/success/

The Bookseller, thebookseller.com

Bradley, L., *Sounds Like London: 100 Years of Black Music in the Capital* (Serpent's Tail, 2013). lloydbradley.net

Ferris, S., *How to Be a Writer* (Summersdale Publishers, 2005)

Grenville, K. *Writing from Start to Finish* (Allen and Unwin, 2001)

Pressfield, S., *The War of Art* (Black Irish Entertainment LLC, 2012)

Watts, J., and Baxter, M., *Writing Erotic Fiction* (Hodder & Stoughton, 2013)

Further help

The Arvon Foundation
arvonfoundation.org
Residential courses

London Writers' Club
londonwritersclub.com
A global networking club where writers can connect with agents and
publishers and get professional help with their writing

Nielsen BookScan Data
nielsenbookscan.co.uk
For ISBNs and book sales figures

Society of Authors
societyofauthors.org
A trade union for professional authors

Susan Moore
mooreva.co.uk
Administrative, book promo and speaking support for authors

The Wheeler Centre, Sydney
wheelercentre.com
Literary and publishing centre – a good source of videos and advice
Writers' and Artists' Yearbook (A & C Black, published annually)

Index